Mixed-Race, Post-Race

Mixed-Race, Post-Race

Gender, New Ethnicities and Cultural Practices

Suki Ali

Oxford • New York

First published in 2003 by
Berg
Editorial Offices:
1st Floor, Angel Court, 81 St Clements Street, Oxford, OX4 1AQ, UK
838 Broadway, Third Floor, New York, NY 10003–4812, USA

Berg is the imprint of Oxford International Publishers Ltd.

Library of Congress Cataloging-in-Publication Data
A catalogue record for this book is available from the Library of Congress.

British Library Cataloging-in-Publication Data
A catalogue record for this book is available from the British Library.

ISBN   1 85973 765 X (Cloth)
        1 85973 770 6 (Paper)

Typeset by Avocet Typeset, Chilton, Aylesbury, Bucks
Printed in the United Kingdom by Biddles Ltd, Guildford and Kings Lynn

www.bergpublishers.com

For my mother

Contents

Acknowledgements

I am grateful to the Economic and Social Research Council for providing the first three years of funding that enabled me to undertake the doctoral research which provides the data for this book.

Firstly I would like to thank all the people who encouraged me to return to Higher Education – and stick with it – including staff and students at the Centre for Research in Education and Gender at the Institute of Education, U. L. In particular, I would like to thank Diana Leonard for her unflagging support in the process of embarking on a Ph.D. and her excellence (and patience) as a supervisor. Debbie Epstein joined in to provide invaluable expertise and guidance; together they made a formidable double act. Both Diana and Debbie have continued to be encouraging of my academic development, as has Shereen Benjamin.

The many children and adults who took part in this research made the whole process a privilege and a pleasure. I thank them for their generosity and enthusiasm, and for their creative input into this project.

Of the many colleagues at Goldsmiths College Sociology Department, who have also provided advice and guidance in all areas of my professional life, special thanks go to Brian Alleyne and Kate Nash for the above and also for reading and commenting on drafts of chapters and other work. Les Back has given endless advice and encouragement and also read the entire manuscript. David Oswell read a complete draft and provided invaluable comments and energising discussion. Kirsten Campbell has not only provided political and intellectual muscle but more personal support than a colleague and friend should have to.

Numerous friends provided resources throughout initial stages, including space to write, washing machines and hot baths. Theresa McGinley provided inspiration in the form of wisdom, strength and mucking about.

Finally I thank my mother, brother and sister for love and tolerance.

Some of this material has been published in different forms elsewhere. Parts of Chapter 2 appear in Ali (2002) and parts of Chapters 3 and 4 have been worked through in detail in Ali (2002), Ali (2003a) and Ali (2003b).

'Where Do You Come From?'

[T]he question, and the theorisation of identity is a matter of considerable political significance, and it is only likely to be advanced when both the necessity and the 'impossibility' of identities, and the suturing of the psychic and the discursive in their constitution, are fully and unambiguously acknowledged.

S. Hall *Questions of Cultural Identity*

Introduction: 'Mixed-Race' Experiences

During the summer of 1998 I was in the middle of collecting the data which provides the material for this book. One day, while I was out shopping in the local supermarket, I bumped into Peggy. I knew Peggy quite well, although you could not characterise our relationship as a friendship. She was employed by my brother as a cleaner and I had lived at his house for a while. A white, working-class Londoner, Peggy had lived in the same area her whole life. Her husband had died many years before leaving her to bring up a son and two daughters alone. She had had a hard life, and though her children were now grown, money was tight and she worked a variety of cleaning jobs to pay the bills. We stopped to chat and I asked how she was, as I no longer lived in the house and hadn't seen her for some months. She said that she was going through a particularly difficult time and explained why. Peggy's big news was that her beloved (white) son had 'taken up with a black girl' and, as a result of his mother's disapproval, had moved out and set up home with her. Peggy explained that although she knew that her boy had some black friends and had even had black girlfriends in the past, this was a serious relationship. Her biggest fear was that they would have children. I was so shocked by what she said next that I remembered the words exactly: 'I'm not racist but two cultures shouldn't mix. Some of those black people are all right, but the half-castes, well they're a breed apart'. (Peggy 56-year-old white, working-class Londoner, 1998).

Peggy had known me for several years (and my brother and sister longer), knew we were at least 'not-white', had met and spoken to our (white English) mother on more than one occasion.[1] In numerous previous conversations, Peggy had alluded to community difficulties living in an area of London that has one of the highest ethnic diversities amongst the population. In particular, she talked about the difference between the 'blacks' or 'West Indians' and herself as a 'white' person. We agreed to disagree; when I challenged her she often said that she was not racist. On this occasion as on others, especially being 'half-caste' myself, I felt she was undoubtedly referring to me and to my family. I was so upset I was rendered speechless. The feeling was as acute as any other experience of racism I had ever encountered when a child. There is something especially bitter about resentments to my mixedness, deep and abiding, indescribably and incoherently *wrong*. It makes not only me invalid as a person, but worse still makes my mother wrong for all sorts of profound reasons. I said nothing, made an excuse and left.

After the encounter with Peggy I went home and wrote it down. It struck me how much that kind of conversation had the power to wound me, even though as an adult who studied in these areas I could rationalise it, analyse it, and to some extent explain it sufficiently for it make some kind of sense. None of those cognitive abilities made the emotion easier to bear. Nonetheless, analyse it I did as it spoke to the heart of the work I was (and still am) engaged with. The encounter reminded me that though we live in the increasingly post-race world – a world concerned with struggles for ethnic, national, religious and cultural meaning – the irrational and corporeal ground of 'race' can still be a powerful force in social relations. It is a clear example of the tenacity of racialisation: 'a dialectical process by which meaning is attributed to particular biological features of human beings as a result of which individuals may be assigned to a general category of persons which reproduces itself biologically' (Miles 1989: 76).

Racialisation is a term which reinforces the psychosocially dynamic processes of 'racial positioning', and is often used in shorthand by talking about the way in which, for example, discourses themselves are 'raced' and often how this takes the form of 'racism'. Such a definition also implicitly underlines the role that 'family', real *or imagined*, informs this dis/identification with mixedness.

In Peggy's (and many others') terms, the language of 'Otherness' is now not only 'racial' but mobilises the 'cultural'. Peggy used the term 'culture' in place of 'race' to prove herself non-prejudiced and so she shows that 'post-race thinking' is filtering into everyday contexts. Post-race thinking is one of the central themes under investigation throughout the book; in this context it signifies a change from old essentialist views of biological races, and hence concepts of 'cultural mixing'. But Peggy also used 'half-caste', a term so outdated in academia that it is only used in historical context. This shows that although language or terms in common usage may change, meanings may well not. Whether Peggy uses the word 'race' or culture the meaning behind it is a 'racist' fear of the 'Other', of the black girl with her rampant sexuality trapping her son.

This succinctly illustrates how discourses of 'race' are also hetero/sexualised and gendered. During one conversation when we talked about a white woman who lived near her, Peggy described her as 'Black man's woman' and asked me if I knew what that meant. I said I did not, and she decided not to enlighten me. I suspect it was a comment on this woman's sexual availability as well as her lack of good taste or judgement. These comments made me think of my mother who had also been a 'Black man's woman' and as a result suffered from abuse and discrimination, as had my father. That had been in the 1950s and 1960s, but for Peggy at least, the disapproval of interracial relationships is still tangible. She expresses a common concern that the children of these relationships are, at best, to be avoided, and, at worst, totally inhuman.

These are discourses that are 'out there' in common everyday usage; they construct and are constructed by a modern multiracial, multiethnic society in which some still believe in a form of white supremacy, fear of 'racial Others' and the contamination that they may bring through 'blood mixing'. Another important feature of this interaction was that the personal relationship between Peggy and myself was based on both a perceived 'race' *and* 'class' difference. She conceptualised or identified herself as white, working class, and positioned me as 'coloured' and 'middle class'. This undoubtedly informed the way that she interacted with me at all times and shows how each part of our personal life histories informs the encounter.

Studying Mixedness

During the past decade I have read a large number of texts in order to try to understand my own position in relation to theoretical and political discourses of 'race' and racism.[2] I found any meaningful engagement with mixedness almost entirely absent from mainstream literature on 'race', and that what material there was that centralised the issue was contextualised in ways that sometimes made translation to my own situation difficult. In this section I will introduce the key theoretical frameworks that inform the rest of the book. I start by looking at the empirical work into mixedness and then move on to consider the key issues about the encounter with Peggy in the light of post-race thinking.

Bad Blood
Foucault (1991) argues that genealogies require us to consider histories of the present, not in a search for an origin or linear trajectory leading us to the here and now but to provide us with details and surprises and possible truth effects from a range of sources. The historical antagonism to mixedness is well documented yet the central concerns within contemporary discussions often still hold echoes of colonial ideologies. Attitudes to interracial relationships and marriage

and responses to fears of miscegenation have varied in different temporal and geographic locations (e.g. Martinez-Alier 1974; Ballhatchet 1980; Alibhai-Brown and Montague 1992; Tizard and Phoenix 1993; Breger and Hill 1998).[3] Cultural and psychological differences categorised as borderline pathological were used to separate colonised 'natives' from the ruling British visitors in places such as West Africa and India (Ware 1992; C. Hall 1992; Balahatchet 1980; Opitz *et al.* 1992). Conversely, in other areas such as South America, miscegenation was a strategy to control the indigenous natives by 'civilising' them through infusions of 'white' blood (see Stoler 2000; Labyani 2000). In Britain, mixed marriages took place as early as 1578, and fears of 'racial mixing' were often disguised by a stated concern for the sad products of this unnatural coupling. Stonequist's 'Marginal Man' thesis suggests that those of mixed heritage will suffer undue psychological harm as a result of possible rejection and lack of 'belonging' to a particular culture or 'race' (Stonequist 1937). Such ideas are tenacious. In 1998 a black woman was refused donor insemination from a London hospital as they only had white donors available. The reason given was for the 'sake of the children' (source Guardian Newspapers[4]). Jill Olumide argues: 'The problems and pathologies of mixed-race are framed in such a way as to indicate that these problems are somehow intrinsic to the group rather than dependent on social processes' (Olumide 2002: 47). Her work challenges this with its emphasis on the role of institutions (such as medical science) in the production of the problematic 'group' of mixed-race people and through in-depth analysis of 'the social construction of mixed-race' (ibid.). Olumide's account is another step towards the 'derecognition' of 'race' (ibid. 157). Her work is still for the most part set within the binary framework of black/white mixing, and again only deals with accounts from adults. It does, though, add more evidence to the argument for recognising how mixed identities force us to reconsider 'race' more generally.

Empirical work from around the world also supports a much more positive engagement with the possibilities of mixedness as an identity. In addition to the USA and British literatures, European perspectives on multiethnic positions are different again in their developing theories on 'racial' and cultural identities (e.g. Opitz *et al.*, Allund and Granquist 1995). There is a growing body of work by indigenous and migrant peoples in Australia and New Zealand that adds to the imperative for a more global perspective on 'racial mixing' (e.g. Ihihimaera 1998; Hartley 1995). In all these accounts, the *experience* of mixedness is seen as potentially positive and counters the psychosocial censuring that is still in evidence in 'common sense' discourses of preferred 'monoraciality'.

It is clear from the above accounts and from demographic data that in spite of the historical and contemporary concerns with 'race mixing', increasing numbers of people are in mixed relationships (see Owen 2001). Even more importantly there is a significant and fast-increasing 'mixed-race population' of whom over 50 per cent are under the age of fifteen (see Phoenix and Owen 2000). In 1997 I attended the 'Rethinking "Mixed-Race"' conference where one of the key issues for discussion was the changes to the upcoming Census which was to include a new 'Mixed' category. Those present felt it to be an important development that needed extremely careful wording if it was to provide mean-ingful data. Although 'we' were happy finally to form a 'we' of sorts, we recog-nised the huge range of potential identifications that were excluded from most discussions of mixedness, focusing as they did on black/white binaries. At a later conference,[5] the general feeling was that our concerns had been well-founded. It was agreed that the Census questions had been flawed as nation, ethnicity and 'race' were confused within the questions asked.[6] Such problems reflect the difficulties in *studying and theorising* mixedness.

David Parker and Miri Song (2001) argue that writing on 'mixed-race' takes three forms, the first of which incorporates diverse formulations that 'recognise "mixed-race" as a viable social category' (Parker and Song 2001: 6). They cite British empirical work by Tizard and Phoenix (1993), Benson (1981) and Wilson (1987) which looked at black/white mixes in support of this position. (I would add Olumide's.) I am not convinced that these authors necessarily argue for or support 'mixed-race' as a *viable social category* that needs no further discussion, any more than 'Black' does. What they do is provide valuable data in an under-researched area, and show that 'mixed-race' can be held as an identity. However, it is the *inadequacy* of 'mixed-race' as a single and coherent category that makes it so theoretically demanding. In a practical sense this is evidenced in the discus-sions over the problems with the British Census questions.

In the USA national identities are increasingly represented as multiracial or biracial (Parker and Song 2001), and this is reflected in the fact that 'mixed' cate-gories have appeared on official forms for many years. Maria P.P. Root (1992, 1996) and Naomi Zack (1993, 1995) have been at the forefront of writing about mixedness in the USA and have put together collections of biracial and multira-cial authors who also foreground their 'American' identities. What these (and other) collections show is the diversity of what can still be loosely termed gendered, mixed, American experience (Camper 1994; Fetherston 1994). Specifically, the authors cited above offer a direct response and challenge to the persistence of the idea that people who are multiracial will suffer more than those who are 'pure' in forging identities (see e.g. Cauce *et al* and Jacobs, both in Root 1992). It is, they argue, most often racism that is to blame for difficulties indi-viduals have, rather than 'psychopathology' or 'dysfunctional families', and in this support the work in the British context by Olumide (2002). These collections include innovative work by individuals who claim heritage from Pacific Rim countries, South Asia, South America and Eastern Europe to name but a few.

Despite the different national identitifications, cross-cultural endeavours focus on possibilities for change: '[multi/biracial/ised identity] provides us with a vehicle for examining ideologies surrounding race, race relations and the role of the social sciences in the deconstruction of race ... the answers are not to be found in a new system of classification, but in deconstruction, synthesis and evolution' (Root 1992: 10–11).

It is the latter part of Root's vision that fits best within the post-race frame-work – the need to *deconstruct* and *evolve*. However, many of the authors featured in their books do not manage to do this as they draw together aspects of the 'comma-ed' or 'hyphenated' identities (Ang-Lygate 1995), that plague multi-plicitous positions and hold to some kind of composite, constructed version of mixing previously singular 'racial' identities.

The problem lies not only with the *idea* of 'race' itself but also within the *language* that constructs and maintains it. Jayne Ifekwunigwe (1997, 1999, 2000) interrogates terminologies and taxonomies of 'race' in her important work with adults of African and white heritage. Through her own experience, reading and the research of others she suggests that: 'Mixed-race people themselves as well as parents, carers, practitioners, educators, policy makers, academics and curious lay people are all hungry for a uniform but not essentialist term that creates a space for the naming of their specific experiences without necessarily re-inscribing and reifying "race"' (Ifekwunigwe 2000: 17). She remains convinced of 'the importance of trying to formulate an analytical scheme that can address multiracialised, biracialised and generational hierarchies of differ-ences within the marginalised spaces of "mixed-race"' (ibid. 18). It is interesting that Ifwekunigwe uses this kind of (American) terminology, because, as Parker and Song note, 'the term multiracial grates on a British ear' (Parker and Song 2001: 8). The struggle to find appropriate names for collective identities whether forced or 'voluntary', coupled with a desire to preserve 'racial' or ethnic distinc-tion, is a common feature of both British and USA literature.

A considerable amount of the work on multiracial identities does often draw upon a notion of multiple 'heritages' or family histories, and with it, unfortu-nately, the mixing or 'blending' of blood (Omi and Winant 1986; Spickard 1992). Both in Britain and the USA there has been a boom in auto/biographical writing, with literary life stories providing the detail of the experiences of mixedness (Spickard 2001). I am not in the least surprised that this kind of writing has become so popular, even with mainstream audiences (e.g. Smith 2000). In response to the ongoing singularity in hegemonic discourses of 'race', and the binary structure that underpins most models of difference and discrimination, it is inevitable that some will choose to focus on narratives of genealogical plurality, more specifically to call on the discourse of 'family heritage'.

Mixed Up Kids and Feckless Families

The sociology of families has been under gendered scrutiny for many years. Feminists have argued that families are a key site for the reproduction of gendered, sexualised oppression.[7] In Britain, families as a site of conflict, and lone mothers (and absent fathers) as a source of concern, both contain 'hidden' discourses of 'race' and/or class. Sociologists have centralised the family when investigating 'race', and responded to the potential racialisation of normative family models (e.g. Phoenix 1997; Lawrence 1982). In response to (white) feminist criticisms of family life as 'bad for women', writing on ethnicity and families has often been linked to an antiracist project which positions 'the family' as *support* in racist society. North American feminists suggested that 'Women scholars of color have mounted the most serious challenges to universalistic theory. They have documented the historical experiences of communities of color, and therefore the differing cultural contexts and material conditions under which mothering has been carried out' (Glenn 1994: 5).

There has yet to be such a concerted effort in such areas in Britain, even though there is writing on ethnicity that does this work.[8] Patricia Hill Collins believes that mothering in racist societies is about nothing less than survival: 'Emphasizing how the quest for self-definition is mediated by membership in different and racial and social class groups reveals how the issues of identity are crucial to all motherwork' (Hill Collins 1994: 62). This approach emphasises the potential strength of ethnic certainty within a family, and the question of racilised identity is taken for granted as a singular one. Centralising multiplicity raises a number of problems for such a position, and can be explored through the debates about transracial adoption.

Coconuts and Bounty Bars

It has been noted that there are high levels of failure in interracial relationships, and there are particular tensions that arise which may not be overcome by 'love knowing no colour' (Jordan 1983; Grearson and Smith 1995; Alibhai Brown and Montague 1992; Breger and Hill 1998). There are also disproportionately high numbers of children of 'mixed-race' in care and awaiting adoption, many of whom may have been categorised as 'black' in the past (Boushel 1996). Throughout the 1980s the debates about transracial adoption in Britain hit right at the crux of the unanswered questions about how we acquire identity, and in particular 'racial' identity within families. Up until the early 1980s it had been acceptable to place black children with white families if there were no suitable black families for them. This policy was challenged on the basis that young children were not being brought up to 'be black'. Specifically, they often had no knowledge of a black cultural heritage and it was thought that this could lead to problems in later life.

I have already commented at length on the discourse that suggests that lack of a *correct* 'racial identity' can lead to poor mental health for those of mixed-race, and, of course, these concerns hold true for the placement of children 'outside' of their 'racial groups' (e.g. Owen and Gill 1983; BAAF 1987; Gaber and Aldridge 1994; Lal 2001). Olumide suggests that criticisms of 'cross-race' placements reinforce 'scientific racism' of the early part of the century, centring as they do on failure and 'pathological bonding' of different 'racial types' (Small, cited by Olumide 1996: 360). However, her research shows that: 'It appears that [families containing people considered to be racially different] do not so much damage one another as receive damaging attacks and affronts to their *social legitimacy*' (Olumide 1996: 355; emphasis added).

Transracial adoption is often bound up with concerns about 'national' and 'ethnic' identifications as it implies that black people (for example) must automatically have a *different* and bounded culture that came from different 'roots' than those of white Britons, and that this cultural knowledge is passed on through 'the family'. Children of transracial placements suffer name-calling – 'Bounty Bar' and 'coconut' were and still are pejorative terms to describe black people raised by white middle-class families who took on those families' values.[9] Such individuals often faced hostility from both white racist society and the black communities who felt betrayed by them in the era of 'political identity politics' of that period of British race history. Despite the abandonment of such identity politics, the discussions remind us of the ways in which some kind of 'colourism' can be a powerful force within identity acquisition.

What seems to me to be of great significance in these arguments is the meaning of 'blackness'. Is blackness only *authenticated* through culture? A person may take on 'white' middle-class *culture* and it is that aspect that can cause rejection on the basis of 'authenticity' from black communities. Simultaneously, they may still suffer racism from whites, which cannot be based on cultural difference, but is about the colour of their skin. There is a very basic fear/aggression towards those who are very clearly *visually* Other. I would be loathe to identify myself with those who are accused by Clive Harris (1996) of 'ocularcentrism'; nor do I believe that we should throw the baby out with the bath water by minimising the power of the visual in motivations for everyday acts of racism. What is important for my own work is that, yet again, these debates were dominated by the black/white binary and failed to investigate *how* ethnicity informs 'race' and vice-versa. This means we are back in the realms of essentialising accounts of 'racial' identity. It is only by taking a deconstructive, post-race analysis to these phenomena that we can better understand how these visual signs work to re-cognise 'race' even as we try to undermine it.

New Ethnicities and Post-race Mixed-Race

> This just might be a suitable time to break the foundational oscillation between biology
> and culture, to open the closed circuit that analyses of what we used to call the New
> Racism have become. (Gilroy 2000: 57)

To understand the possibilities of mixed identities, we must draw upon a range
of terms including 'ethnicity', 'culture' and 'nationality'. My use of the term
'post-race' thinking emphasises deconstructive approaches to identities, and
draws on theories of performativity, passing and new ethnicities which I outline
below. I will show how 'traditional' accounts of new ethnicities still draw on
recognisable 'race', and move on to argue that although poststructuralist
accounts of identities and identification are usefully employed within theories of
post-race 'hybridities', passing and performativity, they seem bound to the
binary frames of psychoanalytic thinking and therefore need further development in order to be useful to the data I work with in this book.

Conventional analyses of ethnicity often emphasise the collective nature of
ethnic allegiances.

> Ethnicity at its most general level means belonging to a particular group and sharing
> its conditions of existence. This will include not only being regarded as having the right
> credentials for membership, but also being able to muster ethnic resources which can
> be used for struggle negotiation and the pursuit of political projects both at the level of
> individuals making their way, but also for the group as whole in relation to other
> groups. Ethnic resources can be economic, territorial, cultural, and linguistic amongst
> others. (Anthias and Yuval-Davis 1993: 8)

It is these, the group constructions of belonging and not-belonging, of being
included and excluded, that are most relevant to the analysis of inter-ethnic,
'mixed-race', inter-national identities, not because they *facilitate* ethnic
belonging but precisely because they are *problematic* in their centralisation of
communities, groups and boundaries. Nick (my brother), Lisa (my sister) and I,
by my mother's admission, received a 'white upbringing' – something that she
says she now regrets. My father had, in his brief time with the family, shown a
desire for Westernisation and Britishness. For him, England was the Motherland,
but when he arrived from Trinidad in the 1950s he experienced prejudice and
hostility. He decided that as we lived in England, we should be as English as
possible in order to avoid discrimination, a position my mother agreed with at the
time. In this, the 'cultural' influences in our lives were overwhelmingly 'white
English', and our ethnic identifications at odds with our 'racial identifications'.
This is another reason for my continued engagement with processes of racialisa-

tion, even when drawing upon post-race thinking.

Cultural Studies has provided a range of exciting developments for examining 'new ethnicities', and with them, the potential for post-race thinking which helps us to consider mixedness in less essentialising ways than in the past. Paul Gilroy suggests that 'culture' is 'a field articulating the life world of subjects (albeit de-centred) and the structures created by human activity' (cited by Frankenberg 1993: 194). Stuart Hall's definition includes 'the actual grounded terrain of prac-tices, representations, languages and customs of any specific historical society' (cited in ibid.). These definitions provide a useful way to consider cultural prac-tices that inform mixedness.

The role of culture is central to Stuart Hall's influential work on 'new ethnic-ities'. Hall suggested that we can no longer identify a unified, simple 'black Subject ... stabilised by Nature or by some other essential guarantee' (S. Hall 1992: 257) He argues: 'it must be the case that they [black subjects] are constructed historically, culturally, politically – the concept that this refers to is ethnicity' (ibid.). Hall undoubtedly moves the debates on, but my impression is that he is speaking to an audience who will still know themselves to be specifi-cally 'black British'. This is in spite of his attempts to reposition (black) Britishness as born out of a kind of cultural plurality that constantly creates new and dynamic forms. While the recognition of cultural translation is useful, I still do not recognise my 'mixedness' in these 'new ethnicities'. 'Black' calls upon an old recognisable 'racial' category and, while not supporting it, interpellates an identification with a skin colour. 'British' tells us that this is a citizen of a country who claims a national identity; however, this subverts not only the hege-monic discourses of nationality as conjoined with 'whiteness' but also that white-ness in conjunction with Britishness implies 'racial superiority' (Anthias and Yuval Davis 1993: 41). 'Culture' in this case is seen as constructing both iden-tity and ethnicity, yet ethnicities that are formed through cultural practices must surely have some claim on being 'cultural identities'. Moreover, in a great deal of work on cultural practices in relation to the term 'new ethnicities' there is an implicit gendering at work that is not made clear. In terms of youth, this is almost always dominated by masculinities (Hewitt 1986; Gilroy 1987; Jones 1988; Back 1996). Finally, I believe that in order for this idea to work a fairly sophisticated 'knowing self' must surely 'choose' and recognise this position over others. Despite these reservations, Hall's analysis provides a useful way of moving on from essentialising (or racialising) theories of ethnicity.

New ethnicities are not simply additions to existing forms, they are evolved and metamorphosed in relation to '*cultural* hybrids'. Homi Bhabha suggests that cultural hybridity develops not from 'two original moments from which the third emerges, rather hybridity is ... the "third space" which enables the other posi-tions to emerge' (Bhabha 1990a: 211). This is a difficult concept to grasp, but

Bhabha goes on to argue that '[If] the act of cultural translation (both as representation and as reproduction) denies the essentialism of a prior given or original culture, then we can see all forms of culture are continually in a process of hybridity' (ibid.: 210). This more recognisable aspect of his work offers great potential for deconstructing multiethnic positions in society and may also be of use in investigating self-claimed 'mixed-race' positions. It is a clear statement of rejection of the biologism of hybridity, and whilst I remain ambivalent about the term, the emphasis on the *process* of cultural change is useful. Bhabha's work also shifts the emphasis from essentialising discourses of 'race' and the kind of 'ethnic absolutism' that replaces 'race' with 'culture' (Gilroy 2000). Gilroy cautions against complacency in language and its use in analyses of hybridity, arguing that

> We do not have to be content with the halfway house provided by the idea of plural cultures. A theory of relational cultures and culture as relation represents a more worthwhile resting place. That possibility is currently blocked by banal invocations of hybridity in which everything becomes equally and continuously intermixed, blended into an impossibly even consistency. (Gilroy 2000: 275)

My autobiographical work supports this caution. Without a strong 'cultural input' from our father, a Muslim with both Indian and Trinidadian colonial genealogies in his family history, my siblings and I had all questioned *cultural* absences and *ethnic* 'belonging' throughout our lives.

Lisa (my sister) said that a lack of understanding about her 'other' family (on our father's side), and more importantly what they represent, is a 'part of me I've missed out on, and I don't hold anyone responsible for that. I never really thought about it before – we lived with Mum, I viewed myself as white English' (Lisa: interview, March 1995). I was shocked that she could say so nonchalantly that she had at one time thought of herself as white. She went on to explain that she had felt extremely confused about her identity before reaching her present understanding. This may seem to bear out the concerns for the 'mixed-race' child as implied by Peggy, or indeed the range of 'experts' as above, but in fact neither she nor I felt that it had been an insurmountable problem. For Lisa it did not overtake other sources of difficulty in life – for example, being female.

My brother Nick said that he had thought about his identity in terms of 'race' but had not felt it 'in a concentrated sort of angst sort of fashion, but it's something as I said before about … discovering yourself and trying a different uniform or different clothes – clothes metaphorically … How you look I consider part of your identity … – I think people prefer attractive people, sad but true.' Nick's sense of himself as someone who can use discourses of 'race' to creatively explore bodily appearance, and his realisation that being a good-looking 'exotic' could work in his favour, was also something that my sister mentioned. The work of 'performing "race"' is particularly clear here. In this case Nick and Lisa both place it in the realm of the cognitive, and both link it to gender. I believe that they also reveal some level of performativity, given that 'performativity must be understood not as a singular "act", but, rather as the reiterative and citational practice by which discourse produces the effects that it names' (Butler 1993: 2).

Butler's work here is focused upon 'sex' and its companionate term 'gender'. Performativity is used by her to destabilise and subvert bodies tied to normative heterosexuality. She argues:

> In other words, acts, gestures and desire produce the effect of an internal core or substance, but produce this *on the surface of the body*, through the play of signifying absences that suggest but never reveal, the organising principle of identity as a cause. Such acts, gestures and enactment, generally construed, are performative in the sense that the essence or identity that they otherwise purport to express are *fabrications* manufactured and sustained through corporeal signs and other discursive means. (Butler 1990: 136)

It may be that in this sense 'race' can also seen to be performative. Butler herself argues later in *Bodies that Matter* that racialisation may be incorporated into what constitutes the performative, and asks 'how might we understand homo-sexuality and miscegenation to converge at and as the constitutive outside of a normative heterosexuality that is at once the regulation of a racially pure repro-duction?' (Butler 1993: 167).

In my own reassessments of my raciality I believe that the normative frame-works of raced gender and gendered race can best be fruitfully challenged in this way and we can then begin to understand the *materialisation* of racial discourses. Butler's writing provides a major impetus into thinking through the possibilities of post-race positions. She explores the issue of 'race' through literary accounts of 'passing'. Her work is limited by two main constraints. Firstly, she outlines her theoretical framework within the binaries of blackness and whiteness, and move-ment between the two, and so limits the possibilities of and for multiplicity. Secondly, she consider the ways in which both gender and 'race' are classed, no matter how problematic a term it may be. This impacts upon her work but does not obviate the importance of the theory as an analytical tool. In relation to mixedness in my sibling's accounts, 'passing' implied room for *choice* – for example Nick's comments above – but a choice to be what or whom, he could not say for certain. This is a direct result of his shifting class identifications, discussed further below.

A Passing Phase?

The incident with Peggy also illustrates how a person of 'mixed-race' may indeed pass as white, or in some way become an 'honorary white' if the rest of their social credentials fit in with that of the hegemonic discourses of cultural and national acceptability. I have in the past been mistakenly identified as Chinese, Japanese, Italian, Greek, German, Spanish, 'white English' and, once, when my hair was bleached blonde, Swedish. Of course at other times I have simply been a 'nigger' or a 'paki'. People have difficulty in placing 'mixed-race' individuals and will often rely on erroneous visual signs to guide them. If one 'passes' for white one may then be privy to the racist beliefs that are held by those in whose company one finds oneself. Either Peggy 'forgot' I was 'mixed-race' or she simply thought I was white enough to make those comments.[10] Whatever the reasons, her basis for racial inclusion or exclusion, to being like or not like, is based at least in part upon physical appearance as well as cultural markers such as clothes and accents. I imagine that the cultural differences between Peggy's son and a young black British woman who grew up on the same London estate are comparatively small compared to many other forms of social and cultural difference, but her blackness is a cipher, a mark of something much deeper for Peggy; it was racialisation in process.

My siblings and I realised that we had at times *been able* to 'pass' as white, but had neither *chosen* to 'pass' through some conscious desire to join the privileged (white) group, nor as 'an avoidance response to the conflicts of dual racial membership' (Bradshaw 1992: 79). We did not think that we were actively 'subverting the comportment line between the dominant and subordinate, and the arbitrary line between white and black' (Daniel 1992: 92). Rather, we found ourselves negotiating identities around multiple influences and being attributed by others to multiple positions. Sara Ahmed writes:

> The difference between the black subject who passes as white and the white subject who passes as white is not then an essential difference that exists before passing. Rather, it is a structural difference that demonstrates that passing involves the reopening or restaging of a fractured history of identifications that constitutes the limits to a given subject's mobility. (Ahmed 2000: 127)

In the experience of the person of multiple mixed origins the binaries of black and white may not speak to their 'passing'. In addition I wish to emphasise that the process of passing is often embedded in encounters that the subjects cannot and/or do not acknowledge as existent.[11] Throughout my life I have '*been passed*' by others as a whole range of possible ethnicities, and it is in these moments that the *structural* elements of the ability to pass are emphasised. That others may pass me without my knowledge is even more possible, and in this too operates as a reinforcement of existing structures of difference. My siblings expressed concerns about 'authenticity', without necessarily using that word, and feelings of 'disloyalty or incongruity'(Bradshaw 1992: 82) – again implied – to our racial and cultural heritages, especially as we had all when younger, even if only for a moment, thought we were 'white'. But both my sister and myself have also thought of ourselves as black. Although passing as 'mixed' is still difficult, some try to achieve this, and are *active* as 'passers' claiming mixed-race identities. Given the colonial history of passing as 'mixed', one important aspect of this work is the necessity to think through the meaning of whiteness as a 'racial' or ethnic identity.

Studies of whiteness over the last decade have largely been set within a North American framework, and David Roediger's (1992, 1994) work has been foundational to the 'New Abolitionist project' for 'the end of whiteness' (Ware and Back 2002: 3). The addition of whiteness as a category for analysis undoubtedly challenges past sloppy terminology that implied ethnic = not-white, and helps with studying the articulation of 'race', ethnicity and culture in gendered and classed individuals and their families. In Britain studies of whiteness have been linked to studies of class, and early cultural studies of class were also male dominated (e.g. Willis 1975; Cohen 1979). By investigating the contextual locatedness of women's lives, their embodied and affective experience and their own accounts of 'mobility' and acceptance, feminist researchers have begun to fill in the gaps left by traditional 'gender-neutral' studies of class.[12] Feminist cultural theorists have shown that '*the experience of class*' is still central to lives of many women (Skeggs 1997: 74; emphasis added). What is most powerful in these approaches are the ways in which women negotiate the complexities and contradictions inherent in any kind of identity work. Thus, the way in which class is gendered is theorised by the respondents themselves and a political cultural validation takes place. A recurrent theme of this work is the uncertain and often transitory nature of class identification, which can be characterised by themes of both stasis and movement. Skeggs (and others) have found Bourdieu's concepts of field, habitus and capital useful, given that 'class' as a term incorporates the economic, social and cultural. Diane Reay offers those unfamiliar with Bourdieu's arguments clear and succinct overviews of his key concepts, and, more importantly, meticulous and creative examples of the theory of practice (e.g. Reay 1995, 1997, 1998). Elsewhere I have discussed in detail the difficulties with looking at the way in which class is *constitutive* of ethnicity, and vice versa (Ali 2003b). This is essential if we are to avoid reinstating essentialist versions of 'race' by simply inserting a word like 'white' in front of working and middle class, without investigating what it is that is 'white' about them. I don't claim to have found the answer to this particular problem but remain committed to the investigation.

The encounter with Peggy was, as I have stated, undoubtedly influenced by a sense of our relative class positionings. It is also true that my siblings' discussions about the performative nature of 'race' are heavily influenced by class, which can also be understood as performative. It is the final part of the puzzle that completes the matrix of identifications. For my own mother, class was central to her sense of social positioning. As a white girl, growing up in a very white and "snooty … fairly rich" environment in post-war Britain, class was important and openly discussed with her parents:

Suki: What would you say your class was?

Mother: Well, [your] Granddad was obviously working class however I think your grandma had delusions of grandeur and I think [laughing] she really sort of put us into middle class. [She explains that my granddad was successful because 'he was a very astute business man despite having left school at thirteen'] so I think Grandma liked to think we were perhaps, by then … certainly lower middle class.

Suki: Why don't you think you were?

Mother: Well, simply because my father was a working-class man. I mean I certainly had the *upbringing* of a middle-class child … [laughs] I don't know.

My mother embodies the ability to shift positioning in both her own mind and the eyes of others. She started by expressing, as have others, that '[c]lass is something beneath your clothes, under your skin, in your reflexes, in your psyche, at the very core of your being' (Kuhn 1995: 98). For her it truly was something in her 'blood', unexplainable but real, inherited from her father. My sister and brother both understand our early childhood as 'poor' and therefore working class. However, they both mentioned that our own and our mother's education moved us into the middle classes. They show a recognition of a 'fractured class background' that I perceived, and that I believe we all described in one way or another, from 'cross-class' perspectives (Spence 1991: 228, 230). Peggy had known something of this history, but in relation to her own life the role of my brother as her employer meant that to her we were unproblematically middle class. We had the right kind of cultural and social capital to warrant that positioning. One of the key markers for both her and my family was education. Education, style and manners – what could also be identified with cultural and ethnic processes – mitigated against our being 'coloured' in some respects, but possibly added to the distance Peggy felt from us. The autobiographical material also points to the ways in which we as children had ideas that may have seemed 'illogical', that we rethought as both adolscents and adults. In addition to the lack of empirical data available, this was a compelling reason for me to work with children in this research.

What binds all of these debates into a theoretical and practical mesh are questions of identity, or more specifically, *identification*. The issues discussed above begin to show that 'identification turns out to be one of the least well-understood concepts – almost as tricky as, though preferable to identity itself: and certainly no guarantee against the conceptual difficulties that have beset the latter' (Hall 1996:2).

The autobiographical material I have used in this chapter is the most immediate way I know to introduce the themes of the book and to explore these connections between the concepts of post-race and the lived experience of mixedness: '[an] autobiography has both humanistic and post-structuralist elements. As a site of interplay between the humanistic vision of autonomous egos and postmodernist decentred selves, actual autobiographies stand at the intersection of the individual and the social, of agency and culture' (Usher 1998: 21).

This book investigates social and cultural processes of racialising ethnicity and class from the position that gender and heterosexuality are central to these formulations in the lives of children and their significant others. In the next section I will outline the structure of the book and content of the following chapters.

Outline of the Chapters

The book follows the themes outlined above through the data collected in schools with children and teachers, and later with families. In the next chapter I introduce the school contexts in which initial encounters with children were made. I will begin to outline how my own engagement with ethical and political practices influenced methodological choices. I wanted the children's voices to be heard above all else because of the ways in which autobiographies and their *representations* are important sources of 'marginalised' knowledge; moreover, 'the ontological and epistemological links between them is a particularly suitable ground for a feminist political analysis to be built on' (Stanley 1992: 3). Children were not asked to 'write' their lives, but to 'speak' them and, given the limits to language as outlined above, to visualise them. This multi-methods approach will be outlined in the chapter, along with some of the key forms of analysis that were used with children primarily but also with parents and teachers.

Chapters 3 to 7 detail respondents' accounts of 'identification' in the social sense, as constituted through everyday cultural processes and practices. Working with children in these areas required innovative methodological interventions. I researched a range of commonplace activities that take place within the home and at school; the use of artefacts, music and cuisine to name but a few. This broad range of everyday experience of culture is used throughout this research, as Richard Johnson suggests that *'All social practices* can be looked at from a cultural point of view, for the work they do subjectively' (Johnson 1983: 581), and that 'reservoirs of discourses and meanings ... are indeed among the specifically cultural *conditions* of production' (ibid.: 583).

The focus of this book is the *production of*, and *conditions of production* of culture as lived by the children. As a way 'into' these areas of study, the children were invited to talk about the way they read popular culture, about their patterns of consumption and their likes and dislikes. It proved to be a rich and interesting vein of the data and will be explored in Chapters 3 and 4.

Chapter 3 details how children understand representations of 'race' in their everyday encounters with the popular. I asked children of 'mixed-race' about whether they were represented in popular culture and began to question how we understand the ways in which children choose to talk about 'racial' identity in popular representations. Children talked animatedly about their consumption and how this in part informed their constructions of self through collective readings and friendship groups. In this chapter, the first interviews with groups of children reveal some of these processes at work, and show how children used these readings in order to discuss 'forbidden topics' such as sexuality.

In Chapter 4 the more personal and individualised readings and imaginings of the children of 'mixed-race' are developed. Throughout, the importance of bodies and emotionally engaged judgements about visuality are interrogated. Through performativity, reading and re-reading visual texts and other cultural practices children are developing identifications by how they present themselves in relation to others, including family. Verbal and visual material from and of parents and families form the basis of analysis in Chapter 5.

In Chapter 5 I will show how mothers provided resources for identity work within familial genealogies as well as wider societies. This chapter details daily cultural practices that take place in the home, and tells some of the family stories that provides such resources. In all cases the ways in which 'family practices' are dynamic and productive provide the central platform for the analysis. In particular, the relevance of class reveals itself to be central to understanding accounts of cultural processes in families.

The meaning of belonging and the ways in which 'home' is conceptualised by the children is developed in Chapter 6. Children and adults reveal the importance of generational and geographical/social changes within the families to understanding multiply identified selves. The research findings suggest that children are consciously exploring the implications of discourses of home and belonging for 'mixed-race' identities. Children's and parent's understandings are investigated in relation to theories of 'diaspora' and 'diaspora space' (Brah 1996), and how we need to think of these with issues of class and gender. Again the importance of the translation of meanings into everyday contexts proves highly heterogeneous.

As meanings of 'race' have changed so too have those of 'racism', and this forms the basis for children's learning in schools. In Chapter 7 I will explore the use of terminology and its importance to children's understandings of how differences (and samenesses) between them include and exclude them from group/social identities. The meanings of 'multiculturalism' and 'antiracism' as perceived by children and teachers show such terms to be problematic for children working with modern multiethnic identities.

Finally, in the concluding chapter, I will revisit some of the writing on 'race' and post-race possibilities which informed the research and writing process, and consider how the findings have implications for these areas and future research. The children themselves show the lack in existing terminologies and the importance of using known family histories to make partial sense of 'racial' selves. The research also shows how fluid the perceptions of selves are and how the dominant 'racial' and ethnic categorisations children face are untenable to their own positions. Children reveal a desire to reject the model of singular 'racial' identity, and the way in which mixedness is a process of negotiation. I argue that the ways in which children work within proscribed discursive registers *are* creative, but often necessarily reinforce existing categorisations. The only way to move *beyond* racialised constraints is to begin a process of deconstruction (one that is often charged with being a-political), and to engage with the possibility of post-race futures. Children and families are often engaged in this process in overtly political and potentially destabilising ways.

Mixed-Race Post-race challenges the tenacity of 'singularity' within the hegemonic 'race' rhetoric, binaried ways of thinking and limits to language which deny possibilities for mixed identifications. I raise questions about the meaning of 'the politics of race' through the accounts of children, and, to a lesser extent, parents and teachers. Like Paul Gilroy (2000) I believe we need 'to free ourselves from the bonds of raciology' and 'compulsory raciality'. This book adds resources to support the process of broadening our understanding of new ethnicities, making better use of post-race thinking in ordinary contexts and raising awareness of their limitations for those who are already engaged with the daily practice of post-race living in a raced world.

Notes

1. My mother is white-English and my father Caribbean-Indian. I know that this description is problematic, and it is this constant reinvoking of biological race, re-racialisation, that the book explores. I imagine that 'Caribbean' will imply both 'race' and ethnicity, and that 'Indian' will imply brown-ness, 'race', as well as nation, culture, and so on. The slippage in these terms is often unavoidable but should not be left unnoticed.

2. Due to limitations of space I cannot review the writings on mixedness in detail. I would refer the reader to Alibhai-Brown (2001) and Olumide (2002) for comprehensive overviews of both histories and theories in the British context. In the USA, the collections by Naomi Zack (1993, 1995) and Maria Root (1992, 1996) contain a wealth of writing which includes that of Paul Spickard, Omi and Winant, Frank Furedi, and other key thinkers. The texts I discuss here have a particular role to play in my own work as contained within this book.
3. In addition to these texts the Zeena Ralf Memorial Fund has produced an annotated bibliography on these issues (Suriya 2000).
4. This incident was widely reported in the national newspapers but I have been unable to find the exact date.
5. 'Mixed: A New Category for the Census', Institute of Education, London, August 2002.
6. Whilst this is being completed, the new Census information has been made available. Initial studies show a continued increase in those claiming mixed identities.
7. See for example Ferri (1976), Driver and Droisen (1989), Phoenix *et al* (1991), Elliot (1996), Jagger and Wright (1999).
8. Again there is a history of responses to the inadequacy of theorising families from white, middle-class research data. For many families of minority ethnic status families are also a source of strength in a racist society, even though the same kinds of micro-political problems occur. See e.g. Lawrence (1982), Bryan *et al.* (1985), Phoenix (1989), Joseph (1981).
9. The term 'Oreo' operates in the same way in the USA.
10. I do not believe that Peggy wanted to insult me personally at that moment. If she had wanted to I think she would have been more open, or simply not talked to me in the first place. My impression is that she did not think of me as black, but as 'coloured' in some way.
11. See Carol-Ann Tyler's (1994) discussion of Adrian Piper's (1998) autobiographical account of her 'passing'. See also Sarah Ahmed's autobiographical work and her theoretical work on 'hybridity' and 'passing' (Ahmed 1997, 1999, 2000).
12. It is not possible to provide overviews of all the feminist work on class. Throughout the book I will focus on selected texts from Hey (1997), Lawler (2000), Reay (1998), Skeggs (1997), Walkerdine (1997) and Walkerdine *et al.* 2001).

–2–

Researching the Unresearchable

It is not individuals who have experiences, but subjects who are *constituted through experience*.

J. Scott 'Experience', emphasis added

Introduction

Researching the ways in which children (aged 8–11) make meaning from discursive repertoires of 'race' and ethnicity presented a particularly difficult set of methodological issues. In the first chapter, I showed how terminology relating to these issues is opaque and often used interchangeably. In addition, the relationships between what can be said about multiplicities is often a list of additive descriptors which brings us no nearer to understanding the experiences of mixedness. In order to try to counteract the potential limitations of verbal accounts provided by interviews alone, I drew upon a range of methods for understanding children and families, including the use of visual methods. In this chapter I will outline the development of these epistemological and practical difficulties and how they affected the methods of research, particularly with children.

One of the most critical aspects of the research process was my own position within it and how it informed what I did. This and an awareness of my own representational power over the children (and parents and teachers) were the main elements of what I would loosely term ethical dilemmas. The research processes developed with a constant concern for the most sensitive way to access children's use of the discourses of 'race', ethnicity and culture as they worked them with and through their gendered, classed identifications. In the following sections I will show how accessing both schools and children in order to explore understandings and discussions of racialisation and identity was inflected by a range of theoretical issues. I will start by introducing the schools in which the research was carried out. Exploring meanings of 'identity' in young children meant encouraging them to speak for themselves. In order to achieve *that* I needed to develop a level of trust that facilitated open dialogue, yet I had a limited amount of time because of obvious pragmatic reasons.

Despite concerns over what may or may not be considered valid in my own responses to the children, the only way for me to access their perceptions and understandings was to use predominantly qualitative research methods. In order to access the data I required to explore the questions outlined, I used a feminist ethnographic framework: 'Whilst ethnography is a theory of the research process, ethnography itself is defined by its relationship to theoretical positions, hence feminist ethnography' (Skeggs 1994: 76). Ethnographic research often employs a variety of qualitative (and quantitative) methods (Hammersley and Atkinson 1983), and in this instance most of the data presented and the ensuing analysis is qualitative.

Data collection was only the start of an ongoing engagement with managing interpretation and analysis of data. After describing access and processes of data collection I will go on to discuss the frameworks of analysis I employed.

> The notion of a theory as a toolkit means: (i) The theory to be constructed is not a system but an instrument, a logic of the specificity of the power relations and the struggles around them; (ii) That this investigation can only be carried out step by step on the basis of reflection (which will necessarily be historical in some of its aspects) on given situations. (Foucault 1980: 145)

In this case the toolkit approach extends to the production and analysis of data as an 'instrument' for investigation of the 'power relations' of mixedness.

Accessing Schools: Getting Started

I have tried contacting primary schools to arrange times convenient to pilot material. I approached ********** school through my personal contact with the deputy head, Julie. She suggested that I send a letter to her explaining what the project was about and that she would speak to the head teacher. I asked if I could video tape any kind of end of school performance that may have been taking place, and if I could pilot some questions before the end of the Christmas term and then possibly carry out some field-work at the school in the Spring term. The head asked to see the questions, which were faxed to her. When I finally spoke to her some few days later, she refused to let me into the school because she said it was too close to the end of term but mainly that the questions were inappropriate. In fact she said, 'You can't ask children questions like that.'

Her objections were that the questions were too personal, that families would object, that I would not know whether the children were telling me what I wanted to hear, that it may be disruptive for them and so on. I asked if I could at least come to video the end of school play and she said 'Oh well we haven't really got one as such, we'll probably just put something together at the last minute.' I took that as a definite 'no'. Later, I spoke to a mutual friend who asked a few things about my work and said why didn't I ask this Head about going into school blah blah. I said that I already had and that she didn't want me in the school and my friend said 'I don't think it was you, I think it was the questions', as though if I just would change my questions it would be alright. I think that changing my questions means changing my research entirely. (Research Diary June 1997)

This extract shows the foundations to my fears that the research was simply not possible on a number of levels, that the question was quite literally 'unresearchable' for a number of reasons, including terminological ambiguity, sensitivity of the topic, children as unreliable respondents, as unable to respond, and so on. Despite the resistance of the first three schools I approached, I persevered until I got some positive responses. I worked with three schools, two in London in a multiethnic location and one in Kent, South East England, in a mostly 'white area'.

The Schools

Christie School (all schools have been given pseudonyms) in London was the first school to which I gained access, and the first from which data was collected. It is situated in a borough of London that has high levels of poverty, and not coincidentally a highly diverse ethnic population. The school is on a small road in an area of mixed affluence and is very close to both a large number of African-Caribbean residents, as well as significant numbers of people of South Asian decent. It is on the edge of a Jewish community, many of whom live and work in the street in which the school stands.

The school had been in a state of crisis for two years since the old head teacher resigned, no new head was in place at the time of the research, and the school had severe financial difficulties. The acting head (who had previously been a classroom teacher in the school) was being supported by a member of the LEA, and she was also heavily involved in the day-to-day management of the school as well as recruitment of the new head and long-term policy development.

The school building, an old two-storey, purpose-built edifice, houses all the classrooms and halls and incorporates the kitchen and dining area, which looked to have been added later. Outside, the play area consisted of a tarmac playground with a section in front of the staff room fenced off for the infants. The building appears to be rather run down, but all of the classrooms and corridors were well decorated with children's work, which provided the light and colour. Posted at various points around the school in the corridors were 'The Golden Rules', which provided guidelines for the behaviour expected of the children. These were produced with the full involvement of the children, working together with staff, and were also sent out to parents.

The school is medium sized compared to many in the area, with approximately 450 pupils from nursery age through to Year 6. The pupil population was approximately one-third African-Caribbean, one-third South Asian, with the remaining one-third being predominantly white 'Anglo' (English, Irish, Scottish or Welsh) and Turkish, with some Pacific Asian and several 'mixed' pupils.

One of my first activities in all schools that agreed to take part was to film the 'Christmas Play'. As an introduction to the schools these provided a surprisingly accurate predictor to the value base, awareness and importance accorded to religious and cultural diversity within the school. These in turn revealed how central concerns about 'multiculturalism' and antiracism were within the curriculum and school policies.

At Christie they presented 'The Late Wise Man', a less than conventional Christian nativity play with some general humanist morals running throughout which were heavily emphasised. The majority of the performers were black and South Asian and Turkish, with only one or two white children taking part. The choir was made up of a cross section of children and the music was provided by a member of staff playing the piano. The performance was held in the School Hall and was well attended by friends and families. It gave me an opportunity to do some rather less participant observation. It provided a fairly safe middle ground upon which everyone could stand. The Christian traditions were balanced with more general 'storytelling' that drew on the secularised themes of good and evil, greed and generosity and so managed to feel more inclusive of a range of cultural and ethnic positions.

Barnlea School is in the same borough of London as Christie, and therefore shares some of the features in terms of pupil profiles. It is a large old Victorian school standing in a playground in the middle of a residential area, which has a wide racial and ethnic mix. As with most areas of London, there are streets containing quite expensive housing very near to those with council-owned properties and high-rise estates. The school reflects this variety in as much that it has some pupils from 'middle-class', higher-income families, unlike Christie, where the vast majority of pupils are from more 'working-class', low-income families.

The school is large, with over 600 pupils. At the time of the research there had been recent intakes of Eastern European refugee children, including some Roma children. Throughout 1998 several Monserratians fleeing the volcano erruption were admitted to the school. Like Christie, the building is old and therefore some of the classrooms and facilities are quite dark, and like Christie every square inch of wall was decorated with beautifully coloured pieces of children's work. There are three floors and several different doors to the building which are kept locked apart for break times. The gate to the playground is unlocked and again there is an entry-phone system in operation (as at Christie), although when I was there the main door, which is overlooked by the reception desk, was often left open. The playground is divided into two areas for infants and juniors (children between four and seven years old), but with no fencing or gate between.

The school concert held at the end of the winter term made no reference to Christmas or Christianity and was a celebration of 'Light'. Every member of every class took part and the sheer scale meant that there were two slightly different performances. The classes all presented some kind of music, dance, song or poetry, with some members taking a more active role than others did. The children, under the direction of the music teacher, provided the choir and music. The whole show had material that came from all over the world and was 'highly multicultural'. Again this approach to the school concert reflected the active engagement with the issue of diversity, and what might be called a more 'progressive' attitude to cultural plurality amongst pupils and their families. It will be seen in the next chapter (and Chapter 7) that in many ways the school had the most successful record and approach to 'racism' and 'race'.

Fairsham School is in Woodvale,[1] a small village near a commuter town in South East England, outside London. The school sits on the corner of a residential road and one of the main roads that runs to the town. It is a modern, single-storey building with several prefabricated huts also acting as classrooms. It has off-road parking for staff and is surrounded by a high hedge. It has both hard playgrounds and lawns surrounding it, as well as a small school garden with a pond. There is also a small covered swimming pool. The head has been there for several years but is still seen as quite new and 'progressive'. He repealed the rule banning female members of staff from wearing trousers two years before the research took place. The staff members are all white and the majority of the children are white and middle class. There are several white children who have one parent from other European or northern hemisphere countries and are therefore 'international', and a handful of children of minority ethnic background. There are two Japanese and two Chinese students, one of East African Asian descent and four who identified as being 'mixed-race'.

I attended the school nativity play, which was held in the local church and was called 'Christmas Throughout The Ages'. It involved about thirty of the children, with more in the chorus, and piano accompaniment by a member of staff. The whole performance was very 'traditional', with the more accomplished members of the cast acting as 'poor Cockneys' and 'Arabs' as well as 'normal English people'. This they did by affecting accents which were unlike their own 'received pronunciation'. This again neatly encapsulated the school view on matters of religion and culture. It was clearly firmly routed in traditional approaches to all things religious and cultural. On reconsideration, I recognise that even though there may have been the will on the part of some of the staff members to offer less traditional forms of celebration, significant numbers of staff and parents would have disapproved. On the first morning I arrived at the school, as I walked through the playground I could hear a cockerel crowing in a nearby garden, which served to emphasise the semi-rural location. It seemed that the differences between Fairsham and the London schools was to be constantly present in all aspects of the research environment.

Developing Research Relationships

My interaction with the children in the schools was extensive.[2] I attended maths clubs, dance clubs, football clubs, sang with the choirs, ate lunch with the children, rode the Vampire train at Thorpe Park, went to the beach and even went on a week-long residential trip to the country with children from Christie. In short, I had a great time. I believe I got to know something of them and their relationships in school and at home. I felt that we had developed some kind of mutual trust and I had come to genuinely like and respect them. Claire Alexander writes about her ethnographic experience and suggests that establishing research relationships fed her 'already well-rooted misgivings about the possibility – not to mention the wisdom – of achieving constructive relationships within formal research parameters and the significance of such research to those on whom it is based and for whose benefit, presumably, it is carried out' (Alexander 2000: 27). This was a feeling I never overcame. I am not sure whether the children always positioned me as researcher. They may have originally intended to, but our sessions took on a form of their own that was a mixture of interview, informal chat or personal confessional, to name but a few. I believe that this fuzziness was in part due to my own failure to 'control' the context, and partly the young age of the children involved, as they showed a very high level of trust once they had understood that the research would be confidential. Despite this I was never just 'one of the girls' (Hey 1997). I also had to struggle to remember that it is 'important to regard the normal as unfamiliar' (May 1993: 119). I often felt a conflict between being a 'researcher' and being 'me', which intensified when I spoke with the parents.

In the final stages of the research I began accessing parents, who were often suspicious of a researcher coming 'from the school'. However, if I presented myself as independent, this appeared to be even less of a personal recommendation and therefore potentially unsafe. There was a fine balance between school affiliations and independent status that was effective in arranging meetings, and in most cases where direct personal contact could be made, parents agreed to be interviewed. I took to 'hanging out' with children by the entrance to each school at arrival and leaving times and managed to engineer many informal meetings. A few times, teachers who knew that I was working with particular children would point out parents for me or introduce me. In three cases at Fairsham I had to 'cold call' and make telephone arrangements to meet. It should be noted that 'parents' in the overwhelming majority of cases turned out to be mothers. It was mothers who mostly came to the schools and therefore presented opportunities for contact (see Reay 1998). Some of the mothers also arranged for fathers to be present for interviews, who then may not have been able to take part for one reason or another. If the fathers were absent from a great deal of the day-to-day interaction with the children they were also unlikely to present themselves as available to be interviewed.

By going into the homes of the children I moved from one of their cultural spheres to another and it was at times very disconcerting. I had been privy to some of their secrets and parents often wanted to know what children had said, and it was an uncomfortable situation to have to tell them that I could not reveal anything. I also felt like a 'snoop'. I went in to talk to these people and in many cases developed a 'research-friendship' with them, and yet I was simultaneously 'observing' them and taking notes that I recorded afterwards about their house and clothes and furnishings, and so on. Although this was all legitimate data, I could not resolve this feeling of 'betrayal' when I later began to transcribe their words, and my descriptions. I felt that I embodied the fragmented self – 'me the researcher' striving to eradicate power imbalances, and 'me the "mixed-race" person' who just wanted to talk to these people and share experiences with them.

The issue of reciprocity was I believe, central to this dilemma. With the children, I wanted to give something back. I told them their words would be used to try and make things better in the school; that they could have some effect on their school. On a more immediate level I got into the habit of helping them with their work, 'lending' (read: 'giving') them little bits of money, bringing in sweets and biscuits, and mediating in fights. I recognise my own behaviour from other feminist ethnographies (Skeggs 1997; Hey 1997). It was not meant to patronise, nor was it an intentional manipulation of their emotions, yet it undoubtedly had an effect. I did not spend a great deal of time 'counselling' them, but when I left one school a child said: 'Who am I going to talk to now?' and asked for my home telephone number. Despite my best intentions, this is a power imbalance in operation. Quite simply, I had the power to shift to being 'researcher' and walk out and leave them. How would I negotiate 'friendship' in a social situation from having met them in this context? What about accusations of favouritism? These kinds of dilemmas were also presented in my relations with adults. My reciprocity in this case was also felt at an emotional level. With the parents I bargained with myself; with my own life story which I offered up to them in the interviews. I could literally be 'like them' in some cases as there were two mothers in their mid-thirties of 'mixed-race'. We exchanged stories, and I hoped by giving them some of my history they would trust me and see that this research was not about 'Othering', it was about trying to 'know' how things are and what they really mean to real people – like *us*. This kind of personal reciprocity had personal costs as it encouraged questions about my own life and at one interview, when talking about my father's death, I nearly broke down. I know that the researcher and I are one, which has informed my choice of research and the methods I have used in the analysis; I know all that intellectually. I do not believe it makes it any easier to deal with these things when you are actually 'out there' doing it.

Frameworks of Investigation

Feminist concerns with epistemology and ontology, and their application to research, have a long and varied history. From critiquing androcentric 'science as usual' to working within feminist postmodernist frameworks the dynamic nature of feminist writing has positioned itself as one of the most important developments in critical thinking in the last thirty years.[3] Feminist methodological debates have centred around the 'subject of knowledge'. Who can produce knowledge, about whom, and on whose behalf? The 'veracity' of data is the basis for some of the most fundamental debates about epistemology and methodology, and even what is deemed a 'legitimate' area of study (see e.g. Oakley 1974). Feminists and others who are concerned with 'emancipatory research' have criticised the idea of a neutral and observable truth that is simply there to be discovered. In particular, they have challenged the limits of positivist research and the *exclusive* use of quantitative data in social science research projects.[4] This they suggest does little to explain *socially relational* phenomena and may in fact be used in ways that are oppressive for those who are researched. Although there is little agreement as to what 'feminist research' *per se* may be, there is support for a 'feminist mode of enquiry' (Maynard 1994: 10). Maynard suggests that there are 'three major related concerns confronting feminists engaged in empirical social research. These are to do with the role of experience, the importance of 'race' and other forms of diversity, and the question of objectivity' (ibid: 23). These are true of this research. It is the lived experience of the children that is important, and how that is understood and filtered through the subject position occupied by the researcher is of critical importance. In an attempt to explore an area that challenges current thinking about a range of epistemological and ontological concerns, feminist praxis was most appropriate to my research. Feminist standpoint theory argues that the particular position one occupies gives rise to unique insights into the social world. Patricia Hill Collins has suggested that black women are often 'outsiders within' hegemonic white cultures and societies and as such offer unique perspectives on dominant paradigms and discourses, and that 'self-defined standpoints can stimulate resistances' (Hill Collins 1990: 28). Other opinions about the difficulties with theorising from one position have been argued about at length elsewhere (see Harding 1991; Stanley 1990; Stanley and Wise 1993). What has been a more fruitful discussion has been recognition of all knowledge as situated and partial, not total and finite (Haraway 1988).

It is particularly appropriate to the lives of those of 'mixed-race' to try to access their understandings of their 'positionalities' (Alcoff 1997) by using biographical data or, to be more precise, their personal verbal narratives and life histories. Children may be added the to list of those who, 'because of their political position, are not placed to conceal the tensions between their consciousness and the social world when speaking themselves' (Swindells 1995: 4).

The research considered how children chose to represent their lives through a variety of means including discussions about images from popular culture, stories, conversations and domestic photography as it represented their homes, their school life, and their relationships. Stories will not be the same at all times in all contexts but we can see 'narrations as social acts, points of public negotiation between self and 'others' which offer insights into the way we negotiate conflicting or complementary subject positions' (Nayak 1993: 127). We may be at a point at which 'we are all of us now living and writing under the autobiographical injunction' (Steedman 1997), but this need not be viewed as inherently problematic when it is imbued with feminist political commitment.

The use of auto/biography raises many questions about 'truth' and knowledge and about the way that the subjective experience of events is continually mediated as memory. Feminists and others interested in such methods are continuing to discuss the implications of these ideas to the data they result in (Ribbens 1993; Rosie 1993; Casslett *et al.* 2001). All events are 'remembered' and therefore reconstructed over time, and as a result there will always be an element of fiction in the way that life stories are told and retold and are constantly reworked through the additional experiences of the narrator (see e.g. Riceour 1984; Bruner 1985). It is possible to say that all responses are 'constructed'. The audience and the motives of the narrator, such as the desire to please or obscure, are always factors in responses given. Common-sense knowledge was until recently based on the idea that women and children could not be counted on as being reliable witnesses in a legal and social setting, particularly with reference to their experiences with violence and abuse (Kelly 1988; Hanmer and Maynard 1987). In this case, the questions about racism could often stray into the territory of conflict, violence and victimisation. For children in particular, what they said must be taken, or so it is argued, 'with a pinch of salt'. Whilst feminists have argued that women and children must be believed as a starting point, the use of narratives and life stories allows for there to be some kind of 'fictional' telling of self.

Autobiography has been conceptualised as a very specific kind of literary genre. Yet since its increasing 'democratisation' it may more usefully be seen as ' "transcending" rather than transgressing categories, generic and cultural' (Marcus 1991: 14). In this research the children spoke of themselves in autobiographical terms, as did their parents, yet it was not a coherent, chronological description but was indeed transcendent of such constraints. Two related terms are used throughout this book to understand the biographical tales told to me. The first is 'narrative', the second 'discourse'.

The use of the word 'narrative' can have a wide variety of meanings in qualitative research (Polkinghorne 1995, Riessman 1993, Lieblich *et al.* 1997 and Berger 1997 offer extensive overviews of the usage of the term). Narrative can denote any prosaic discourse; that is, any text that consists of complete sentences linked to a coherent and integrated statement (Polkinghorne 1995: 6). I do not intend to use the term this loosely, nor do I wish to use the term 'discourse' in this way. In this book, I will use the Foucauldian notion of discourse as texts that create and construct the fields and institutions they seek to explicate and serve:

> Indeed it is in discourse that power and knowledge are joined together. And for this very reason, we must conceive discourse as a series of discontinuous segments whose tactical function is neither uniform nor stable. To be more precise, we must not imagine a world of discourse divided between accepted discourse and excluded discourse, or between dominant discourse and the dominated one; but as a multiplicity of discursive elements that can come into play in various strategies. (Foucault 1978: 100)

Discursive matrices are not monolithic impenetrable stuctures, but allow agency, subversion and transgression. In conjunction with the term 'narrative' they provide a way of understanding the power of social structures and knowledges and the ways in which they may be deployed by children. A more definitive term for use is *'narrative stories'*: 'Stories express a kind of knowledge that uniquely describes human experience and actions and happenings contribute positively and negatively to attaining goals and fulfilling purposes. The knowledge carried by stories differs from that which has been promoted by Western Scientific tradition' (Polkinghorne 1995: 9). In this research the children construct knowledge through 'both paradigmatic and narrative cognition (ibid.).[5] The connections (discourses) inherent within stories told, and the use of scraps and snippets of data, may inform a less coherent narrative of self on the surface but construct stories in co/representation between myself and the respondents. Ken Plummer (1995) argues that we should begin to think through a new sociology of stories in which we look at the *role* of stories in society. One of the roles he suggests is that of *community building*. Perhaps some of the reasons behind my use of stories is to start work on producing some kind of 'community of thought' in relation to mixedness, no matter how many differences may be contained within it. My interactions with children and parents show how the collection of data followed the form of *dialogic process* which will be discussed below.

Bakhtin's theoretical work has very important implications for the ways in which we try to understand the narratives the children use in particular locations.

Both in form and content the interviews can be seen as a kind of 'speech genre' (Bakhtin 1986). These genres are noted for their 'extreme *heterogeneity*' (original emphasis), and certainly the conversations with the children reflected this fact as they were not set in a particular form, and in differing locations became different genres (ibid.: 60). There was a more formal interview genre in which children talked of 'racism' to me in a way that showed they understood both the rhetoric that was expected and the power relation that positioned me as adult/teacher. However, our relationships in the playground, where the relational boundaries blurred, provided different kinds of responses. The term 'heteroglossia' is most helpful as a way of understanding how children come to 'speak' themselves into complex subject positions (Bakhtin 1981). The term reveals how each dialogue, speech act, or utterance is imbued with meaning from previous encounters. There are multiple meanings encoded in the language and these are called into play by the dialogic processes of the interview, or informal talk or game, and so on. For Bakhtin, we 'assimilate' genres just as we learn language, and many people may be eloquent in one sphere are less so in another where they do not have a practical command (Bakhtin 1986: 78). I believe this is a useful way to consider the varying forms and styles of response I got from the children in different settings.

The term 'genre' has also been developed in educational contexts where social processes are recognised as generic interactions. They are also a form of discourse. The strict structural linguistic beginnings were moved on by the work of Bakhtin and others into a debate about teaching children writing, and how they need to understand the generic form expected of them (Threadgold 1988). The implications for using genre in more diverse spheres of social enquiry are used to consider the way children talk about issues such as 'race' and racism in schools. Kress goes as far as to suggest that '[g]enre is the term that describes that aspect of the form of texts which is due to their production in particular social occasions' (Kress 1987: 36).

We can see that the generic forms of production of the children's 'texts' about themselves in relation to discourses about 'race' endorse Kress's view that:

> [Consequently], in that individual's participation in the production of texts a large number of discourses, several of them all bearing on a particular subject-matter and its formulation, are available to her or him. Where institutional constraints are strong only the legitimated discourses will appear; where the constraints are weaker, several discourses may make their simultaneous appearance. So texts are the site of the emergence of discourses, most usually several at once; they may be complementary in their meanings and tendencies, or they may be quite contradictory. (Kress 1987: 37)

The multiple meanings, discursive and imagined, their histories and their futures are all embedded within the choices of language used in the narratives the children tell, in particular about their families. They may appear to contain contradictory discourses, but the children did not perceive them as doing so, as will be shown throughout the book.

In some instances the voices of the children were indeed uniquely unsettling of dominant meanings. All of these interactions (interviews, lunches, games, etc.) and the production of all texts (verbal and visual data) are dialogic (Bakhtin 1986), and they are all a site of contestation and struggle for meaning given the available material. In some cases the children showed that they resolved their struggles for expression by completely subverting given outcomes, and utilising seemingly unrelated information, as the extract below shows:

Suki: If I asked you to describe yourself [in terms of 'colour'] what would you say?
Tito: I love yo-yos.
Suki: You'd say that you loved yo-yos?
Tito: That's the only way I can describe myself.

Tito was a boy in Year 5 of a multiethnic primary school in London (Barnlea School, described on pp. 24–25). He was positioned as black by the school, having a white English mother and a black Jamaican father whom he saw on an irregular basis, as his father no longer lived with the family. Tito had a twin sister, Talia, in the school – a hard-working, thoughtful and intelligent girl. When I talked to Tito outside of the interview setting in more informal ways in class, the playground, and with other people present he was happy and loquacious. As can be seen from the extract above, when it came to talking of himself in the terms of my choosing he simply could not and would not do it.

On another occasion he and his sister were trying to describe to me one of Talia's classmates:

Tito: … and she always got these Hi Tec trainers.
Talia: … she's got Hi Tec …
[both talking] …
Talia: … she sits she sits ah … near uh …
Tito: … Talia, she's Talia's colour, black and white …

In this context he was happy to, and able to, refer to someone in terms of skin colour.

Speech genres are ostensibly about difference. Furthermore 'single speaker and writer texts are no less constituted in difference and constructed around its resolution than are dialogues. Indeed the task of the author/writer is precisely this: to attempt to construct a text in which discrepancies, contradictions, and disjunctions are bridged, covered over, eliminated' (Kress 1989: 15). I believe this is a very helpful way of understanding how children try to talk about 'mixed-race' identities and offers a more constructive way of understanding the struggle Tito is having in talking to me. It would be tempting to suggest that he just won't talk to me, or that he does not have the language to deal with this concept in relation to himself. Perhaps a combination of the two is more likely. The one-on-one interview causes him sufficient difficulty to result in him switching from talking about himself in the context of 'colour' to talking about himself as someone that he knows he 'is' and, I believe, likes. He obviously felt that he was required by the power relations to give some kind of answer and yet he did not feel that he had the language to do so in the terms I wanted. So he resolved his struggles by describing himself in relation to his love of yo-yos, something he had already mentioned and an area of achievement in which he shone.

Tito still tried first to describe Talia's classmate as someone who has the right kind of trainers, a common form of cultural currency among the children. Recognising the generic and discursive constraints upon Tito allows for a much more nuanced understanding of what is at stake in his statement rather than just dismissing it as uninformed. He has, in resolving this difficulty, carried out a political act, and thus we may see in it ways that it challenges the hegemonic political positions available to him

From my conversations with Tito, his sister and later his mother I know how important his family is to him. His mother's view about her children is that they are 'mixed-race' and not black and they should be 'proud of who they are'. Tito is showing that he *is* proud of who he is: lover of yo-yos, best yo-yo player in the class, recogniser of style and trends, identifier of good trainers, and so on. He had also said earlier in his school career to his mother, who is white English, that she should go to the club for black mothers at his school. She said that she thought that was funny, but added, 'He knows I'm white.' Tito is obviously trying to subvert the meaning of 'black' and 'white' for his own gains in this context, and not recognising the discursive limits upon doing so. This tension between what the children desire in terms of positionality and what is available to them runs throughout the data, and Tito's tale shows the importance of multiple methods in data collection and analysis.

Visual Narratives

In the process of this research it became clear that the verbal resources at the disposal of the children failed to deliver the kinds of detail they wanted to express about themselves, their lives, or others connected to them. We can see from Tito's accounts there are many reasons for using non-verbal, visual forms of communication. Discussions of 'passing' inevitably highlight the relationship between the 'visible and the articulable' in that they are precisely discussions about the disjuncture between those two (Deleuze [1988] 1999: 47). The disjuncture reveals how both the visible and the articulable fail to provide basis for knowing or knowledge acquisition in relation to the ambiguity of mixednesses. There is no language for what is taken to be visible, no way to articulate 'mixedness' that is truly meaningful. By using popular images of the stars of mass media the children were able to show how these representations impacted upon their understanding and discursive manipulations in producing subject positions. The images that were used in the research were not simply tools for research, although that was a major reason for their use; the family photographs held their own (varied) narratives. Although there are important developments in the ways in which subjectivities are produced through visuality, this was not explored in depth here (e.g. Lury 1997 works through the idea of seeing 'photographically'). Simply put, by allowing children control in creating and reading and re-reading such images I was able to access those aspects of their sense of home and family that may have been harder to verbalise, or not chosen through verbal means. In short, the visual representations of 'mixed-race' positions illuminated different ways of seeing the positions of the children *vis-à-vis* hegemonic discourses of 'race'.

Popular Culture

Tito's identification of trainers as currency shows the role of style in the lives of children. He has access to many forms of 'advice' on this matter through the media he consumed. The way in which the children read these media, and in particular the ways in which these readings and the discourses they identified played a part in their understandings of themselves, show, that the relationship that the children have with the texts is dynamic, and they are often not confined to the 'preferred' readings of the texts. Stuart Hall has described how readers are presented with polysemous texts which contain preferred readings: 'There can never be only one single univocal and determined meaning for [such] a lexical item; but depending on how its integration within the code has been accomplished, its possible meanings will be organised within a scale which runs from *dominant* to *subordinate*' (Hall [1974] 1993: 30).

Multiple readings of the same text allow for oppositional and counter-hegemonic readings and as a result 'connotative and contextual "misunderstandings" are, or can be of the highest structural significance' (ibid.: 34). This form of reading and re-reading is part of a 'circuit of culture' in which individuals and groups are in constant relationship with the production and consumption of culture. They are interpellated into positions which they also seek to disrupt and in doing so reposition themselves (Hall 1997: 1 and ch. 1). Van Zoonen (1994) takes up Hall's work as a framework for feminist media theory and research (see Figure 1):

In institutionalised processes of media production media is 'encoded' in discursive forms that do not constitute a closed ideological system but in which the contradictions of the production process are enclosed. The thus encoded structure of meaning serves in another 'moment' of meaning production, the decoding of practices of the audiences. Encoding and decoding need not be symmetrical' Van Zoonen (1994: 8).

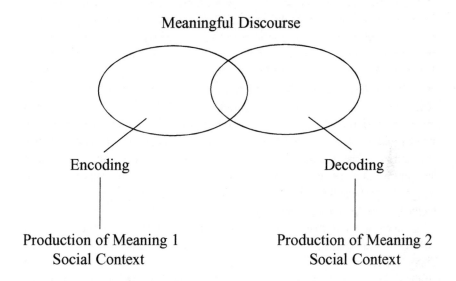

Figure 1 Hall's encoding/decoding model (in Van Zoonen 1994)

Such processes are some of the most interesting ways that the children appear to be actively involved in constructing gender, 'race' and sexual identifications through their readings of popular culture. Certainly, during the research process this was often a way in which children manipulated the situation in order to raise issues about what bodies mean, how they understand the ways in which not only 'race' but also culture and ethnicity are embodied practices and how these are sexualised.

The desires and dislikes of the children in this arena provided ways for them to talk about the 'forbidden' that is heterosexuality and homosexuality, and also to play with the newer narratives available to them of relationships and dating and marriage as they sought to stabilise gendered positions. In addition, it was clear that using the image of a famous person (Scary Spice) as representative of someone of 'mixed-race' helped with understanding the way the term may be lived. In a sense it did interpellate the children of 'mixed-race' to claim that identity. The use of images from popular culture was supplemented in the next stage of the research by children using domestic photography.

Domestic Photography

As was mentioned above, the children produced their own images of 'family' and 'home' as well as choosing to bring in favourite images that already existed. The reading of family photographs provides us with another prompt for memory work that also forges very strong links with the rest of the social world. Family photographs follow extremely strict conventional codes; they take a generic form. It is both true that '[T]he personal histories they record belong to narratives on a wider scale, those public narratives of community, religion, ethnicity and nation which make private identity possible' (Holland 1991: 3), and that paradoxically the collection held within families, be it in albums, envelopes or cardboard boxes, remains a 'personal treasure, while so much of it was part of a shared flow of common socially determined events' (Seabrook 1991: 178). It is this combination of the distinct personal narrative and its intersection with the wider social history that will be explored. Stanley concludes that a photograph is not 'simply a frozen "slice of time", but also a tool to travel both into the past and future and construct multiple, flexible meanings' (ibid.: 27). In this way the images do not simply 'amplify biographies' but become ways of facilitating memory work (Seabrook 1991: 172).

In the original formation of the term 'memory work', a group collective writing and analysis is worked upon from memories triggered by a suggested theme (Haug *et al* 1987). My own work has more in common with that of Annette Kuhn (1995). I did not require the respondents to really *work* on the photographs unless they wanted to. The photographs (the images themselves) may be 'read' but the narratives, narrators and 'narratees' may also all be implicated in unpredictable ways in a form of 'memory production'. Memory is a process that constantly invokes and reinvents past events through the lens of the present and the imagined future. The social and the self are linked in a continuous co-productive venture (Ricoeur 1992). Parents and children were invited to look at the photographs and talk about them in a number of ways. From their comments and observations other questions would arise in a more spontaneous fashion than from rigid preformed questions. This spontaneity was also a way to reduce the rigidity of the interviewer/interviewee positions, and for the interview to take a more informal generic form.

In Tito's case, not only were the interviews surprising compared to my interactions with him out of that context, but so were his photos. He took one picture which included his mother in it, and all of the others were of his belongings. These included trophies handed down to him from his maternal grandfather, his own football trophies, the family television, video player and hi-fi. This boy wanted me to know that his home had things. Valuable things, precious things and desirable things. The images also showed his own football. These were no accidents, they were carefully arranged and staged. In addition to his speech acts, these visual narratives told a story of a boy who would undoubtedly know the value of trainers and the use of yo-yos.

Within the research process the confidentiality of the data was of great importance to the children and families who took part. The photograph collection that I now have represents a rich source of data that is only partially represented in this book due to issues of confidentiality. The analysis of the photographs is limited to a written description of the ways in which children and mothers talked about them, not of the photographs themselves. I did gain permission from some of the participants to reproduce some of the images as they are a most powerful medium, conveying a depth and complexity which eludes us in written language. Yet, if they are seen as 'illustrating' the text they bear a huge burden of representation, as well as increasing the likelihood of respondents being recognised. For these reasons, and despite the loss to the book, they are not included. However, the issue of representation was only one part of the ethical dilemmas I faced.

Mediating Textual Ambiguities: Ethics and Politics

Feminist research ethics foreground the need to minimise traditional power imbalances between the researcher and the researched. When asking children to talk about intensely personal issues this plays a major part in the need to try to develop a relationship of trust which would minimise the chance of deliberately misleading data. Such ethical issues have been discussed at length elsewhere, and they were ever present in my thoughts throughout the process (Mayall 1994; Alderson 1995; Alldred 1998; Maybin 1993; Mauthner 1997; Epstein 1998).

Feminist research ethics and politics are not easy things to deal with. I have been relating events from relationships in the fieldwork, but the process of analysis and writing sets up the next set of ethical 'tripwires'. These tripwires may be represented as a set of questions:

- How can one take the words of these children, and in some cases their siblings, friends and parents, and transform them into data that remains true to their intended meanings?
- What interpretation may we place upon their intended meanings?
- How will this interpretation actively 'empower' them and others?

These questions may be seen as a matrix of concerns that guide a heuristic process. They are, of course, unanswerable as there are no guarantees in this kind of research. The ambiguities are the sites of most interest and potential, both positive and negative. The fieldwork generated huge amounts of data in a variety of forms. I centralised the interviews and conversations and interactions with the children for the reasons explained in the first chapter. I transcribed the interviews with the children myself and listened to them more than once in order to refresh myself of the verbal nuances in the speech.[6] I read through all the transcripts once and identified the main themes which were then coded. But with further listening and reading the coding was refined and expanded:

> Working with narrative requires dialogical listening (Bakhtin 1981) to three voices (at least): the voice of the narrator, as represented by the tape or the text; the theoretical framework, which provides the concepts and tools for interpretation; and a reflexive monitoring of the act of reading and interpretation, that is self-awareness of the decision process of drawing conclusions from the material. In the process of such a study, the listener or reader of a life story enters an interactive process with the narrative and becomes sensitive to the narrator's voice and meanings. Hypotheses and theories are thus generated while reading and analysing the narratives, and – in a circular motion as proposed by Glaser and Strauss's (1967) concept of 'grounded theory' – can enrich further reading, which refines theoretical statements and so on in an ever growing circle of understanding. (Lieblich et al 1998: 10)

In doing this kind of formal analysis I felt that I had to guard against imposing structures of meaning, fixing the stories and narratives that I was engaged with: 'traditional, empiricist narrative methods represent an approach to storytelling that must be avoided. They turn the story told into a story analysed' (Denzin 1997:249).

The desire for intellectual rigour can lead to an oversimplification of the processes of narrative analysis. I believe that my own connection to the stories of the children meant that some of my decisions in questioning and response were intuitive and emotional, based upon the integration of the theorising of my own 'mixedness'. This, and the length of time I spent getting to know children, meant that the dialogic process was one that extended beyond the confines of the interview itself. The data could be analysed by drawing upon all of these resources in ways that other qualitative research (i.e. interviews alone) cannot.

These dilemmas are best illustrated by looking at an extract from one of the interviews I held in a gym at Barnlea school one day near the end of my fieldwork there.

John had taken part in some of the earlier general discussions and had not offered a great deal about himself, other than he was from Nigeria and not long in England. A friend of his suggested he should be interviewed because he was 'half-caste' and had a white dad. John agreed to be interviewed, and after some reluctance, which I judged to be guardedness in the one-on-one situation, began to talk more freely. At first it was hard to follow what John was saying as I had made assumptions about his family, and it took a great deal of discussion to understand the situation. John had a father in Nigeria whom he saw occasionally, and a man also called his father who had been with his mother for several years and lived with them as a family. In the extract I echo back what he has said to me, in part to clarify that I have understood, and also for the practical reason that he spoke quite quietly and I wanted to be sure his answers were clear:

Suki: Have people ever talked to you about racism and stuff like that?

John: Yeah.

Suki: What have they said to you?

John: They said 'Oh no, look at that boy, his Dad is white!'

Suki: Have they?

John: Yeah ... and ... and some people cuss me because my Dad is white.

Suki: Do they?

John: Yeah.

Suki: That's nasty, isn't it.

John: Yeah.

Suki: What kind of things do they say?

John: Like ... um... Like look at this half-caste boy, he doesn't look like a half-caste he looks like a Yoruba, and stuff like that, and they cuss me and say f-words to me ...

Suki: Oh no that' s awful!

John: ... And all those things.

Suki: Yeah. And how would you describe yourself though?

John: Ummm ... I would describe myself like ... I, I don't mind what they're saying, but ... but it's quite nasty

        [...]

Suki: Do you mind being called half-caste?

John: Um no.

Suki: You don't mind?

John: No.

Suki: So you think that's right, would you call yourself that?

John: Yes.

Suki: You would?

John: Yeah.

Suki: Umm, do you know what it means?

John: Yeah, like your dad is white and your mum is black and that would make you in the middle and that is what half-caste means.

Suki: And do you think that is what you are?

John: Yeah, 'cos my dad is white and my mum is black.

Suki: Right.

Later, when asked about his family in Nigeria, he said:

John: That would make me Yoruba.
Suki: Yoruba.
John: 'Cos my mum's boyfriend was Yoruba.
Suki: Uh huh, and do you think you are Yoruba?
John: Yeah, but I like people calling me half-caste.

He explained that this was because his new dad treated his mum well:

Suki: … You want to be with this dad and you like being called half-caste then?
John: Yeah I would like to be called half-caste.
Suki: Yeah.

John talked about his mother, and Nigeria as his home, and described his favourite foods as Nigerian; he had strong familial and cultural links to Nigeria that affected his 'cultural' identity. His 'family' were crucial. And although he missed his family in Nigeria, the tie to his step-father led to him choosing to incorporate his father's whiteness into his own ('racial') identity. The children rarely knew that the term 'half-caste' was considered, as another child said, 'rude'. John had used it with such frequency that his friend knew that he would not mind being interviewed for the research. With such a complicated history, it is no wonder that John chose to hold two clear 'racial' identities – that of Yoruba and implicitly black African, and of half-caste that is, 'mixed-race'. His logic was impeccable – his new father is indeed white.

Discourses of 'family' that are increasingly available to young children allowed him to play with his own familial complexities. As his new father is *family*, then he is undoubtedly half-caste. Further, if race is untenable, and biology and skin colour erroneous choices for categorical positions, why should John not choose to be 'mixed-race'? One might argue that this would be a question of politics, the politics of identity, but maybe more importantly the politics of 'race' in a society which insists on perceiving 'white' as the norm and desirable. For John families are a site of resistance to the constraints of racialisation.[7]

I believe it unlikely that John's family would be unaware of his desire to reassess emphases on 'blood' in his family history and thus his identity, although perhaps they do not know the exact language he is using, such as 'half-caste'. The way the family perceives the 'politics of race' is hard to gauge, but the family structure and interrelations themselves, with the attendant movement and relocation, have obviously been the major factors for John. Is he attempting to 'pass' as 'mixed-race', with its attendant connotations, or is his decision based upon his narrative dexterity? Is John showing some psychic rupture with his social world? Is this 'irrationality' that needs to be explained away by psychoanalytic theory of introjection of the dominant views on whiteness? I don't think so. I believe he shows a desire to organise his social world to maximise his sense of belonging to his current emotional, social and spatial geography. He shows this generic and discursive 'closure' by the ability to manipulate the discourses of family to resolve the questions of difference presented by racist attacks.

In this case I think it inappropriate to attempt to 'solve' the riddles of John's claims. I have had to simply 'suspect' what the intentions of this choice of naming were. Researching children's identifications requires a respect for the ways in which they are both 'fictional and "real"' (Katz 1996). In all their dealings with the research process, the children remained enthusiastic and engaged with talking about themselves and their lives. The children are not only creating meaning through the talk they have with their friends, but also building upon that in their retelling within the research process. They often showed the way in which 'person-hood is constructed … through the reporting [of dialogue] and taking on of other people's voices' (Maybin 1993: 148). This way of talking seems to me to show that John is both of and not of a time and place. I believe that his identifications are 'fragmented', but coherent and cohesive in narrative form, neither diffuse nor destabilising. There is an important locationally driven naming process at work which will be explored in later chapters with other children (see Ang-Lygate 1995; Simmonds 1996). John shows a form of 'ethnic identification' which is 'operationally situational'; therefore flexible and malleable even at this age (Okaura, cited by Ifekwunigwe 1997: 129).

The methodological decisions that have been outlined in this chapter continued to be negotiated throughout the research. Using ethnographic methods and theories of narratives, life history, discourse and speech genre proved useful in accessing and analysing the responses of children and parents. Using popular culture and family photographs played a major part in constructing the narratives of selves which John and Tito were not articulating. Not all of the children show the same levels of dexterity as John, but many have an awareness of the ways in which they have to solve some disjunctures in their positions. Tito represents the other end of the spectrum. In his own way, he showed resilience to my probing and then a strategic response to a difficult question. Others I spoke to have, at this stage in their lives, no such struggles with speaking themselves, having claimed (for the moment) non-problematic positions. As the two transcript extracts have shown, there were inevitably some children for whom talking about such matters was easier and others for whom it was a struggle. A *partial* perspective of this complexity is evident in the following chapters.

The analyses that follow are not representative in an *equal* fashion of *all* the children and parents with whom I spoke. During the research process three children whom I had interviewed changed schools, and not all parents who were originally contacted took part. In order to develop an analysis I have picked up on the themes raised in dialogues and interviews, such as John's and Tito's, and used them as ways that illuminate and advance the theoretical concerns of the research. This process and its representation is of course limited by constraints of the space and form of the book.

In the next chapter I will analyse how the themes of gender, sexuality and appearance articulated with the development of 'mixed-race' identities. I will show that there are a range of discourses from which the children learned, but that they also manipulated for their own purposes, in their collective and individual use of popular culture. This proved to be a most powerful form of cultural capital and was one of the criteria for including or excluding children from friendship groups. The types of cultural material available to the children were heavily influenced both by their immediate environment (school and home) and by their connections to other social (ethnic) groups. I will consider the ways in which the children of black/white interracial relationships were offered membership to black British culture, and how they used this to 'choose' a 'racialised' identification. But I will also begin to analyse the ways in which black popular culture has become most influential for *all* of children in the multiethnic primary schools, regardless of racial, ethnic or cultural identifications.

Notes

1. This is also a pseudonym.
2. The overview of children, teachers and parents from each school who took part is contained in Appendix A.
3. Obviously the texts that cover these developments are too numerous to list. My own reading has been guided through collections in Women's Studies collections by James and Busia (1993), Humm (1992), Robinson and Richardson (1993), Tong (1992), Evans (1995), Mirza (1997), Nicholson (1997) and more specific texts on epistemology such as Code (1991), Fox Keller and Longino (1996), Tanesini (1991) and Nicholson (1990).
4. This is not a simplistic rejection of 'quantitative' methods, which have their place in all research, and have been used successfully in feminist work such as Kelly *et al.* (1992) and the return to such methods by Haraway (1997) and Oakley (2000).
5. Polkinghorne offers a thorough analysis of the development of paradigmatic and narrative forms of cognition drawing on the work of Bruner (1985) and Ricoeur (1984). He continues to suggest that there are two main forms of narrative analysis: 'paradigmatic analysis of narrative' and 'narrative analysis of eventful data'. The latter was used in relation to Ifekwunigwe's work in the

previous chapter. My own work will occasionally use aspects of both, but more usefully, Norman K. Denzin's later work (1997) which takes these two concepts and develops them into the storied, performative approach to narrative that will be used in Chapter 6. Some of the more structural approaches to narrative analysis are, I believe, unhelpful, totalising and proscriptive (cf. Riessman 1993 on 'how to do' narrative analysis).

6. I transcribed the group interviews that were conducted on videotape myself, as I did with all of the children's materials and those of the parents. Some of the teachers' interviews were transcribed for me, and I listened to them again after I received the transcriptions, reading them through and checking them against the spoken word. All transcripts were also cross-checked against my notes taken at the interviews, and taped debriefs after.

7. This analysis has been developed from its original form in Ali (2000).

–3–

Reading Popular Culture:
Same Ideas, Different Bodies

The experience of pop music is the experience of identity

S. Frith, 'Music and Identity'

Introduction

In this chapter, the children's use of popular culture is used in order to show how the themes of the research were analysed. I will explore the relationships between popular culture (particularly visual culture), learning about racialisation and racism and how these inform the development of identifications. Children show that they often use popular culture to learn about discourses of 'race', ethnicity and gender; in particular how to 'read' bodies and style with sexuality. They do this not through passive acceptance of what they see, but through collective critical rereading of texts in their own social circles. This is part of a 'broader process of constructing social relationships and thereby defining individual and group identities' (Buckingham and Sefton-Green 1994: 24).

In the first sections I will show how children from *all* backgrounds have some kind of pleasurable relationship to popular culture, if they are allowed access to it. Although the schools were located in inner-city London and rural Kent,at first glance the findings look to be very similar; however, upon closer investigation regional differences become clearer. It is not merely spatial but social geography that impacts upon the way children relate to 'racial' sameness or difference, and in the way that they deal with concepts such as 'racism'. Using the phenomenon of the popularity of Will Smith, I consider the acceptable limits to black masculinities and how some form of class is again central to all of the children's identity work.

The most popular area for debate was the heterosexual relations between stars and their alleged sexual orientation. (Hetero)sexuality was of major importance to the way the children chose their favourites and attacked others. Significantly, I found there was no clear correlation between the sex and 'race' of the child and their enjoyment of particular stars. Finally, I will discuss the ways in which the Spice Girls.[1] provided some interesting divisions of opinion that crossed stereotypical gendered lines, with both girls and boys expressing love/loathe discourses. However, construction and maintenance of friendship groups revealed gendered differences in the use of power/knowledge.

Valerie Walkerdine suggested that 'Cultural Studies has had almost nothing to say about young children' (Walkerdine 1996: 324). In the last few years that has begun to change, but it is true that there is still very little on the young and middle years child as compared to the teenager. The findings here offer unique insights into the ways in which young children use popular culture. It reveals that they do so in ways that are quite different from those in the older age groups, showing less concern about 'authenticity' in 'race' and more concern about sexuality and character. The children grapple with the impossibilities of 'reading race' and untangling the problems with the visualisation of 'race'. They do this through the limitations of their discursive repertoires and show how '[t]he paradox of subjectivation (assujetissement) is precisely that the subject who would resist such norms is itself enabled, if not produced by such norms' (Butler 1993: 15).

Seeing, Reading, Thinking through 'Race'

I began the group video sessions by showing children images of celebrities, and from there led the discussion into the area of 'race' and 'racial' identity, thus smoothing the way into investigation of children's active critical individual and group re-readings in these areas (see Appendices for details). The focus of this method was not simply to look at 'representation' or 'children as audiences', it was to use the popular as a tool for talking about the unspoken and unspeakable. It also inflected data analysis, as popular culture is both constructed by and constituent of social identities. Using this type of material served several purposes:

- it allowed children to talk freely about things they had some interest in, thereby encouraging confidence in the research process;
- it helped to identify social groups/friendship groups;
- it facilitated children's self-definition of their 'racial' and ethnic positions;
- it provided preliminary data about the relevance of media readings and their influence on identification in children who described themselves as 'mixed-race'.

This was successful on many levels, and even the problems that emerged provided further fascinating data. It was, on a very superficial level, a form of 'photo elicitation', but by taking a creative and interpretive approach I encouraged children to work in a much more subtle way with the conceptual relationships between the visual and verbal narratives of mixedness, and gender and ethnicity more generally. This part of the process therefore showed the limits to the kind of proscriptive visual method that imposes structured questions and responses (Banks 2001).

One afternoon after lessons, I saw several children in a huddle in the play-ground at Christie School. In my role as ethnographic snooper, I strolled over to investigate and discovered them to be bartering stickers. Children are notoriously passionate about their 'crazes' in school, and adults find it hard to keep up with trends. At the time of data collection there were two main obsessions – yo-yos and stickers. The stickers in question were 'head-shots' of famous film, music and television personalities from a pre-teen pop music magazine. The stickers were collectable and thus valuable. They represented a range of capital for the children – cultural, symbolic and economic. These stickers were collected, swapped and sold throughout all of the schools, and in some cases were stolen or spoiled. After careful negotiation, I took the sheets, photocopied, enlarged and laminated them and returned the originals the following morning. I continued to collect stickers throughout the research process and by the end of it my tape recorder was covered with favourites which I kept, and I gave away the rest of my collection in the last week.

In addition to using stickers I bought several magazines that covered a spec-trum of interests such as football (*Shoot*), black women's fashion and beauty (*Essence*) and pop music and television news and gossip (*Smash Hits* and *TV Hits*). I included *Black Beat* which specialised in British and American pop stars, both male and female, but there appeared to be no equivalent specialist magazine for South Asian mainstream stars (of whom there are few) in newsagents.[2] The children in the schools confirmed this and told me that most of the popular (South Asian and Turkish) magazines were about film stars. I realised later I could have used computer game magazines; however, the materials did what they were intended to do – namely, they 'broke the ice' amongst the groups and facil-itated discussion. Using images of famous people allowed the children to speak freely in both direct and *indirect* ways about issues. Despite them being 'real' and not characters, they were protected by distance, a sense both of familiarity and of closeness yet separateness. This echoes the 'oscillation between involvement and distance' between soap opera fans and their favourite stars (Geraghty, cited by Buckingham and Sefton-Greene 1994: 14). The children often talked about the most intimate details of the lives of the stars that they believed to be the truth, having read about or seen these titbits in popular media.

Despite the project being about children of 'mixed-race', this first part involved all of the children in the target classes. It provided a fuller picture of the educational context in which the further work with the children of 'mixed-race' was to be set. After discussion about the meanings of terms connected to ethnicity, including 'mixed-race', any children who self-identified as such were invited to take part in the second, more detailed one-on-one interviews.

Using images of 'Scary Spice' to talk about 'race' proved especially successful. Mel B, as she was also known, had been featured in a special edition of the BBC television programme 'Black Britain'(1998) in which she revealed that her mother was white British and her father black Jamaican, and that she was 'mixed-race' but identified with black people as a black woman. The Spice Girls, complete with Geri Halliwell, were all very well known and usually prompted some kind of comment from children even if it were negative. This was especially true of Mel B.[3] The fact that she had called herself of 'mixed-race' introduced the term and I could then ask children about it and also about the implications of having such a 'racialised identity'. This led on into general discussions about the importance of 'race' and racism, both in meaning and in everyday experience and practice. Importantly, discussions showed how children gained pleasure from their objects of desire and fantasy, and offered some insight into how 'race' and ethnicity are interconnected with sexuality and status in the processes of identification.

Getting out of Lessons and other Initial Reactions

I was most struck by how this method was overwhelmingly successful in all three schools. The children in all of the locations responded positively and enthusiastically to the visual materials. At first glance there were few differences in the likes and dislikes held about pop stars and actors, and in the kinds of programmes watched on television, in hobbies, magazines read, and so on.

All the children were familiar with at least some of the faces that were presented to them on the headsheets. There were three children from the whole sample who were not able to put names to faces but they at least *recognised* famous faces. All these children came from homes in which their consumption of the popular was heavily controlled. One child watched Turkish television through cable TV almost exclusively, another Bengali child was not allowed to listen to a great deal of pop music, and the third Bangladeshi child also had his television, radio and computer game usage limited because of 'religion'. In the first week of the project I acquired two more sheets of stickers which also had pictures of cartoon and Disney characters on them. Even those who were not so familiar with music and soaps seemed to recognise some of these characters, such as the traditional Mickey Mouse and Donald Duck, as well as the more contemporary Glenn Close as Cruella de Ville.[4]

None of the children had significant visual or other physical impairment and their reaction to the initial sight of the materials was unanimously energetic and noisy. They all leant forward to the materials and picked them up, looking at each other's sheets and suggesting swaps, trying to snatch ones they wanted. They exclaimed 'cool!' and 'wicked!' or similar phrases, and began naming their favourites or listing those they could see and recognise, all without any prompting. Many recognised the images as altered stickers and asked where I had got them from. The children were happy to talk amongst themselves about the celebrities and were only slightly more reluctant when questioned about their individual habits. Once they realised that this was not some kind of test to name the most, they relaxed. If they appeared to find it hard to name anyone, I offered other sheets or asked them to talk about their own preferred leisure habits.

After the headsheets, the magazines were passed round. These were less recognisable and interesting to the children. In Fairsham, four groups of children said that they did not recognise any of the magazines I showed them; however, the vast majority of children were familiar with the mainstream pop and television magazines. Black British children, both girls and boys, were the most likely to be familiar with the black music magazines. Despite fairly obvious gendered divides concerning familiarity with football magazines, girls expressed interest in the football magazine and boys in the pop magazines, even if they did not actually buy them.

On a *superficial* level the likes and dislikes of the children were also similar in all of the schools. The Spice Girls were guaranteed to provoke responses in the children, some negative, some positive. In fact, there were often extremely strong attacks on every aspect of their public personae: it was the 'love/hate' response that was typically expressed in the analyses of responses to Madonna's music (Brown and Schultze 1990). There are many similarities in the way that the 'Girl Power' of the Spices and the original 'Material Girl', Madonna, can be read. Both have had phenomenal success despite the fact that they are constantly criticised. The Spices, like Madonna, signify the 'low-Other of popular culture' (Schultze *et al* 1993). Some critics have accused Madonna's music and performances as highly offensive in their appropriation of black cultural forms (e.g. hooks 1992b). Others have have reclaimed Madonna's work as a sympathetic tribute to the complexities and difficulties faced by African-Americans (Scott 1993). Despite the disagreement about some aspects of her work, she remained a successful if controversial figure. Much of the hype and debate about both Madonna and the Spices was centred on their physicality and, more specifically, their sexuality.

Children were interested in the physicality of the Spices (see below) but it was not just the female artists whose appearance was questioned by all the children. After a general talk of people showing off their 'pecs' (pectoral muscles) too much, Clive, a black Jamaican boy in Year 5 at Christie (London), told me that Peter André (a white, male, 'boy' artist) had had a lot of plastic surgery. He revealed that André had had 'meat taken from his buttocks and put into his pecs', and concluded this was disgusting! Three young white British girls in Fairsham made unanimous decisions of:

Rebecca: Urrghh, naked men!
Val: Urrgh, They've got their pants showing!
Suki: Isn't that supposed to be trendy?
Rebecca: Yes it is, but it *isn't* though [they point the photograph of the three young black men in the group Damage at the camera].

However, this same picture produced squeals of delight from other girls of all 'racial' backgrounds during the research. These expressions of disgust and delight are revealing of the ways in which such emotions are highly localised to specific groups and individuals who are motivated by different understandings of acceptable stylised behaviour and how that is linked to attractiveness. This theme remained dominant throughout the sessions.

The supposedly intimate knowledge of the celebrities' personal lives, such as who has had plastic surgery, was also a repeated theme which impacted upon the readings of the sexuality and sexual orientation, and thus desirability, of the stars (see also Chapter 4). Clearly there are many factors in play when the children are choosing whom they like and do not like, and the actual music that they play is but one element. In all of the groups the general sentiments of the 'love them or loathe them' type were repeated across all ages and locations, and regardless of gender and race and class.

Music was very important to the children as a way of negotiating friendship groups, as it is with older children and teenagers (Back 1996; Buckingham and Sefton-Greene 1994; Willis *et al* 1990). It is also evident that the children are not split along stereotypical lines in their preferences. Across all age groups, and across gender, 'race' and class divisions, the Spices were both vilified and loved. The children in London schools in particular enjoyed performing for the camera at the end of the group interviews and many of them chose a song by the Spice Girls. Likewise the children in Fairsham who did perform chose the Spice Girls first. It was notable how *few* of the children in Fairsham *did* perform. In London I often had a struggle to stop the performances! Another more compelling difference between the locations was the initial understanding of 'race' as a concept.

Understanding 'Race'

'A race is something you run in'.

Larry, Year 6, Fairsham

I often began to lead the questions into the area of racialised identity by asking if any of the interview group knew anything about Scary Spice. Responses usually started with things that described her appearance or her character, such as 'she's got a tongue ring', 'she's got her tongue pierced', or 'she's got bushy hair' or 'frizzy hair', and 'she's very loud', 'she's weird, 'she's wild', and, of course, 'she's scary' – which also describes her appearance. When asked 'Do you know how she describes herself?' the same responses would be given.

The question was not explicit enough for the children to equate this with the earlier contextualising that had explained that the session was to be about 'race' and 'racism'. The children also forgot or did not see the significance of the fact that they had also given short descriptions of themselves in terms of self, family, place of birth, languages spoken, etc. at the beginning of the sessions. So they chose to talk about the things that *they* thought were the best descriptions of her. Further prompts were required, such as 'Do you know anything about her family?' Answers ranged from 'she's got a sister' to 'she comes from Leeds'. If these oblique prompts did not lead to discussions on the area of 'race', I would explain that Scary had described herself as 'mixed-race' and ask if anyone had heard of this term. There was no pattern as to who had heard of this and who had not. In London schools they were more familiar with the term 'half-caste'.

For example, Dawud, Raizwan (both South Asian) and Arle (Zaïrean), three Year 6 boys, discussed her in the following terms:

Daw:	She's kind of Scary and she's got her tongue pierced and everything.
Suki:	Do you know anything about her background; could you describe it?
Raiz:	She's black.
Daw:	She's kinda weird.
	[someone unidentified says 'crazy']
Suki:	Could you describe her family?
Arle:	Her mum's white and I think her dad's white too.
Suki:	So you think both her parents are white?
Arle:	Yes.
Suki:	So how is she black then?
Raiz:	'Cos her mum is white and her dad is black.
Suki:	Have you heard of the expression 'mixed-race'?
Daw:	Yeah, I knew she was 'mixed-race' 'cos of her skin colour.
Suki:	Because of her skin colour; is that how you can tell if someone is 'mixed-race'?
Raiz and *Ar* together:	No.
Suki:	So its quite confusing as to how you would tell?

(Group interview: Barnlea, February 1998)

Raiz picked up on 'race' quite early in the discussion, but I still needed to guide this further. Arle seemed to want to follow that theme and, from his hesitancy, he clearly knew that at least one of Scary's parents is white. He cannot quite make sense of the fact that if both parents are white it would be fairly unusual, though not impossible, for her to be black. Dawud showed a very typical response to my question about the term 'mixed-race'. He said that not only did he already know the expression, but that the visual sign of skin colour is the main way of telling if someone is 'mixed-race'. He wanted to present himself as knowledgeable and aware of the issues, but the other two boys tried to show that the subject is not that simple. This may be a sophisticated understanding of the fact that I queried Dawud's assertion, possibly implying that I thought his analysis was wrong. All three in turn went on to attempt what they hope are satisfactory answers to questions that cannot really be worked from the information available.

Mapping Racialised Genealogies

I also asked children if they knew where certain celebrities 'came from'. In many cases this was answered by a straightforward knowledge of the person in question. In cases where they were unsure, they would resort to the same sorts of processing to work things out or just guess. For example:

Suki: Do you know where her [Scary's] father comes from?
Reb: Tasmania.
Val: No I think it's somewhere like Africa where she went to dance ...
Reb: Oh is it J ... J ... J ...
Val: Jamaica.
Reb: No, I think its somewhere Muslims are.
Val: Japan.
Reb: No.
                   (Rebecca and Valerie, Year 4 white English girls, Fairsham 1998)

There is so much that could be said about this extraordinary exchange. What is most prominent is the association of Scary and her brown skin with all things 'exotic' and thus 'foreign', and the 'logical' attempt to make connections and answer the question for me. This group of girls cannot be expected to have a wide command of geography, but the way they associate nation, ethnicity and culture is indeed indicative of a very uncertain connection between them.

With another (all white) pop group famous for its quirky style, there were similar problems.[5] These children of colour living in a predominantly white country found the range of possibilities extensive:

Dawud, Raizwan and Arle went through a range of possibilities:

Ar: England.
Daw: Somewhere else in Europe.
Raiz: Sweden? Iceland?
Ar: Russia!

Suki: I think it might be Belgium.

Daw: I think I heard them on '****' [a Saturday morning children's television show] say Yugoslavia or something.

In this dialogue the children went through their repertoire of 'European' countries which echoes the 'white' children with their 'exotic' countries. The definitive answer comes of course from the television and the band themselves. At the time of the interviews Yugoslavia was long gone, so it seems highly unlikely that they would be claiming it as a homeland. However, this account satisfied the rest of the children as it had the unmistakable stamp of authority, even though Dawud was actually very cautious, and qualified his remarks with 'I think' and 'or something'. For the others who had no better information, it was good enough. This method of processing diverse pieces of information about stars could also be used in other locations.

Visual Clues: Racialised Ethnicities

Children would often try to fix people into categories which they understood, or provided analyses that meant that they could pass on and negotiate information within frames of reference that others could understand. One group of children at Barnlea tried to describe a boy (Zane) who came from Somalia:

Gery: Its [He comes from] that kind of Indian country, kind of ...

Meli: He looks like he's got kind of part black inside of him, kind of, but he doesn't know ... kind of ... he looks Asian.

     (Meli (mixed-race and black), Gery (white English), Year 5, Barnlea 1998)

In this example, where the children have a wider understanding of the range of ethnicities present in the school, they struggle to place the child using nation and 'race' in terms of appearance. So Gery's 'kind of Indian country' gets taken up by Meli and developed into a notion of Asian-ness. Interestingly she also uses the term 'black', and this is the way that the adults in the school would loosely categorise children, so that those with genealogies that originate from the Indian subcontinent would be deemed 'Asian' even if they were African-Asian or British-Asian. Likewise all children who may lay claim to African heritage, i.e. have black skins, may be subsumed, at times, under the heading 'black', regardless of nationality. Meli was highly aware of the politics of race and her own mixed-Polynesian, New Zealand, English mixedness made her a particularly interesting member of the research group. She was a very articulate girl, yet struggled with these generalisations when trying to describe Zane purely by appearance. Interestingly, this boy was also frequently cited in discussions about racism because he often 'cussed people's religion', particularly Christianity. He was a

Muslim and this undoubtedly cut across all of the discussions about him, and from his perspective about his own sense of movement and belonging.

Researching the Researcher

In order for children to make the move from the 'unreal' or distant personalities such as Scary Spice to the everyday relations with friends, the children would sometimes use my own 'racial' identity as some kind of a stepping stone from one area to the other. I was quite closely scrutinised during these discussions:

Jack:	Where do you come from?
Suki:	I'm English.
Jack:	Do you have any relatives who are African or ....
Suki:	Yes ... my father came from Trinidad and my mother comes from England.
Larry:	Where's that?
Adrian:	Is that South America or somewhere?
Jack:	Trinidad and Tobago.
	[After a discussion about the meaning of 'mixed-race']
Jack:	I couldn't describe myself as mixed-race.
Adrian:	Its like ...
Jack:	[exclaims, smiling] Coffee coloured! Coffee Coloured!
Larry:	[to SA] Well that's the same as you!
Suki:	Er ... yes ...

(Interview: Fairsham, June 1998)

Jack had lived in France for much of his childhood and liked to claim an international background, even though he couldn't use the label 'mixed-race'. However, when it came to talking to me about my own background he was clearly interested in trying to locate me in relation to the current discussion on 'race' and its meaning and relevance to his own life.

I have had similar questions asked to me so many times that I responded to the first question in a way that I knew would obstruct him from finding out what he *really* wanted to know. The fact that I responded in the affirmative to the question of whether I have any African relations is revealing. I knew that Jack wanted to know why I have brown skin. That is why he mentioned Africa, which is where he believes black people come from. I knew that this is what he wanted to find out, so I said 'yes' despite the fact that my father's family is predominantly Caribbean-Asian. Finally, Jack managed to make sense of me by making the connection to the phrase 'coffee coloured', something he believes to be safe, aesthetically pleasing and apolitical. I have indeed been told how lucky I am to have 'coffee coloured' skin on many occasions.[6] Jack's use of this phrase shows his delight in finding a happy resolution to the 'problem' of talking about 'mixed-race'.

Seeing or Believing

The way the children think that they may be able to tell where people come from breaks down when there are no 'obvious' visual pointers. In the case of Zane and myself, the children struggled with a mixture of ideas about 'race', nationality and ethnicity. These are imbued with a notion of embodiment, of physicality and racial phenotypes such as Meli talking of Zane having 'black in him'. But they are also about histories and genealogies, the way that we tell the stories of our families is what gives credence and truth to our own versions of 'race'. In the absence of such information the children could not and (I believe, to their credit), *would* not try to fix people.

In all of the pop magazines the way that the lighting and reproduction were used often made skin colours fall within a range of golden browns that made black people look paler and white people look darker, reminding us that all of these discussions about 'race' are indeed spurious. During the course of the interviews we often talked about this, and that if you really looked at people in these pictures it became harder to ascribe 'racial' type on skin colour alone. Increasingly 'boy bands' fall outside the simple black/white divide. The make-up of the groups reflects the demographic changes in Britain, showing, for example, young Mediterranean men (Greek and Turkish), though there are still very few of Pacific Rim or South Asian origin. 'Girl bands' are still more likely to rely on the black/ white dynamics, with 'variety' being shown in having white girls with different hair colours and one or two black women – like the Spice Girls.

The media tendency to 'white out' the black stars and 'exoticise' the white stars proved too difficult for the children to read, and so they resorted to guess-work or a refusal to engage with a patently impossible and wholly undesirable task. I explained that we were talking in this way about appearance only in order to consider the ways we categorise people, or how we feel about those categories, and that they are indeed often inadequate or 'wrong'. In the case of 'ambiguity' the way in which children responded was directly influenced by their *environment*, which meant that those in Fairsham were lacking both a language with which to talk about these things as well as an understanding of the issues.

Media Edutainment: Learning Racism

In recent years there has been increasing interest in the way that children behave as audiences and in the kinds of influence various media may have on them, particularly visual media such as television, video and computer games. Berry and Asamen (1993) suggested that television plays a role in 'helping developing children (and adults) learn about themselves and an array of people, [and] places' however, 'events are not fully understood' (Berry and Asamen 1993: 1). This ambiguity about the ways in which children manipulate media is central to many debates about the educative, negative or even negligible effects media have on children. We perhaps no longer fear 'the disappearance of childhood' (see Postman 1994) through exposure to adult materials in media, but recognise the need to understand how the role media play in young children's lives is profound and varied and increasingly imbricated with education (Buckingham 2000; Kenway and Bullen 2001).

The distance that the majority of children in Fairsham felt from the questions asked them coincided with the lack of experience most of them had with dealing with people from 'minority' ethnic groups, who were in the majority in the schools in London. As a result, in Kent, the few children (Years 5 and 6) who knew about racism had, in the majority of cases, learnt about it from the television – not from any kind of children's programme but from the adult news. Several mentioned that it was coming to the anniversary of the death of Stephen Lawrence, and that they had heard about that on the news and about the then ongoing inquiry into his death. This again appeared as racism in a realm far removed from what they believed to be anything to do with them.

Giles told me how he had learnt about racism from a comedy programme. The programme had come under fire for reinforcing anti-Irish prejudices, featuring as it did three very highly stereotyped Irish Catholic priests. In the episode Giles described, the main character was accused of being 'racist'; in a 'comedy of errors' about history and culture he had offended the local 'Chinese community'. Despite the self-conscious ironies of the script, Giles took this as unproblematic information about racism. Another Anglo boy recounted how he called one of the Japanese pupils in the school 'foo foo' and 'begola', which were, he claimed, 'Chinese food'. He knew this because he had heard it on the children's cartoon *Scooby Doo*.

These two children, and others, were emphatic that they had not heard of 'race' and racism at school or from their families; they 'learnt' about them from entertainment programmes. These are small and very obvious examples of the way in which the children use television and then manipulate what they hear for their own use in school. They are taking material from fictional lives and using it in their own 'real' narratives. This is not a new phenomenon and is hardly sinister in most contexts; however, it shows the amount of discernment required to make 'preferred' readings of texts as seemingly 'innocuous' as a Hanna Barbera cartoon.[7]

How Hip to be Black?: Gendering Authenticity

Amongst urban and semi-rural children, African-American culture represented all things 'cool'. In 1994 a small piece of research showed that many more black British teenagers than white were watching 'black' programmes such as *The Cosby Show* and *The Fresh Prince of Bel Air*, and within that, girls were more likely to say that they 'always' watched (Buckingham and Sefton-Greene 1994: 21). By 1998 *The Fresh Prince* had moved from being a specialist programme to being watched almost universally by the children. They also enjoyed other comedies featuring young African-Americans such as *Sister, Sister*, *Moesha* and *Keenan and Kel*. During the course of conversation children repeatedly named American artists as their favourites, and when asked directly, agreed that they were better but could not say why. Les Back noted that 'urban black American speech is also being incorporated into the linguistic repertoire of black South Londoners. This development is closely related to the emergence and popularity of black American youth culture' (Back 1996: 145). It is also true that *all* children in this study were enamoured of the same sorts of black culture.[8]

Will Smith for President

For the children in this study the most universally popular artist was undoubtedly Will Smith. The film *Men In Black* had raised him to Hollywood superstar status. He had had several hit records, including the theme from the film, and his sit-com *The Fresh Prince of Bel Air* was being re-run on television. Those who may not have seen him on TV may have seen the film, or if not seen the film may have heard his records, and so on. Children would often spontaneously break into song when his name was mentioned. His appearances in all media had obviously been highly saturated (as had those of the Spice Girls) but he remained popular – a good singer, stylish, and funny, and a good comic actor.

It seemed that one of the factors that allowed for his popularity was the fact that he was such a well-rounded performer; he had a wide range of abilities. Some of the girls thought of him as 'good-looking' and attractive. Hilary, a very confident middle-class white girl in Year 5 at Fairsham commented: 'Will Smith looks gorgeous without his moustache.' The forbidden interracial element of sexual attraction in previous rerearch was clearly not a problem in this case, and may even have been an enticement. This shows a shift from the histories of race and sex where whites are encouraged to see black men as sexually predatory and dangerous, and black women as voracious and insatiable with whites and blacks needing to be kept distinct (see e.g. Davis 1982; 1990, Hill Collins 1990). A few girls knew that Smith was married and had a son whom he loved – he had released a song about him. This fact raised his credibility with them because being a 'good father' and 'faithful husband' made him a 'nice person' – specifically 'in real life'.[9] The boys liked the fact that he was funny.

Smith's self-claimed and common-sense positioning as a black man is, in some ways, the most remarkable thing about his popularity. He showed the ability to transcend most of the limitations placed upon black performers to achieve this phenomenal level of success. He was sexy, but not too sexy, funny and smart and a good mainstream singer and actor. In all, he was *non-threatening* to the children regardless of their own personal location.

The Politics of Black Masculinities

Despite Will Smith gaining immense success and being firmly stationed in the mainstream of pop and appealing to all other ethnic groups, he still maintained his credibility with the black students. The children did not discuss Will Smith or other artists with the level of critical distinction about the politics of 'race' and the incorporation of the artist into the mass production of the popular in the way that teenagers do. There was a vague and barely articulated understanding of the notion of artists 'selling out'. Clive (black Jamaican boy, Christie, Year 5) was surprised at the fact that Shabba Ranks was, to his mind, endorsing homosexuality and therefore had lost some credibility.[10] Black British teenagers enjoy distinguishing between 'hardcore' and 'commercial' rap. Hardcore is authentic with higher status; it is often more underground and only available from specialist shops. Commercial is 'a cop out' and much less valued by true fans who can accumulate capital through showing specialist knowledge of rap (Buckingham and Sefton-Greene 1994: 65) . When talking about Shabba Ranks, Clive showed a greater critical knowledge of black music. Through questioning Ranks's hetero/sexuality/masculinity, he implies that Ranks has in some way 'sold out'. Clive knows that 'hyper-masculinity' and homophobic lyrics are the required credentials of 'real' hardcore rappers. In rejecting those ideals Ranks must be moving towards acceptability in mainstream music. The other children were impressed with Clive's knowledge and he was seen as something of an expert in the area of rap music.

The fact that Will Smith was non-threatening aesthetically, in terms of his style, music and acting, made him more popular, and rendered him a-racial/non-racial in the white children's eyes; yet he was not seen as a 'sell-out'. Will Smith is not a controversial figure. His music and lyrics affirm a new form of black *middle-class* masculinity that is at complete odds with the more 'hardcore' rappers who are often criticised for their espousal of separatist politics, and violent and misogynist lyrics. Many have discussed the inherent fear of the black male that critics of rap have invoked (Back 1996; Buckingham and Sefton-Greene 1994; Gilroy 1993b). Rose (1995) suggests that the particularly negative responses to rap concerts represent a similar fear of African-Americans, teenagers in particular, to the fear of slaves who threatened to revolt if allowed to organise into large groups. Whilst cultural investigations into teenagers show an understanding of the implications of these debates on the development of black identities, the children in this study did not express any concern at this level.

The black children in London schools had, on the whole, greater 'specialist' knowledge of black music and a greater interest in the less mainstream R and B, rap and soul groups. Likewise, many of the South Asian children listened to more traditional and modern music that was grounded in their own ethnic heritage, with only one of the black Caribbean children in Barnlea claiming to listen to 'Indian' music. The only children who listened to 'classical' music or jazz were white, middle-class children from Fairsham, one of whom was North American. This rough guide to the pattern of listening was broken down upon fairly predictable if not quite stereotypical lines, whilst mainstream pop was listened to by all. Will Smith represented the acceptable face of pop, despite and because of being a black man, and in this way was remarkable.

Sex and the Stars

Despite their age, the children had extensive knowledge of the stars going in and out of fashion and how quickly this could change. They delighted in showing their expertise and in telling me when I was wrong about who was 'in'. There did not seem to be a pattern to this though, as was evident from the variations on the love/loathe Spice Girls, and the fact that children would justify their own liking of someone who was 'not in' if they were a true fan.

The capacity for gossip amongst both girls and boys was huge, and the more shocking the gossip the better. The most scandalous and therefore interesting topic of all was SEX. It was also not always easy to talk about directly, but could be talked around, using language that was in common usage – hence 'I don't say s-e-x but I say the f-word though' (Jamal, 'mixed-race' boy, Year 4, Barnlea). Sex often had to be spelt out, despite the fact that 'lesbian' and 'poof' could be said freely; they counted as 'swear words' or insults, rather than as something to do with sex. The common concerns were with who was going out with whom, who was a lesbian and who was gay. The sexuality of stars was a source of conflict amongst friends, as much as who someone liked. Indeed the two were inextricably linked. It would be impossible to like someone who was lesbian or gay, as reporting alleged sexual deviance was done in order to devalue the star in question.

When talking about the Spice Girls, a group of Year 4 children from Barnlea, both girls and boys and from a variety of ethnic backgrounds, became quite heated:

Alan: She's a … they're all lesbians, Miss.
          [Cain and Jam together, 'Shut up!']
Cain: Don't talk about Emma like that.
Jam: Yeah I told you not to talk about Baby Spice like that.
Cain: Don't talk about Baby Spice like that.
          [All talk at once]
Suki: Where did you hear that?
Alan: I saw it in …
Cain: … 'cos everyone's saying it innit?
Becky: Victoria's getting married isn't she?
Cain: Yeah! So is Scary Spice!
Suki: And Scary?
Alan: And then on 'Tricky' I saw Baby Spice and Posh kissing on the lips.
          [Cain hits Alan on the arm]
Suni: Shut up, don't say such rude things about girls.
Cain: But Baby Spice got a boyfriend, innit?
Suni: Innit!
Suki: Does kissing mean anything much?
Jam: No, my mum kisses …
ALL: No!
Cain: But they was … mmmmm … [mimes a big snog].
          [They all laugh a bit and someone says 'Shut up' again.]
                    (Interview Barnlea, February 1998. Alan (black British),
                 Cain (Anglo/Turkish), Jamal (Kenyan Asian/ black African),
                     Sunita (South Asian), Becky (white British), Year 4)

At Fairsham some of the girls in Year 5 had also seen an interview with Ruby
Wax the that Spice Girls had given. They said:

Hilary: Mel B and Geri kissed right on the lips.
Lena: Disgusting!
Suki: They 'snogged'?
Hilary: Basically it was a really embarrassing situation which I'm not going to
          tell you …

Presumably it was too 'disgusting' to repeat. It was also a way that Hilary took
control of the interview and avoided having to say anything that may have been
embarrassing. Being lesbian was a terrible insult to the Spices, as was being gay
for the men. One particularly worldly Year 6 boy at Christie told me that Gianni
Versace was killed because he was gay and his family had found out that he was
dating Giorgio Armani! The whole group erupted at this piece of information and

wanted to know all the details and where they had come from.

Peter André was described as 'gay' because of his style in his clothes and hair. The appearance and style of Peter André was crucial to his success, and conversely his limited time in favour. He was (in)famous for revealing his torso on stage and having in fact a very 'masculine' muscle-bound body. His macho display is a mirror image of the kind of 'hyper-femininity' used by the Spice Girls. He was therefore open to the same kind of attack as they were. This group also bemoaned the fact that 'there are a lot of people turning to gay', 'even Shabba Ranks is turning to gay' (Clive, see p. 58).

Within the school context the term 'gay' had many meanings and acted as a way of regulating heterosexual masculinities (see Kehily and Nayak 1996; Epstein 1993; Epstein and Johnson 1994, 1998a). The multiple meanings can be seen in the comments about the men but not so clearly in the label 'lesbian' for the women. The way in which the children perceive these sexual orientations, and their sexualisation of stars, is developed in the next chapter. The discussion above reveals that the children are using sexuality as a form of regulation in normative gender acquisition, and that they are linking this to attractiveness and character in a person. Therefore, you cannot be 'nice' *and* 'pretty' *and* 'a lesbian'. These value judgements are imbued with issues of style and identification for the children. For boys, you can be too good-looking, and that makes you 'gay' and therefore 'nasty'. *All of these processes are formed with and through a recognition of racialisation, but only within particular textual contexts.* These contexts were often negotiated through friendships and collective re/readings of popular images.

Friendship and Fandom

The way the children negotiated their friendships was often linked to their likes and dislikes of particular artists. For Frith, despite the fact that musical taste is guided by something outside of oneself (social conditioning, history, and so on), the experience of music is something which is itself performance, and as such creates social identities.

> What I want to suggest ... is not that social groups agree on values which are then expressed in their cultural activities ... but that they only get to know themselves *as groups* (as a particular organisation of individual and social interests, of sameness and difference) through cultural activity, *through* aesthetic judgement. (Frith 1996: 111)

The friendship groups of the children were often formed through the processes of musical affiliations. Through collective readings of music in particular, and the more extreme pleasures of fandom, the girls especially moved in and out of groups with a fluidity policed by an agreement of what taste they shared, particularly in music.

Pop stars were still the dominant 'pin-ups', with television actors and film stars coming a close second. With the expansion of the electronic media, the experience of music is no longer exclusively aural supplemented with static images from magazines. It is now more often experienced through video, music programmes and music channels on satellite and cable television.

The girls at Fairsham in Year 6 mentioned above (Hilary, Lena and Angela), were led by Hilary, who was a very dominant character. Hilary was particularly 'in love' with Ronan Keating.[11] When Lena had the audacity to suggest that he was not very good-looking, Hilary said, 'Yes he is! We *all* like Ronan, don't we, Lena?' in a mock-threatening manner. In her introduction to the discussion, Hilary often used the collective voice to speak for her friends in the group, as if their musical taste were identical.

> Power is employed and exercised through net like organisation. And not only do individuals circulate between the threads; they are always in the position of simultaneously undergoing and exercising this power. (Foucault 1980: 98)

Lena was positioned on the outskirts of this group and Hilary used her knowledge/power in ways that the girls, particularly Lena, readily acquiesced to. They colluded with Hilary's style of group leadership and enjoyed the privileges that came from the gang.

These girls showed that fandom was certainly not pathological; rather, it was simply a heightened form of appreciation for stars. Yet 'fans' were always female as girls were the only groups to use the term, and they were also all white. Other girls in Year 6 in Fairsham banded together in the face of considerable opposition and ridicule from other groups to enjoy the Spice Girls, despite it being covert enjoyment. The image of the fan as excessive, hysterical and dangerous with some kind of psychological dysfunction is one that is well known (Jensen 1992). Yet both groups of girls used the term in a more positive way; and their pleasure in the term and its attendant practices was similar to that one would expect to see in older fans.

I noted in my field diary that some Year 5 and 6 girls at Fairsham, who formed two 'gangs', were constantly writing, talking and singing about their favourites. Being a fan involved a considerable investment in time and energy. The superior knowledge of the objects of desire was a form of cultural capital that resulted in status within the groups (see Fiske 1992). Within this age group in the microenvironment of this school, liking the Spice Girls was, if not quite 'counter-hegemonic', certainly an oppositional reading to the majority in their class and year group. However, the terrain of the debate was superior knowledge. Those girls who didn't like them claimed to know better, that their knowledge of music showed the Spices were overexposed and therefore over.

The way the boys in Fairsham used their knowledge and pleasure was markedly different. The girls were very open about stars they saw as attractive, describing them in 'romantic' ways as 'gorgeous' and 'good-looking'. This parallels McRobbie's (1991) work, but it was not true across all locations as will be discussed later. The boys barely talked about the physical appearance of female artists, other than to comment if they were 'pretty'. (The exceptions were a group of boys who made up a set of names for the Spice Girls based around the fact that they were 'ugly and fat'.) Instead, boys often formed allegiances around the fact that they *disliked* particular things, discussing at length how 'bad' people were and who they 'loathed'.

A typical interaction about the Spice Girls in Fairsham, a primary school in a predominantly white, middle-class, semi-rural area in Kent, follows. The virulence of these boys shows the possible level of dislike of the Spice Girls. The boys were all in Year 5: Jack, a white English boy; Larry, a white boy with one Swedish and one British parent; Adrian, white English, and Lance also white English:

Suki: Do you like the Spice Girls?
Jack: I like their music but don't like them.
Adrian: 'Cos they have taken over the world now.
Larry: I want to go to one of their concerts with a bomb and blow them up.

This group were extremely critical of the Spice's clothing and appearance, and there seemed to be an awareness that this was to do with them having no 'taste' and also no 'class', although they did not use these words themselves. The strength of their responses prompted me to ask:

Suki: Do you think they are horrible people or not?
Jack: Their personalities are all right.

Jack's comments, which separate the idea of the personality of the girls from their music, and even perhaps their public image, is one of the more sophisticated readings of the group. Larry's desire to 'blow them up', on the other hand, is in keeping with alternative analyses of them as 'ugly', both literally and in terms of being unpleasant, loud, noisy, and talentless, and of concern about their overexposure in the media.

Even if boys' allegiances were not initially formed around 'loathing', this was often the basis for debate and negotiation. This was less true for the girls in the school who were more likely to debate and argue about what they *did* like. The use of consumer goods and knowledge/power was equally in evidence with boys, but was more likely to be tied in with football stars and computer games. Here, status was accrued by the number of games they had, and how up to date they were, as well as how skilled they were at playing.

The ways that the boys and girls in the London schools spoke about the strength of their feeling for particular artists were similar but a great deal more explicit. The girls in Year 6 in both schools talked about who they thought was attractive in a much more overtly sexual manner; so too did the boys.

Some of the boys in the first group in the first school, Christie, actually started enhancing a photograph of the Spice Girls, showing some cleavage with a pen. But the girls also talked about the fact that many of the stars they liked were 'fine', and they would pore over the images in the magazines, touching the photographs and begging me if they could have certain pictures for themselves. This again was a communal activity. The talking and touching took place in the group setting, and the shared aspect of the reading with contemporaries undoubtedly enhanced the levels of enjoyment gained from the materials.

The fact that the initial interview groups consisted of peers or indeed friends was crucial to the experience. It would have been significantly different in a one-to-one setting with me as research-friend. There were many reasons for this. The children stated that they enjoyed talking to me, but this was about the research and general school gossip. I did not have the necessary expertise to talk to them about the music that they liked, and with the age difference between us the problems were more marked. It was even harder to imagine having any kind of free talk with the boys about these things, as the issue of expressing sexual desire for the stars and their attractiveness was hampered by the fact of my being female. The way that they sometimes objectified the female stars made me feel uncomfortable and doubtless this showed in some way, despite my best efforts to disguise it. They were often doing this to shock and they sometimes succeeded. The relationship I had with the older girls in the schools, in contrast, did resemble the research-friend as I got to know them better, and resulted in greater freedom in their speech.

Making Meanings Make Sense: Asking Difficult Questions

The use of popular culture alone was not adequate to uncover the more subtle distinctions about how understandings of 'race' and ethnicity worked in the immediate social environment of the children, but as the interviews progressed it emerged that conversation about the celebrities was partially useful. Fairsham was outstanding in this way, but all schools had groups which needed explicit guidance to take the conversation into particular areas by asking direct questions. In the discussions about media stars, the idea of 'race' seemed at first to be abstract and removed from reality. The way the children moved from the distant to the involved at Christie and Barnlea was quite smooth. In Fairsham, this conceptual shift required more negotiation, and often utilised my presence as researcher and co-discussant to bring the concepts into some kind of concrete reality in an everyday form. The social geography of the children and the demographics of the area showed themselves to be of paramount importance. For most of these white children there were no minority ethnic children in their immediate sphere of peers, and the few that there were, were located entirely within the school context.

Making 'Race' Matter: 'Reading Race', Talking Racism

It is clear that one of the ways the children conceived of 'race', even when talking about people they knew, was by visual signifiers. Skin colour, facial features and hair type were most often invoked. Judith Butler has argued of gender that '[If] the body is not "a being", but a variable boundary, a surface whose permeability is politically regulated ... gendered bodies are so many "styles of the flesh". The styles all never fully self-styled for styles have a history, and those histories condition and limit the possibilities' (Butler 1990: 139). In this context the children show that the same is true of raced bodies and that they were learning the historical and contemporary limits to racialising bodies. The children show the fluidity of the surface of the racialised body and the discursive limits to 'mixed-race' are bound to crude binaries, or listing comma-ed genealogies of family and nationality. Clive was the only child in the sample who expressed a preference for being 'monoracial' during these discussions. Generally, the groups were well versed in the idea that it made no difference to Scary's dancing or singing if she was black and/or 'mixed-race'. It made her no better and no worse; it's just who she is and 'how' she is. They responded to questions about the hierarchies of 'races' in a very predictable way, quite blatantly repeating the mantra of 'equality despite difference' that had been presented to them by schools. Those who had a more sophisticated understanding were those who had had additional information from outside the school context. This shows that the discourses of multiculturalism were inadequate to children (see Chapter 7).

Sexuality and Morality

The children were less likely to want to talk about 'race' *in the first instance* than they would about sex and sexuality. The research gave them the opportunity to discuss with an adult the way they perceived (hetero)sexual relations. Using media to talk about people at some distance from their own lives provided them with a safe environment in which to do so. It was difficult to make generalisations about the ethnicity of children, and their responses to these debates about sex, but it is important to note that these conversations were often tempered with discussions about what was *morally* acceptable to the children, and they were often conservative in tone. A notable number of African-Carribean children in London showed greater confidence in talking about the issues in my presence, but I am not suggesting this reveals evidence of greater sexual awareness. It does show that there was a greater confidence for many of these children in expressing their own ideas, desires and pleasures verbally.

Despite a certain amount of gendered appreciation that revealed an active development of heterosexual identities, the discussions showed that 'race' remained 'unreal' to most of the non-urban children. It would be hardly surprising that they would continue to talk about this as something forbidden, just as they talked about sex as something forbidden. In contrast, the children in the multiracial schools had immediate and endless experience of racism in their lives and although they were happy to talk about it, it was not as exciting as talking about the other forbidden topic: sex. For them 'race' took precisely the opposite meaning as it did for the majority of children at Fairsham. It *was/is* part of their everyday experience.

Learning Mixedness?

Van Zoonen (1994: 41) suggests that '[o]bviously all media are central sites at which discursive negotiation of gender takes place'. The same is true of sexuality, 'race' and class and dis/ability. Children are most often engaged with reading meanings of gender and heterosexuality and this shows that 'race' is not always the most *consciously* salient factor in the way that children read popular culture. The children from all backgrounds are involved with interracial, intraracial, racial and ethnic questioning, but as part of the all-important business of girling and boying. Readings of popular culture are certainly, in part, responsible for a sense of the Black Atlantic (see Gilroy 1993a) diaspora that involves the 'black British' children in a strong cultural identification with black artists from the USA, and the reading of the specialist black music magazines. There were exceptions to the rules in all cases and generalisations were hard to make, but, unlike teenage responses, the children in this setting did not claim to be concerned about 'authenticity'. Older children can be hostile to those who are 'trying to be black', who listen to black music and take on black styles of talk (Back 1996; Buckingham and Sefton-Greene 1994). *All* children who took part in this research showed an appreciation of 'African-American culture', which shows a change from earlier studies, and a common form of black-British-speak crosses all ethnic groups.[12] However, the question of *authenticity* is most certainly evident when the children use racist abuse during arguments, particularly towards 'mixed-race' children (see Chapter 7). Within the privileging of cultures of style and sex, the children who claim mixed identities have to work with both the disavowal and reclamation of the authentic in their everyday encounters with others. The ways in which these children negotiate their sense of mixedness in relation to hegemonic singular models of racialised identity, and how they relate their own (raced) positions to celebrities, peers and family members, are explored in detail in the next chapter.

Notes

1. Pop is a particularly volatile arena for 'stars'. They come and go with reassuring regularity, and it is those who have real staying power that are notable. In this chapter, it is inevitable that some of those who were 'huge' at the time of data collection are barely remembered today. I believe that despite this, the ways in which children talk of these artists is still relevant and recognisable. The same types of analyses could be made with different artists today.
2. This was before the explosion of interest in Bollywood and all things 'Asian' that happened in 2002.
3. Mel B was later married and changed her name to Mel G. She has separated from her husband and then became known as Melanie Brown. I have used 'Scary' throughout as that is what the children called her, and this is still the way in which she is most often referred to.
4. The first real action *101 Dalmatians* (Disney) was very popular at the time of research.
5. Aqua are now defunct – another casualty of the fickleness of fans and short shelf-life of 'manufactured pop'.
6. I immediately relate this term to the film *Coffee Coloured Children* (Non-Aligned Productions 1988), an autobiographical film showing the misery of being the only two black children, living with a white mother, growing up in a village in the north of England in the 1960s.
7. Another child also showed how influential these cartoons could be, as she picked her favourite 'people' exclusively from cartoon characters (see Chapter 4).
8. Children in Years 5 and 6 in all schools also revealed a passion for adult white comedies such as *Friends* and *Third Rock from the Sun*. They were still shown after the nine o'clock watershed on terrestrial TV. Children from Year 4 claimed not to like such programmes.
9. See also Chapter 4 for a discussion on sexuality and morality.
10. The meaning of 'gayness' is discussed in 'Sex and the Stars' (pp. 59–61).
11. Ronan Keating was lead singer with a (then) popular white Irish 'boy band', Boyzone. He has since launched a successful solo career.
12. However, the term 'whigger' has been used by white supremacists for those emulating black cultural styles and in this context implies 'race' traitor (see Back 2002).

–4–

Ambiguous Images:
Relating 'Mixed-Race' Selves to Others

> The visual is simply one point of entry, and a very strategic one at this historical moment, into a multidemensional world of intertextual dialogism.
> E. Shohat and R. Stam, 'Narrativising Visual Culture:
> Towards a Polycentric Aesthetics'

Introduction

In this chapter, 'mixed-race' children articulate their ideas of what constitutes sexual desirability in others and the importance of a form of reflexive embodiment to acceptability. The children show an acute but only partially expressed concern about 'attractiveness', which is about style but also incorporates notions of class and sexuality, though not always explicitly 'race'. In the following sections, I will introduce some of the ways in which the children who identified as 'mixed-race' took up the reading of popular materials and used them to form part of their identifications. I will argue that children do this when available discourses of 'race', ethnicity and culture are not allowing 'accurate' readings of themselves; when language fails them, they utilise readings and performances of visual signs that accord them positional flexibility.

The children show that their awareness of their embodied positionality has value judgements attached to it which play a part in where they 'fit' in their social networks at school and outside. Children are engaged in making sense of their world in the everyday through what Paul Willis calls 'symbolic work' showing considerable symbolic creativity (Willis *et al.* 1990). Symbolic work involves language, body and drama and the creative use of these resources. He states: 'It's also a cultural sense of what symbolic forms – languages, images, music, haircuts, styles, clothes – "work" most economically and creatively for the self.' (Willis 1993: 209) The acquisition of 'racial identity' can be achieved through the 'creative' though obviously constrained mutability of physicality and skin colour (Ahmed 1999). I will look at the possibilities and limitations of 'passing' arising from 'social antagonisms', and how it can problematise the pre-given positioning of both 'whiteness' and 'blackness'. The value of this approach is highlighted in the ways children avoid binaried either/or, black/white starting points and work with 'animated borders' of style, speech and food' shifting the terrain of debate from binaries to pluralities (ibid.).

Children's readings of the 'stars' drew on physical appearance to assess sexual orientation. In the first section I show that these 'moral' responses to representations followed no obvious patterns relating to gender or age, or to location. Individuals were guided by their own 'grounded aesthetics', which I can only assume were informed, in part, by their home environment, as well as by the hegemonic 'popular' within their friendship networks and in the 'particularness' of their own dynamic locations (Willis 1993: 211).

In the second section, the way in which children perceive themselves, their appearance and their attractiveness will be explored in some detail. It is clear that for many of these children the established hierarchies of colour in beauty are not relevant to their readings of what is beautiful and attractive in self and others. For the children in this study, there is an acknowledgement that claiming blackness is desirable and desired, but without using essentialising discourses, or, even overtly, identification. How they are positioned by others indicates that these assessments still operate at a (sub)liminal level, as popularity seems to be based on an 'attractiveness' which is in part physical, even if it is not based on 'whiteness'. This provides an interesting opening into assessing how children think of themselves as being like or unlike others, and how that may be differently experienced in relation to family members who are (whether in real terms or not) biologically connected.

In the final section, I will show how family identifications influence children's understanding of their physicality, and how this is often gendered and constituted through relations of distance and closeness to other family members. I conclude that the way in which children understand their bodies as both gendered and raced may be read as a form of 'drama' (Willis *et al.* 1990) or 'performativity' (Butler 1990, 1993) in which they are exploring subjectivities which are both constrained, yet liberating and dynamic.

Morality and Appearance

The sexualisation of stars through reading embodied style was an important aspect of social interaction amongst children in the study. Celebrities' popularity and was also informed by, and informed, children's perceptions of their character, which was entangled with understanding them as sexually desirable. The children often made decisions about who looked 'nice, 'good' or 'stylish' based upon some perceived notion of 'decency'. Being pretty or handsome or (reasonably) good-looking was equated with being a 'nice' person. They rarely talked about one without the other, even if their comments about the person were critical. People could have quite flamboyant style and be perceived as attractive by some children and 'disgusting' by others. These kinds of polysemous readings of bodies-as-texts pervaded the interaction within and across children's friendships.

These unstable and volatile interpretations of style are reminiscent of both Skeggs's (1997) and Hey's (1997) ethnographic work with girls and women that explore the relationships between heterosexuality, class, race and gender. In both cases the research showed the importance of respectability to maintaining correct levels of acceptable femininity. Whilst children in this research are also trying to manage the same demands on femininity, they do so from a much more loosely interpretative framework. The work of masculinity also requires translation of both femininities and masculinities, *not* into respectability based on controlled and invisible sexuality but into the right form of visible sexuality relational to both – that is, heterosexuality.

Reading Sexual Desirability: Too Spicy

The ubiquitous Spice Girls, as we heard in the previous chapter, were especially open to this kind of style/character interpretation. Many of the attacks on them centred on their 'style' and how that expressed a type of character that was somehow very decadent and very sexual. Meli from Barnlea (London) thought that the Spice Girls did not look 'decent'. She repeated at a later interview that she thought that Lauryn Hill had really good style and that she looked pretty and 'nice' and 'decent'. In this case there are clear links between decency and niceness. The girls in Hey's (1997) study were acutely aware of the dangers of oversexualised behaviour. The ways in which the girls managed this tightrope of sexual attractiveness and acceptable levels of sexual activity, with the constant spectre of ostracism due to slaggishness, was subtle and in most cases highly skilled. Hey says of Carol: 'Being a proper dressed up young lady was the respectable form of heterosexuality within Carol's community. She had ferocious rows with her mother about "suitable" appearances which in essence were arguments about Carol being thought "improperly" that is, too sexily dressed' (Hey 1997: 93). Like Carol, Meli and other girls were all interested in cultivating femininities which, at this stage of their lives, draw heavily on resources from popular culture. Scary Spice was one of those most likely to provoke strong feelings of pleasure or disgust in appearance.

Jamal (Barnlea, black-African/Asian-African, Year 4) said that the Scary wore 'too many see through clothes'. In a later interview with him and his friend Cain (Year 4, Anglo/Turkish) he got quite enthusiastic about this theme which took on surprisingly racialised tones:

Jamal: She's ugly and she's got curly hair and a big earring stuck in her lip and she got one in her belly button and it so nasty. I can't stand her bush hair! [...]

Suki: I like big bushy hair.
Cain: Uuurgh if you had it I wouldn't sit next to you!
Jamal: She got spider hair!

As the conversation continued, Jamal told a story about a 'crazy' man who lived near him who went out wearing dreadlocks, a skirt and lipstick. The man had, so local myth went, 'killed his wife' and if you went near him he would 'rape you'. I believed that he was talking about a black man, as the story was a response to my asking if he liked dreadlocks. He began to describe the man, and said he was 'kind of tall' pointing at me:

Suki: Tall like me? But I'm not scary though!
Cain: When you talk in that voice you are!
Jamal: And you look a bit scary with that earrings running down ...
Suki: Did you think I was scary when you first saw me?
Jamal: I thought that when you get upset you shout.

This conversation shows yet again the dominant discursive positions that are on offer to and being explored by the children. Jamal reveals his concerns with sexuality and 'race' and gender, and how he connects these to respectability and attractiveness.

Firstly, Scary Spice is seen as too flamboyant in a very sexual way and that makes her 'nasty'. Part of this nastiness is her hair and her clothes. Her hair was (at that time) in a large 'Afro' style, which Jamal sees as 'bushy' and horrible. This is a raced position, but it is mediated through a particular cultural/ethnic location that interprets hair in that style as unkempt. He similarly rejects dreadlocks, which are most commonly embraced by black Caribbean men and women.[1] As a West African/African-Asian Muslim these are not desirable or attractive styles for him. This sets him to thinking about a 'crazy man' who sports dreadlocks. We can tell he is crazy because he wears a skirt and lipstick. This equation with non-normative gender representation and madness is common, hence the loud unsexy Scary is masculine and 'crazy' too. More explicitly Jamal mentions the fact that this man is a 'rapist' and a murderer, both sexually and violently uncontrollable.

In returning the conversation to our present location the children used my own physicality to further explore the nasty/scary/crazy matrix. I was perceived as scary in part because of my physical size. I had extremely short hair at the time and often wore trousers, but with 'earrings' (facial piercings with jewellery) in my face. These gave out mixed messages about my gender to the children, one of whom asked me 'Miss, are you a man?'! For Cain and Jamal I was potentially threatening as I was not presenting myself as typically 'feminine', and this was a transgression they found difficult to position in their own desire to develop successful masculinities. These are fragile and partial positions, as will be shown below.

Both of these boys thought that Baby Spice, Emma Bunton, was very 'pretty' and chose her as their favourite person, as well as their most attractive female. They clearly read her style in a wholly unproblematic way. Baby wore short, 'feminine', low-cut dresses, a lot of pale pink, and frequently had her long blonde hair in two bunches to make her look young; hence 'Baby'. For these boys she was 'nice' and 'sweet' as well, despite the fact that she wore clothes that were equally as revealing as those of Scary. Her style is in fact a form of 'hyper-femininity' which distorts and exaggerates the fetishises of young female sexuality through a middle-aged white male gaze. It is clear that for these boys the readings were multilayered and informed by normative sexualised gender aspirations which read Baby as cute, unproblematically feminine, infantilised and sexy, and Scary as scary, 'masculine' and therefore of necessity independent and assertive and as a consequence unsexy.

Not all the children read the Spice Girls this way and for some she was the 'prettiest', along with sporty Spice. Miranda (Year 6, Christie, white English/black Jamaican), said that she was one of the prettiest women in the media.[2] There was nothing remarkable in this except that Miranda is a Jehovah's Witness who had quite strong views on sex, relationships and gender. She was quiet, studious and very intelligent. Her best friends were based around a group of self-defined black girls, and she joined in with their group readings of the popular in the school playground. When I asked about her favourite playground conversations, she said 'music, groups, people, songs' (Miranda, Christie, 1998).

Miranda's reading of Scary was that she was a good singer and dancer and very pretty. She also chose Shola Ama, another black soul/R and B artist who is mainstream and non-threatening. It is clear that the children of 'mixed-race' are sharing as many diverse readings of the popular as any others. The love/loathe factor in relation to Scary traversed to Fairsham where Ella, a girl in Year 4, also loved the Spices, in particular Scary who she thought was the best in the group. Ella raised the issue of 'reality' or 'authenticity', as she did not like people who were 'plastic', yet she did not read the Spice Girls as 'fake' and liked the idea of their Girl Power.

Show-Offs and Fakes

Meli: I don't like Mel B [Scary] 'cos she shows off.

Being 'nice' and being decent were tied to the notion of being 'yourself' and being 'natural'. The 'natural body' was a powerful discourse amongst the children, yet they were all beginning consciously to engage with disciplining their own bodies in striving for gendered heterosexed identities (Foucault 1998). It is of course an irony that the achievement of naturalness was so artificially produced in the representations of bodies of popular stars.

As Judith Butler comments: 'As the effects of a subtle and politically enforced performativity, gender is an "act" as it were, that is open to splittings, self-parody, self-criticism, and those hyberbolic exhibitions of the natural that in their very exaggeration reveal its fundamentally phantasmic status' (Butler 1990: 147).

One of the most censured behaviours was the use of plastic surgery. This is an arena which is rich for the kind of parodic (self) criticism of gender and 'race' performativity as exhibited in the readings of the children. Ella had an extensive, though rather confused, knowledge of such matters:

Ella: Michael Jackson, he looks like a girl, not that girls don't look good, but he's like ... and plastic surgery and I don't like Pam ... Pam ... Pamela Anderson either.

Suki: Same reason 'cos she looks too plastic?

Ella: Mm.

Suki: Have you seen her in lots of things?

Ella: I've seen her in some magazines, but my friend my best friend liked her and he said that she had had plastic surgery on her nipples and his ... then his dad walked in and said 'He means he that she blew them up in the car ... in the umm ... car what's it called, where you put oil in your car? Where is it?'

Suki: Garage.

Ella: Yeah that's it – garage [laughs].

Suki: Her nipples or all of her breasts?

Ella: Her nipples and her stomach.

Suki: So you don't like people who do that kind of thing?

Ella: I like people for what they are not for what they want to look like.

These words introduce the idea that what we look like is not simply about style and character, as such; rather, it is about *choice and aspirations*. In this she reveals the signs of having understood that her development as 'girl' has to be achieved, and is still open to failures. Ella is aware of the need again for a certain authenticity even in the appearance of/representation of one's 'self'. Despite the knowledge on the part of some of the children that the Spice Girls had been manufactured, Ella liked them so much that her best job in the world would be being a Spice Girl. Yet with Michael Jackson, again his 'gender bending' is seen as problematic. Although Ella did not mention it, others had talked about the fact that Michael Jackson had reportedly tried to bleach his skin. This was unanimously perceived as being a bad thing by the children.

Attractive appearance was clearly tied to ideas of 'naturalness'. Despite the fact that children clearly recognised that stars were given to quite radically altering their style, there was a notion that there was some underlying 'self' who was either acceptable/nice or not acceptable/nasty and whose 'essence' was unchangeable. Yet how that could be discerned was open to multiple interpretations. Miranda told me that a white, female TV presenter got on her nerves because she was a 'show off'. Yet she loved the less-than-shy Scary. Could this be in part alienation from the presenter's 'white' sub-cultural image based in the dance and club music of predominantly white youth. Miranda's tastes were guided by black music, yet also included reading white, middle-class-school-girl stories.

In a few cases the children could recognise that good style/looks did *not* equal 'nice person'. One of the more sophisticated responses to these questions came from Lola at Barnlea (Year 6 Chinese/white English):

Suki: Who do you think is good-looking?

Lola: Michael Owen. Yeah Michael Owen except he's a bit eeuughh [mimes sticking her fingers down her throat] sickening!

Suki: In what way – a bit full of himself?

Lola: Yeah, *I* think so.

Lola's emphasis on the word 'I' shows that she is aware that she is in the minority when expressing this opinion. But both she and Sima (boy, Year 6, white English/black Jamaican) were adamant that looking good and being good were placed in relation to each other.

When talking about being good-humoured, Scary came up again:

Sima: That's who I was thinking of, 'cos she seems like a really good person to know and she's not like all in love with herself.

Lola: Yeah, she helps people. Like Diana she helped people but unfortunately she died, boo hoo.

Sima in particular is very concerned with people being 'nice to know', and here Lola elevates Scary to the role of pseudo-saint on the same level as Princess Diana, whom they both decided was a 'really nice person'. Being vain or arrogant, 'in love with yourself', is undoubtedly a bad thing, yet many of the children expressed views that showed that they were at least content to be/look like they did.

For example, Lola said:

Lola: I'd look like, I like Denise, but I don't think I would like being her.
Suki: You would? Denise who?
Lola: Denise Van Outen.
Suki: So you think she looks good but don't want to be like her.
Lola: I ... she's pretty but I wouldn't like to be her.
Suki: Why not?
Lola: Umm.
Suki: [using clues from previous interviews] You just want to be yourself?
Lola: Yeah.

Again, Lola shows that she can separate the person from the image and the lifestyle, and in doing so asserts the idea that there is a 'self' that she would currently rather be than someone famous. This is a key way in which children expressed the narrative of a self in process, a level of reflexivity in the process of imagining themselves.

There were occasions when children suggested that they would like to be someone that they knew who was a friend from school or home. It was always girls who did this, except for one boy who chose a classmate who was always smiling. In this sense the responses were likely to be gendered, and the girls were more likely to be able to articulate aesthetic pleasure from looking at other girls than boys were from looking at boys. This ties in with the normative power of the heterosexual masculinities for boys. It made it impossible for them to reveal a 'male gaze' being turned upon another male. It was more dangerous for boys to talk about men as attractive than it was for girls to talk about women, as girls could be expected to enjoy looking at women within the generic popular productions of fashion and beauty on television and in magazines. Boys often claimed to want to be like footballers or musicians that they admired for their talent rather than their looks. Boys could talk about appearance through style, which was constructed through musical style, or by using the voices of girls who had positioned men as popular.

Gendering Pleasures in Looking

There were some differences in the emphasis on readings which boys and girls made that crossed location and class. The ways in which men and women 'read' visual texts, it has been suggested, are in part determined by the scopophilic position which is gendered. Mulvey's (1975) influential work from a psychoanalytic perspective suggests that 'the gaze' is male, and that women and girls are only allowed problematic identifications and that they are denied pleasures of looking (at). Others have argued that this position is context-specific and needs some revision (Van Zoonen 1994: 90). Certainly girls in this study, as seen in the previous chapter, *are* enjoying the pleasures of spectatorship (as feminists have found: Winship 1987; Gamman and Marshment 1988; McRobbie 1991). In this section, I will show that the ways in which the boys and girls chose to talk about their readings, and how they used these in gendering identifications, reinforce a more complex view of the pleasures of visual culture.

Boys and Masculinities

Thomas is a boy of white English and black Jamaican parents in Year 6 at Christie School. He lives with his mother, who is white, and sees his black father rarely. He has a reputation for being naughty and difficult and was in the past labelled as having 'emotional and behavioural difficulties'. He is by his own admission a 'pretty boy', a term he used with knowing irony, and he admitted or boasted that he was 'vain'. Miranda, who is also 'mixed-race', told me that she did not like him because he was 'always talking about sexual relationships'. It is true that he was more than happy to talk about his girlfriend with me in the interview context. When he was in conversation with his best friend Onal, he told me that his favourite all-time character was Jackie Chan. He and Onal spoke animatedly about Jackie Chan movies and managed to draw Chan back into the conversation at every opportunity:

Suki: So who do you think is a great person?
Onal: Jackie Chan.
Thom: Jackie Chan.
Suki: Would you like to look like that though.
Onal: No.
Thom: Yes.
Onal: No.
Thom: You'd rather be a film star and showing off too much.
Onal: Actually, no, I'd be Jackie Chan.
Suki: So what's so good about him?
Onal: Jackie Chan does his own stuff, and every time when he breaks his leg he still does his own stuff, 'cos in this film *Lost in the Bronx* and he jumps from roof.
Suki: So you like him physically, how he is …
Onal: Yeah.
Suki: Do you actually think he is good-looking then?
Onal: Yeah.
Thom: He gets all the girls in the films, all of his films.

This identification required some negotiation on the part of the boys, and Jackie Chan certainly was an unusual choice. They went on to talk about physical strength, which was another thing they admired and wished for themselves. The text reveals how surprised I was at their choice, and the fact they would like to look like Jackie Chan who, as an Asian man, is outside the hegemonic boundaries of acceptable good looks. Onal also had to change his position after being led by Thomas. Jackie Chan was deemed to be good-looking on the basis that he got all the girls in the films, therefore he had to be good-looking, and so they would be him and also get all the girls. This is another clever piece of manipulation of some difficult areas on their part. By using the utterances of others, or rather, the actions and visual texts of others, they are able to negotiate the dangerous ground of homoerotic fandom into which they had strayed.

Thomas was also keen to represent himself as expert in the area of martial-arts films, and also claimed to watch a lot of Japanese 'manga' films. His expertise in this area is again gendered as he claims it as status and reflects the status of Clive when he talked about his knowledge of Shabba Ranks, and how that fitted in with dominant readings of hardcore rap. This is different from the rather more 'feminine' form of fandom that is characterised by the image of hysterical teenage girls, and which is not imbued with the same status as 'expertise' within peer groups. Thomas is able to form a purely heterosexual story out of his same-sex reading, and in doing so maintained a *sexualised* reading.

Girling: Looking Beautiful, Wearing Hair

For girls the reading of attractiveness and whether it was 'raced' or not was often articulated through hairstyles. Debbie Weekes (1997) studied the attitudes of young 'Black' women between the ages of 14 and 16 to beauty and attractiveness.[3] Her findings showed practices of exclusion by those of darker skin against those with paler skin and more European features, including those of 'mixed-parentage'. She argues that the discourses of 'colourism' and 'essentialism' have become intricately woven, resulting in a form of essentialising as a means of claiming a position of power in face of the normative standard of European beauty (Weekes 1997: 122). For authors investigating such issues there are a number of reasons for the operation of these norms and how they are mediated through bodies. In the mid-range of skin tone, femininities take on a vague form of indeterminate exoticism. Skin colour, hair texture, and facial features such as thickness of nose and fullness of lips, are invoked as the markers of blackness.[4] Young women appear to be resorting to such narrow 'definitions of Blackness' as a form of strategic essentialism. She suggests that: '[a]t one extreme there is a rejection of European ideas of womanhood and at the other an assumption that these qualities are desired. However, what these issues highlight is the underlying influence of Whiteness as yardstick for beauty' (Weekes 1997: 123).

Many of the girls in this research did *not* use whiteness as a yardstick for beauty. Miranda's reading of her mother with her 'gingery' hair was a rejection of whiteness as a preferred standard of beauty:

Suki: What does she look like your mum, tell me a little bit about her.

Miranda: Mm well, she's got gingerish-brown hair and she's white (mmm) and I sometimes say that she looks a little bit like Ginger Spice.

Suki: Does she? [Miranda nods] Is she really pretty?

Miranda: Mm.

Suki: Do other people say that as well, that she looks a bit like Ginger Spice?

Miranda: No.

Suki: No? Just you think that?

Miranda: No, I'm just teasing her really.

Suki: Oh – does she not like to be like Ginger Spice?

Miranda: Not really no.

Miranda describes herself as 'mixed-race' and can see herself as different from her mother, who is 'white'. She also positions herself as a discerning reader of the popular in that she teases her mother about looking like Ginger Spice, whilst preferring Scary herself. She acknowledges gender in the way that she also claims that her sister looks more like her mum, but when pressed about who she would like to look like herself, in common with many of the girls, chose a black woman, 'Tamara' in 'Sister, Sister'. She has turned the beauty standards Weekes describes on their head.

In common with other theoretical works, Weekes's analysis leaves us with no room to explore 'the Thing' (ibid.) that 'does' the constructing; despite a desire to reclaim the work of the young women as active responses to cultural hegemony. As Butler (1993) suggests, in taking this position, discourse becomes the subject of the sentence, and in the process creates the passive object. The tension between activity and passivity within a knowing subject is one that plagues discussions of racialisation and Othering processes in general.

Conventional studies of racialised beauty standards produce results which, I suggest, form a constraining continuum for both conventional *and* so-called counter-hegemonic readings (see Figure 1). This model means that for black women ('natural') blackness is the only possible counter-hegemonic form of *authentic* beauty and anything that utilises so-called whitening processes is inauthentic. It also means that those who are also 'naturally' pale are automatically inauthentic. Either end of the 'natural' scale are the essential positions of white/black with no room for other Others (for example 'Orientals' *sic*) or mixednesses which become automatically 'exotic' and inauthentic as well.

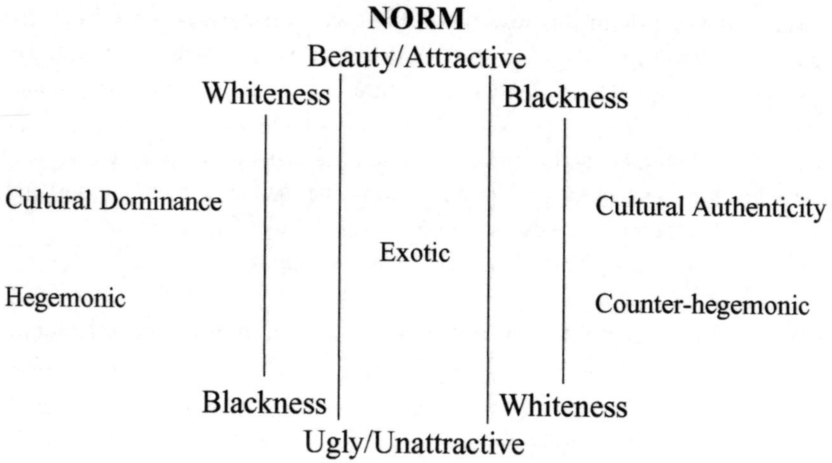

NORM
Beauty/Attractive

Whiteness | | Blackness

Cultural Dominance | Cultural Authenticity

Exotic

Hegemonic | Counter-hegemonic

Blackness | | Whiteness
Ugly/Unattractive

Figure 2 Normative Racialised Beauty Standards[5]

Kallie and Hannah (both white English/black Caribbean, Year 5, Christie) also chose a black girl who was in their class at school as their 'ideal person'. They said that they thought that she was really pretty, but also that she was funny and a good dancer, linking her abilities and talents with her looks, her character and her popularity in much the same way as Onal and Thomas did with Jackie Chan. But they chose to see such popularity in a non-sexual way. This choice had more to do with the gendered aesthetics of beauty and popularity. Kallie also experimented with many different hairstyles. When I was at the school she too chose plaited styles over 'straight' and 'inauthentic' styles.

Dinease (Christie, Year 5) was another of the girls who had naturally curly hair, not 'Afro', yet chose to wear it in 'black' styles:

Suki: So you didn't have long, the style it is now, you had it in extensions before didn't you?
Dine: Yeah.
Suki: When did you change it?
Dine: I don't know.
Suki: Do you like a change?
Dine: 'Cos my mum thought it was getting a bit tatty and so she took it out.
Suki: Your mum does it.
Dine: Yeah.

Dinease's mother is black, originally from Montserrat.[6] As a black woman and a mother, she has the ultimate say in the acceptability of Dinease's hair. She has also passed on some of her expertise with hair to her daughters:

Dinease: Yeah sometimes we mess around with G's hair [her baby sister] and like plait it and cane row it and put in Chinee bumps. Yeah you can like plait it, or you can plait it and then twist it round and tuck it under or you can just get the hair itself straighten it out and then just do the same thing ...

Despite this identification with blackness, Dinease calls herself 'mixed-race', as does her mother. But the importance of good hair is not lost on her. A friend of mine used to talk about being at school and being able to tell the children who had white mothers because they were 'the one bunch kids', the ones whose mothers could not do their hair properly. Liesbeth de Block, aware of her position as a white mother of a 'mixed-race' daughter, is determined that this should not happen to her child:

As I have had to learn about the complications and intricacies of caring for black hair I have met astonishment and denial from black and white that I have cane rowed or plaited Daniella's hair. Meanwhile Daniella's father is especially concerned about the appearance of her hair when she goes out with him because he does not want to be accused by black women of not caring for her properly. (Block 1997: 14)

Hair is not just appearance; it is values, caring, kinship and culture. I asked Talia about her new plaits:

Suki: Did you get your hair done before you went on holiday?
Talia: Mm hm.
Suki: And your neighbour did it?
Talia: Yeah.
Suki: Do you do Talia's hair? [to Mrs Farmer]
Mrs. F: I can do all this. Once it's parted I can pick it out and ... Its a necessity I think when you have 'mixed-race' children to be able to care ... There are too many English women have mixed-race children and you see their hair all ... [Tito and Talia giggle] No it's not funny.

So not only are the parents aware of this need for a statement in hair, so are the children. For the children who are 'racially' ambiguous, this is a powerful statement of allegiance to their blackness. It also shows the way in which they begin to write their identities upon their bodies, and perform their blackness.

Boys could of course use the same kinds of processes of identification through hair, but were not as heavily invested in their appearances at this stage of their lives. They had to negotiate the fine line between being good-looking without being vain, which as Thomas revealed was aligned with gayness. Mrs Farmer (Margaret) also told me about an incident involving Tito when he was subject to racist abuse when they were in Yorkshire, because he had the 'Adidas' symbol shaved into his hair. This was, she suggested, a strongly 'black' sign, as are dreadlocks. 'Curls' are not. Yet Lesley told me how disappointed she was when her son Jacob cut his hair short and greased it down because he 'looked like a white boy, he lost his curls'. In fact, short, shaved hair is a dominant form of black British hair for men (and to a lesser extent, women). Lesley did not read it as such, and was disappointed because she thought that Jacob was aspiring to whiteness.

This performance of 'race' and 'ethnicity' was not taken up by other children, who did not have such an obviously powerful sign of a racial/cultural marker as 'blackness' and black 'Afro' hair. The children of Chinese and Polynesian and Indian heritage could not achieve the same ends through hairstyles.[7] Just as Weekes (1997) criticises the use of hair and skin as markers of racial authenticity, so too girls subvert simplistic images by both accessing and rewriting simple equations between beauty and 'race' in order to claim a unique space for themselves.

For others such as Meli, her cultural affiliations to her grandmother's blackness took the form of identification with *black Britishness* as well as to her Polynesian heritage. At her house her mother had hung traditional clothes and accessories that Meli could name for me. She also used to quite literally perform her traditions and genealogies as her mother was a dancer who had worked with a traditional Polynesian dance troupe, and Meli often performed with them. She negotiates her positionality in fluid and dynamic ways which are ethnicised and cultured and to an extent 'raced', and are of her own making within the limitations of the discursive registers offered to her.

What the girls show is that their readings of popular images of race and gender are not governed by the same kinds of fears as the boys. They manage their readings of other girls and women in non-sexualised ways that also help to construct their ideas of beauty, but they do not fear the stigma of homosexuality enough to problematise these identifications. For girls, they are part of the enjoyment of same sex reading and are acceptable positions to occupy. This kind of identification is developed in the next section.

Being Myself

The children often had a very well developed sense of pride in themselves, which showed that if there was any kind of conflict in their positions they could often rationalise it within this particular form of conversation/interview. Although children could often identify things about themselves that they did not like, they would still say that they would rather be themselves either in appearance or character, or a combination of the two. These children showed that despite the unstable aspects of identifications, they are using 'narratives of selves' to create their own positions in their daily social relations. In doing so, they asserted confidence in being 'happy with who they are'. This is one of the discourses that I came to hear as having a basis in the liberal humanist principles of the schools. Just as we are 'all the same under the skin', so we need to learn to be 'happy with who we are'.

Both Meli and Jacob, who were friends, said immediately that they would not be someone else:

Suki: So if you could be anyone who would you be.

Jacob: Me. Me, its stupid to want to be someone else.

Meli: Me. You are lucky to be alive and have a face that is not burned or scarred or something.

Meli linked herself to beauty and physicality, and was the only person to mention the fact that she was healthy and able-bodied. The possibility of disability was seen as a legitimate reason for wishing to be someone else, and reveals how the discourses of desirability, whether in white or black terms, were always predicated on physical 'perfection' – though not too perfect as that is 'fake'. Both these children at Barnlea were able to articulate the position of self-contentment in a direct way, whereas for others, such as Jamal, the need for self-pride was tied in with the ways in which others positioned him in positive and negative ways:

Jamal: Yeah, like M has said 'How comes your mum's white how come your dad's black and how come you're brown and how come your brother's brown? There's lots of pink and black pigs in your house and you don't know which one is your mum and your dad and which one's your little brother!'
[...]

Jamal: I think its disgusting to say things like that. I'm a Muslim and I'm not supposed to say 'pigs' and all of that stuff and I just ignore them.

Suki: So how would *you* describe yourself or your skin colour?

Jamal: I'm brown, I'm pretty. And my little brother's cute and he's brown like me and my mum is white and she's a Muslim too and my mum is sweet, and she's kind and she buys me lots of clothes and my dad is good to me and he buys me pets and guess how many pets I got?

Suki: How many?

Jamal: Four. 'Cos I got a dog, a puppy I mean, I got a little toad, I got a tadpole and I got a bird and next I might get ... what they called?

Gerbils. Holly's [teacher] got them and she's got baby ones too, they
had about seven babies.

Suki: Wow, that is a lot. It would be lovely to have one of the babies. Um.
Have people talked about racism in school?

Jamal: Yeah, just that boy M.

Suki: Have people ever said nice things too, like you're lucky?

Jamal: My best friends, and my friends they say 'You're so sweet, you look
nice', and when I'm like sad they say like, 'What's wrong?' and if like
something bad has happened they go to the teacher and they tell.

What is shown here are the contradictions and complexities that are lived and
resolved for children of 'mixed-parentage' every day. Jamal has a series of
'voices' in play at any one time, some oppositional and some conciliatory. He
uses them to perform a poetic of identity, which he suddenly disrupts with his
desire to share his list of pets with me, showing how much he is valued by his
parents, and gaining 'status' from his ownership of them which adds to my sense
of his identity.[8]

Jamal *is* a very 'sweet' boy. He is physically quite small, and very good-
looking with a beautiful ready smile. He dressed in the ubiquitous sports casuals
favoured by boys; yet they were, he told me, 'from the market' rather than
branded. He was a popular child with a lot of friends. He had been confused by
my earlier question about religion, and said he had none, until he later explained
that he did not celebrate Christmas because he was Muslim. In this extract he
begins to talk about himself as he was defined by another boy, M, who was being
'racist'. Jamal is not so worried by the slur against his family as about the fact
that it challenges his position as a Muslim. This was not perceived as 'cussing
his colour' but 'cussing his religion'. The boy who insulted him is black British,
of Caribbean heritage, noted for being something of a bully.

Jamal claims to ignore people who are trouble, but in another conversation he
admitted that he sometimes lost his temper. He did go on to talk about himself in
terms that his mother uses, as she tells him that he is 'pretty'. This seems to be
an odd choice of words for the super-macho boy who laughs at the mad man who
wears a skirt (see p. 72). It also reveals how his self-esteem is negotiated through
the language of beauty, and that it is articulated with popularity, being sweet and
brown and, in the case of his brother, 'cute'. He is almost infantilised by his peers
who also perceive him as 'sweet', and will come to his defence if he is picked
upon. I believe his physicality has a great deal to do with this, but also that Jamal
himself presents in this way as it gains him benefits.

Although there is a view which positions South Asian boys as holding 'invisible' masculinities, or as quiet and 'feminised' (Gillborn 1990; Mac an Ghaill
1996; Connolly 1998), I am not convinced that this is an analysis that fits with

Jamal. He is concurrently actively constructing heterosexual masculinity in other contexts, but neither is he 'demonised' in class (Mac an Ghaill 1999). He is at present able to utilise discourses that sound feminised in an unselfconscious fashion, in ways that seem to be directly related to his age. At secondary school level, young men are much more consciously engaged in 'expelling femininity and homosexuality from within themselves' (Mac and Ghaill 1994: 90). Jamal does this, but it does not take the form of the totalising regulation of self that it does for older boys (see also Connell 1995). Jamal also utilises his whole family in order to describe himself. His mother is Kenyan-Asian, and by most people's reckoning would be seen as brown or 'black' in the political sense, yet M sees her as 'pink', and Jamal endorses that by saying that she is 'white'. He then qualifies her acceptability by saying that she too is 'sweet' and a Muslim, which makes her like him. Of course, most importantly she is 'good to him' – she cares for him, as does his father.

In the section of the conversation in which he talked of his family, Jamal was speaking in a very lyrical fashion, listing these people in a stylised way, which was completely disrupted by him switching into 'himself' and talking about his pets. When I tried to steer the conversation back, he misunderstood, thinking that I was asking whether people had talked to him about *dealing with* racism, and he repeated that the boy M was racist to him. This was balanced out by the fact that his friends like him, think he's sweet and 'looks nice', which is clearly what his family have said to him as well. This is not the only version of Jamal on offer, but it is a very powerful one. I know that he was often quite cheeky and naughty and was quite happy to tell me that he used 'the "f" word'. Jamal said he would like to look like Will Smith, yet he knew that ultimately he could still take pride in being himself. However, he did say that the best thing he could imagine was to be a king so he would have lots of money and do what he wanted! I am not surprised a small child from an impoverished home would aspire to a position of such power and wealth. But in his daily encounters he manages to work with his assets so as to maximise his power over and through his friends.

What is apparent from the interviews is that being happy with who you are also requires one to know which or what kind of 'who' the 'you' might be. The way in which children often operationalised this knowledge was by telling genealogies of selves. They did this either directly or through reporting on the words of others, as shown above. This was particularly relevant to the way children placed immediate and extended family into their discussions. These accounts of likenesses to family members provided a fascinating insight into their developing intimate bodily and emotional identifications.

Looking Like My Family

A major finding of my earlier work, confirmed by this field experience, was that children often had to negotiate themselves through telling stories and histories of their families. Focusing on this provided a crude method of assessing the ways in which they identified, in terms of race and gender, both with parents and other older family members.[9] Just as the question 'where do you come from?' is posed by others who need to fix one in a recognisable social position, the questions about looking like a family member encourage children to try and answer unanswerable questions. In many cases they had to resort to going back generations:

Lola: I don't really look like any of them [her family] … like my nan a little bit, she's my dad's mum, so I think I look like my dad a little bit, I don't look that much Chinese, like my mum, all my brothers and sisters do though, and my little brother though … he looks very English he's doesn't look Chinese at all.

I did not ask Lola directly about whether she perceived her appearance as Chinese, she raised that herself. As she does not look Chinese, in her opinion, it ruled out her mother and her mother's side of the family completely, obliterating the usual visual gender identification. She began by making the gendered connection to her white Scottish grandmother, and from there worked hesitantly back to her father, 'I think' and 'a little bit' revealing her uncertainty at this cross-gendered identification of looks. Sima explained the conundrum perfectly:

Sima: Both. Yeah, 'cos, it's strange really, 'cos I'm a boy and that's my dad, and I'm black and that's my mum. So I sort of like I look like my dad even though I look like my mum. But it's just 'cos, my dad … I have my mum's legs definitely, because my dad's got big calves, and I've got … and little thighs, and I've got big thighs and little calves, and my mum's got little calves and big thighs. So I think I look a bit like, a lot like my mum.

In this case Sima finds the ties to his mother more powerful than to those of his father, and it is interesting to note that he identifies as black, not as 'mixed-race'. His mother is a black woman who, in her interview, made it clear that the 'politics of race' do not allow for any negotiation on this question. Sima has taken that as a primary source of identification, but he also sees *gender* as a more logical and perhaps *necessary* form of identification. He is a boy, therefore he is/will become his father. He does not specify that his father is white; that is unnecessary, as the most important aspect is that they are both male. Again the hegemonic discourses of gender acquisition are interrogated and manipulated by the children. He does go on to work out quite conclusively that there are also other ways in which he is 'physically' his mother.

The negotiation of body parts and blood and genetics is a complicated matter for the children and they manage to resolve the complexities in many ways. When asked directly about looking like her family, Meli said: 'I look like my sister and my mum mostly.' These were her immediate family who she lived with; she saw her father on an irregular basis. Her mother's mother was black and it was from her she claimed blackness. She simplified the whole process into a form in which all contingencies were resolved. Meli had told me a more problematic story of appearance in an earlier interview when we were talking about her experiences at school:

Meli: When someone's angry with me and they're not my friend, they'll go behind my back and they'll go, um, 'oh, she's white!' and they'll like say 'oh the white b-i-t-c-h' something like that.

   [...]

   Yeah, um sometimes when someone would ask me my colour and then they'll see my Mum and they won't believe me. And they'll go, 'she doesn't look it though'. And sometimes when I say that I'm that colour [black], something like that and then like I'll go up to them and say something like 'Excuse me! You don't know my family and ... you haven't seen my grandma, you haven't seen like my grandfather, you don't know nothing about my family, my background or nothing!'

This shows the emotional perils of not looking right. Meli's presentation of herself as black – her attempt to 'pass' as black – has failed when she cannot offer the correct credentials; that is, a black parent. Here we are told that Meli's mother is not recognisable to others as a black woman. Meli's grandmother is black and it is that 'fact' which gives Meli a stake in blackness. More importantly it is her mother's ongoing education about her ethnic and 'racial' heritage that allows Meli to claim and perform blackness, which she did through use of clothes, make-up, hair, music and dance. Her gender identification with her mother means that she also reads her as black, when her mother, Mala, describes herself, at times, as 'ethnic', 'mixed' and 'black'. Narratives of family and belonging helped to construct differing versions of her self-image as the focus of the interviews changed. Meli shows how the rhetoric of post-race is strained by the challenges of her own embodied encounters.

Jacob had a different story of reconciliation between body and family. I also asked him who he resembled in his family:

Jacob: I can't say anything; people say I look like my brothers and sisters and my dad but …

[…]

Suki: So do you think you look like your dad, what do you think?

Jacob: I don't know. I can't exactly compare myself with my dad.

Suki: Why?

Jacob: Well, 'cos his face is bigger than mine, I've got the same colour eyes as my dad I think, um part or one of my eyes is lighter than the other and you can really only see it if there's light, and um my nose is the same as my dad's but otherwise … and my mum says that I'm built like my dad … and my mum, my mum just thinks I'm more like my dad than her, but too, the good thing is that I might come taller, 'cos my mum's got long legs and my dad's got a long body!

Jacob lived on his own with his white mother, and the brothers and sisters he mentioned were half-siblings, many of whom he had never seen. He also explained later in the conversation that he had not seen his father for nearly three years. He first chose to report back the ways in which others saw a resemblance to his father. When I said I thought he looked like his mother he was surprised and rightly responded, 'Well you haven't seen my father though!' Still, his 'required' gender identification with his absent father was stronger than his immediate relationship with his mother. He used *her* description of his father's body shape to make a real and physical connection with him in spite of his absence. He managed to include his mother in the happy probability that he would 'inherit' her long legs (he was at the time one of the smallest boys in his class)! His father's blackness and his shape were the things that kept him close and immediate in Jacob's life. However, his mother, politicised in issues of 'race', was the most influential figure in Jacob's developing understanding of his racial identity:

Jacob: I'd just say I'm black. Really can't believe … You can only be black or white.

Suki: Has anyone like your mum or dad ever talked about that?

Jacob: Yeah. My mum, she says really you can only be black or white and only one colour and that's black.

I find this quote rather moving. It seems to me a no-win situation for the white mother of a black son. My own memories of struggling with a black identity were that I *could not* deny my mother. She was there, *in me*. It is as though Lesley, Jacob's mother, has had to sacrifice her stake in him as her child to the politics of a racist society that will position her son as black. She is not alone in her assessment of how society will position her son (Jordan 1983) and offers to eradicate her very physicality from him. As Ifekwunigwe acknowledges: 'The well intentioned political mandate encouraging *métis/se* people to identify as solely black renders their white parent invisible, but not forgotten' (Ifekwunigwe 1997: 140).

I believe that the interplay of 'race' and gender may operate in far more complex ways than might first be imagined. What is at stake is a recognition of a politics of 'race' (and gender of course) that is based on boundaries, purity and exclusion, and the need to come from out of the borderlands into a place of security. There are no such certainties that do not involve loss and erasure for the children in this study, despite the exciting potential for dynamic bodily performances and re/presentations.

Becoming Whom, Becoming What?

Children claiming positions of multiplicity use popular images to help them interrogate racialised discourses of beauty, attractiveness and thus acceptance. In the face of unacceptable 'racial' simplifications they use strategies in presentation of themselves that allow for the fluidity of their positionality to be expressed in their bodies, clothes and hair. The children are engaged in producing embodied accounts of themselves that can accommodate their own familial identifications, their need to refine gendered positions that are conceived in relation to Others and the collective popular. They recognise their own ambiguous positions and the potential limitations of fixity. In addition, the necessity for correctly heterosexualised identifications requires boys in particular to begin very careful gendered and gendering readings of the popular at young ages. They are given less opportunity to talk about themselves as sexual beings in relation to other men than girls are in relation to women. Girls are required to make the same kinds of choices, but their aspirations are much more likely to be mediated through same-sex readings in popular culture as the female gaze is acceptable to and accepting of readings/representations of femininities.

Appearances of Attractiveness

Research has shown that attractiveness takes an important role in the gendered relationships of *girls* (Connolly 1998). I believe that this research shows that the same kinds of discourses are beginning to have salience to boys, and this is particularly true for boys of 'mixed-race' who utilise their positional fluidity in 'raced' relationships. Both boys and the girls are quite heavily invested in the presentation of themselves as attractive physically and in their characters, and this is reflected in their readings of popular culture. The ways in which bodily texts are read are, however, complex and more likely to be mediated through the hegemonic cultural readings in the school.

In Christie School in London, the 'mixed' girls and boys, who were all from Anglo/African-Caribbean backgrounds, were invested in presenting themselves as black ('passing' as black as Ahmed (1999) would suggest). In Barnlea, the girls were less likely to do so. At Fairsham, none of the children activated 'raced' readings based on hair, style and music. For children such as Lola and Meli, there were undoubtedly choices in the way in which they chose to represent themselves in narratives and in their embodiment. For Meli this was to claim a black identity despite a strong 'coloured' Polynesian identity. Lola did not have a strong enough resemblance to her Chinese mother to allow her to 'look like her'. Lola's family were also middle class and her mother, Jung, talked to me about how hard it had been to come to England as an outsider from such a 'foreign' culture. I believe she was quite happy for her children to claim a multiracial identity that was based upon acceptance. Jane Ayers Chiong (1998) also recorded the fact that her 'Anglo/Asian' (white Anglo/Korean/Chinese) children were treated differently at school according to which of them looked more Asian. Her younger child, who looked white, was never interrogated in the same way as her older daughter. This particular kind of 'mixed' physiognomy sits comfortably within the 'exotic' paradigm, and Lola has gained credibility as a model by appearing in magazine and television adverts for several international companies.

The analysis of representations of blackness by writers such as bell hooks (1992a) holds to, and, I would argue, *reinforces* the 'centrality of whiteness' position. hooks's (1991) use of the terms 'black folks' and 'brown folks' who often become 'nearly white' in her analyses of film, authorises and even reinforces the hierarchical additive models of racialised oppression. In her account, the only worthy folks are black, and those who are brown inhabit a twilight zone of disidentification and inauthenticity, resulting in their alignment with the dominant whites. Whether this is a matter of choice or the fault of the film-makers is unclear; the illegitimacy of the position is stressed regardless of intention.

Emotional Embodiments

The processes of reading the popular are supported by children invoking their inheritance of physical similarity to parents. In order for children to acquire gender identities that are based on identifications with parents (including those who are absent), they subordinate aspects of developing 'racial identities' but do not occlude them completely. The children (such as Jacob) also showed how they rely on being told the ways in which they favour family members who are absent or who they do not know very well. Children do not always choose to take up all the parts of their cultural identities that are offered to them and read them through the lens of the dominant cultural positions.

The children reveal very complex and dynamic subject positions and it is hard to see a pattern in them, but I believe that social geography and class play crucial roles. The middle-class families seem to be making choices based upon both cultural acceptance and politics. The working-class families were all positioning the children as 'mixed'. Walkerdine suggests that '[b]eing looked at still presents one of the only ways in which working-class girls can escape from the routines of domestic drudgery or poorly paid work into the dubious glamour industries' (Walkerdine 1997: 143). She does not include 'race' in her analysis, but the children show that the readings of the 'mixed-race' girls were also aspirational by the way in which they valorised the women of 'mixed-race' who were counted as 'dubious' by others. I also believe that 'being looked at' within 'glamour industries' is becoming more acceptable for boys, but only when tied to some form of talent or agency. Footballers and actors were two of the preferred professions for boys, both of which now require glamour and image consciousness.

There were only three children who talked in an unequivocal way about having a black identity, and they were all based in London. These were two boys with politicised mothers (Sima and Jacob), and Meli who would describe herself as 'mixed-race' and also claim that she was black. Meli saw no conflict in having both these identifications in play at the same time, whereas the two boys were aware of some loss in the position.

What these children show is that there can be no easy discussion of 'racial' performativity. That we may aspire to 'pass' as a racial type is partially true, as the whole area of mixed-raceness is often about desiring and holding *multiple* texts of belonging and mis/re/presentation. Children in this study reject hegemonic whiteness, the possibility of joining an 'invisible and privileged community' (Ahmed 1999: 94). They equally reject 'passing' as Asian, South Asian or Turkish. Whilst such an analysis is useful in that it looks at the ways in which bodies, effects and affects are mobilised to situate selves in particular collectivities, the children negotiate positions of much greater flexibility, *as they conceive of them in their own terms*. The ways in which we may choose to interpret their actions might challenge this, but I believe it is essential that we respect their own choices of positioning whilst remembering

[to] question any assumption that hybridity constitutes *in itself* a basis from which to theorize resistance and transformation. The traversing of racial distinctions ... can easily be recuperated into the identificatory practices of the master discourse. The danger of the hybrid – the loss of clearly demarcated identities – may be read, in the terms of the master discourse, as constituting the necessity for new forms of policing and surveillance. (Ahmed 1999: 96; emphasis added)

In theorising the ways in which children are dealing with their own embodiment we must at all times remember the temporal specificity of the research. As children learn more about current 'politics of race' they will undoubtedly shift their ideas and behaviours, as they will also do upon reaching a more sexually mature embodiment. The way in which they choose to identify themselves will undoubtedly change, motivated by many different factors. In conversation, a colleague working in 'the new' South Africa's Higher Education system has talked about how she covers her hair so that people cannot easily position her when they meet her.[10] Her *masking* of her 'roots' is the opposite form of strategising from that of others who embrace the visual for their politics. As Kobena Mercer argues, all kinds of black hairstyling, including those which come under criticism for imititating 'white hair', need to be 'depsychologised' and recognised as cultural activities and practices (Mercer 1994: 97).

Jayne O. Ifekwunigwe notes: '[In fact], those who have known me over the years can trace the emergence, the lapses and the resurgence of my political consciousness by the particular hairstyles I have sported: relaxed, curly perm, short and natural, braids with extensions and the ultimate – almost bald' (Ifekwunigwe 2000: 37). This revealing section shows the intentional aspects of politically and socially informed style, with some kind of arbitrary yet powerful policing process of what is allowed. The styles Ifwekunigwe lists are inflected by an Anglo/American middle classness and so require by her use of the phrase 'the ultimate' to describe a close-cropped head. So the extract that reveals the author's struggles are contextualised in her desire to belong to a politically aware community of blackness. In the next chapters the importance of such imagined belongings will be discussed further.

Notes

1. Hair is another main form of display which will be considered further in the next sections.
2. Miranda's story is explored in some detail in Ali (2003b).
3. In her first footnote, Weekes writes that of the thirty-one black women she interviewed thirteen of them were of mixed-parentage. 'All mixed-parentage women interviewed categorised themselves as such, and many of the sample considered their ancestry African' (Weekes 1997: 125). However, having established separate categories the conflation of them becomes problematic, with black and 'mixed-parentage' becoming interchangeable.
4. Numerous 'black feminist' writers have written about this phenomenon, such as Hill Collins (1990), Mama (1989), hooks (1992a), Morrison (1994).
5. This diagram and discussion appears in a longer discussion of visualisation and race in Ali (2003a).
6. Sheila, Dinease's mother, gives accounts of her ideas of home in Chapter 6.
7. There are ways in which these children could choose more 'traditional' styles over more 'Western' styles, but in this sample the children were using

the kinds of styles that were common to all ethnic groups.

8. A fuller discussion of ownership of pets takes place in Chapter 5.

9. The importance and meaning of family to the children will be explored fully in the next two chapters. This is an attempt to look at the same processes from a different angle: that of the importance of 'looking' and belonging.

10. Personal communication with Gail Smith, 1998.

–5–

Creating Families Through Cultural Practices

All the theorists including Benson and Tizard and Phoenix, who see the interracial family as the microcosm of race relations are only seeing one aspect of a multi-faceted phenomenon. Race and ethnicity are not monolithic features of society which are reproduced in families, and racism is not irreducible within families ...

> I. Katz 1996: The Construction of Racial
> Identity in Children of Mixed-Parentage

Introduction

In the previous chapter I began to explore the importance of visual and verbal narratives to the children's identifications and formations of family. Children tell and retell stories of themselves in slightly differing ways in varying locations. They tell stories of what families are to those in schools, and to researchers who ask, and in doing so construct more or less coherent histories that attempt to contextualise their current positionalities. How the children do this is not always easy to follow to those unfamiliar with their situations.

Children use narratives that were provided by families in order to develop a sense of 'self', which has the beginnings of genealogical trajectory. Again, this arises from the failure of the current discourses of 'race' and ethnicity, which are based upon collectivities supposedly sharing (racialised) cultural practices. I found that parents showed a more highly developed sense of the diachronic in creating families, and they incorporated 'home' as a concept and a place into narratives of translocation. Children were more inclined to think about the synchronic meanings of 'family' in the first instance, and had to be prompted to develop trans-temporal perspectives.

Parents and children are engaged in the construction of family histories, but the ways in which they do this change over time. The concept of 'family traditions' is passed on, but its meaning is flexible and evolving. Families also use secrets to create the desired family unit. The 'family practices' (Morgan 1996) which form the relationships within families show gendered patterns of parenting, with mothers having overwhelming responsibility within the domestic sphere and fathers taking a peripheral yet powerful role, even if only in the imagination. Family narratives reveal the ways in which constructions of 'class' are deployed by mothers in particular, and the way these are imbricated with ideas of 'race' and ethnicity.

Talking to Families

In order to build a partial picture of the 'home life' and family of the children, I sought interviews with other family members. Of all the children that took part in the research, only twelve sets of parents agreed to be interviewed, and of those, only two sets were conducted with both the father and the mother present. In all the other cases the mother was either the only parent living in the home, or the father was away working or too busy to attend the interviews. In Chapter 3, I discussed the difficulty of making contact with parents when one is seen as an outsider with no connection to the school or to others who are in authority. However, when I did get to see parents it had advantages, as it allowed the mothers and two fathers[1] to speak more freely knowing that I was not reporting back to the school or local education authority.

Once the project had been explained the mothers were not just agreeable, they were interested and enthusiastic about the idea and wanted to know more about what I was doing. I believe that my own 'mixed-race' background was a key factor in this. Being obviously sympathetic to the children and their families and having a very personal interest in the work overrode initial concerns about what I may do with the often very private information that they gave me. In fact, one of the most striking things about talking to mothers was the open and generous way they invited me into their homes and told me about the intimate details of their lives. These were often obviously very painful to talk about and may have only been recently discovered. In one case, there had been a family suicide; in another the man who had been referred to as a 'father' was finally revealed to be, in fact, a step-father; and in a third, a mother revealed she had been raised in children's homes until her teens and had barely known her own family. Feminists such as Finch (1984) have noted that interviewing women can be difficult in the way that boundaries become unclear during the process. To be precise, sensitive information does not make an easy transformation into data (Mauthner 1998), and the issue of family secrets will be dealt with below.

The ways in which the children and mothers narrated their ideas of families using domestic photography and 'well-worn stories' form the basis of this chapter (Kehily 1995).[2] In all cases, the questions about the relevance or not of the problematic terms to this work ('race', culture and ethnicity) are imperative to the narratives the families told, and the discursive registers they re/produce and subvert. It is by no means clear with multiethnic histories, and multi-locational, generational changes, quite how important these terms are to the way that family is constructed. It is often not an overt factor in forming collective familial identities or creating a 'family-like structure' for want of a better term.[3]

Kinship systems are often barely known and are constructed and maintained despite hardship such as family breakdown and forced movement across space. Increased geographical distance often puts additional strain on kin relations, and to cultural stability as constituted through traditional practices such as language, food and religion. These have been described as cultural 'ways of thinking' and 'moral systems' (Dove 1998: 7). I used the *everyday* 'family practices' of children and parents to explore these aspects of kinship. Whether or not one sees disparate cultural systems as conflicting and in need of resolution, cultural reproduction has cognitive, emotional, philosophical and material dimensions.

One of the major reasons for talking to parents was not simply to link 'home' as a 'separate', potentially conflicting or complementary sphere to education. It was also to see whether parents and children had shared understandings of the children's developing identifications. Discussions with parents offered an insight into the places and helped to construct a sense of ethnicised family.[4] In some cases, the mothers were overtly politicised, and, as mentioned before, this was often passed on to the children (e.g. Jacob and Sima). In other cases, the parents had a common-sense approach to their politics of 'race' and they talked in much more general terms about 'racial identity'. This was often in response to 'racism' and was about having a sense of 'pride' *in spite of* having a minority 'racial' identity.

An interesting finding was the number of parents who displayed a very limited form of 'political' awareness about issues of race and who in some cases expressed views that may well be considered 'racist' by some. This may be seen to be the equivalent of the kind of internalised racism of white people that black writers such as Fanon (1970) and Young (1996) have analysed; parents have not externalised this onto their children but onto other 'Others'. This kind of 'denial' of the 'racial' position of the children is something that I experienced from my own grandmother, who would express a racist view and then when challenged about my own position she would say, 'But you're lovely darling.' Parents sometimes seemed to privilege 'blood' over skin – kinship and family over all else. So whilst they may appear to be 'colour blind', they do not deny connection to their 'racialised' children and can still characterise them as such. Mr G (father of Lola, Barnlea), called his children 'Chinglish', but talked about the 'refugees' bringing down the level of schooling. I believe it is a variant of the 'some of my best friends are ...' syndrome, where personal knowledge (and love) of individuals refutes universal racism. It echoes the colour/power evasiveness of the white mothers who had 'mixed-race' children in Ruth Frankenberg's study (1993), and the way in which they privileged being the same under the skin. This is more forcibly illustrated when the 'Other' is one's own child.

Picturing Families

Both adults and children used a variety of images to evoke 'home', which often included some favourite family members. Pares was the exception amongst parents who first chose to talk about the landscape of her home, her birthplace, Cyprus. The narratives of colour and texture of the land described during the interview was most evocative of the differences between the two countries: Cyprus and England.

Pares: Another of my favourite places … umm … collecting some thistle flowers … and … I wore this green dress, and everything else apart from my green dress because of the season is actually yellow. So that there's this thing, people called it an 'Out of Africa' photograph, you could just see tons of landscape behind me and I was right in the foreground, and then … this just … I don't know, there's just something about it. And I always go on about yellow, I used to when I did my art in the beginning, I've gone a bit conservative, but … every time I started everything it would have to be yellow. And it was really funny and I didn't even know why and somebody saw that picture like years afterwards and said 'I know why you talk about yellow or why yellow is in your work because, you know, look at the landscape where you come from.'

This extract also indicates how family and 'home' are intertwined in the consciousness of the families and individuals that have experienced some form of relocation in their lives. It is particularly striking that Pares refers to the film *Out of Africa* which is about a white woman writer who spent her adult life in Africa. Although the film is about displacement, its central character embodies the archetypal colonial representation of white womanhood as the ultimate feminine. Pares is a Turkish Cypriot, but also a black woman, who does not see her diasporic roots (at the time of the interview) as being 'out of Africa'. Such complicated cultural vocabulary is typical of the interviews, but many women wanted to simplify the processes. This was done by controlling the choice of photographs and whether they presented them visually.

In all cases mothers and children already knew which ones were their favourite photographs even when they could not find them to show me. In some cases mothers and children would just talk about photographs they could not find. I am still unsure in two cases as to whether the photographs were actually lost or whether they were just not for my eyes. Significantly, the spoken texts were equally revealing in different ways.

Holidays and Other Special Occasions

Very few children or parents chose formal family portraits taken in photographic studios. However, school portraits of children were most prominently displayed in homes. Several images of the same child showing their development over time as they progressed through the school were displayed in houses in London and in Kent. Although there is still a tradition of having children's portraits taken by professionals, the use of studio portraits has decreased with the number of people owning their own cameras and the frequency with which they are used. I would suggest that in place of these professional portraits which portray an especially precise, formalised image of 'immediate family' groups, we now see 'special occasion' semi-formal images holding the same special meaning in the construction of the family groups. These are often partial or incomplete as they may have been taken by a member of the family. This is usually a male such as the father or older brother who are keepers of the technology (Seabrook 1991). This is still the case even though there is often more than one camera owned by family members.

The photographs that will represent the family group are taken by the father, and it is as though they are not needed in the photographs, just as they are often absent for much of the time in the lives of the children. In this way 'family' comes to be represented by mother and children, whilst 'father' retains a distinct identity and an external and active subject position. In many cases these semi-formal portraits are taken at special occasions such as parties, religious celebrations, school functions, and so on. In these the family members are typically in their 'best clothes' – they will be dressed for the occasion; they will also be lined up either standing or sitting (by height order), to show the group to their best advantage.

Holiday photographs were another favourite way to show families and, in particular, children. The images in the holiday shots showed both similarities to and contrasts with the semi-formal poses described above. They were often of children in swimwear or colourful casual clothing, near or in water, such as the sea or swimming pools. They were still in that sense 'special' clothes; things that would not be worn on a day-to-day basis in England. It was most usual for the people in the shots to be captured in relaxed and spontaneous positions, 'caught' behaving naturally, and this is in stark contrast with the often very stiff, awkward looking posed images of the special occasion.

It is not surprising that these two types of photographs were seen as the most popular as they reinforce and document the 'ordinary' (family), but in extraordinary circumstances:

1. They will often show the majority of the family together, including those who live at some distance from the immediate family group. In these cases they are showing something close to the concept of who 'makes up family'; in the wider sense they are 'documentary'.
2. Holidays may be one of the few times that the immediate family spend any length of time together, with father (if present), mother and children for a period of days or weeks rather than just hours. Again, this warrants special notice.
3. They show people in their most attractive and best physical form. Special clothes, hair, make-up, and so on, showing another ideal. In the case of holidays, the locations may be unusual, spectacular or beautiful. The people within the pictures may be particularly healthy looking, being more rested and 'tanned' and relaxed and happy. In this sense they are also out of the 'ordinary', certainly not showing the mundane of the everyday lives of those who used photography. These are the more perfect or idealised images of the physical selves who are valued by those who do the choosing.
4. These are all appropriate times to have taken photographs, and thus make them easy for those choosing. None of those who took part wanted pictures shown of them at inappropriate moments, in inappropriate locations or not looking their best.

Pets Mean Families

Recent research showed that children drawing 'maps' representing 'family' often chose to include their pets (Wade 1999; Brannen 1999), and many photographs of pets were brought in for me. In a way, what the children chose to show was who they loved and who they thought loved *them*. So pets, in particular cuddly and furry pets, were often shown to be very important to a sense of home and family. This supports the notion of 'kinship' and 'family' changing from a clearly defined notion of blood ties to known and unknown relatives, into a set of relationships of care (Brannen 1999).

Children showed an enormous amount of pride in their pets and were very articulate in describing the way that the pets behaved, favourite foods, programmes of care, and so on. Obviously the caring for animals as pets has many different cultural manifestations in locations around the world, but the choice of cats, dogs, rabbits and guinea pigs were most common within this project. It would seem that there could be some fairly obvious reasons for choosing these particular animals:

- Cost – these are animals that can be bought and kept fairly cheaply.
- Space – these animals require little space or looking after.

- Availability – they can be bought from pet shops, friends or even given free of charge through rescue and charity organisations or word of mouth.

How different would it be if the children were in other locations? In other locations there is little tolerance for animals that do not work. A truism suggests that average Britains and North Americans have a cultural tradition of being more caring of their animals and pets than they are of other human beings. This is supported by the strength of the Animal Rights movements in these two countries. To gauge accurately how much children are responding to animals in the home, based on cultural values passed through the family, through experience of diverse cultural attitudes or based on the hegemonic views about pets in Britain, would be impossible. However, conversations with the children again revealed the kinds of discourses about animals they were drawing upon, and from which cultural positions they had been informed. Marita was quite clear about the different ideas her parents had to her having pets:

Marita: Yeah. This is a picture of my cat on my bed, having a sleep.
Suki: Does it sleep on your bed often?
Marita: Yeah sleeps on my bed every night, by my pillow [laughs].
Suki: Does it ... aaaah!
Marita: Yeah, my dad doesn't like it he says it will suffocate me, 'cos you know the Trinidadian people they think that animals are so ... mm ... he doesn't like animals because, he thinks they've got diseases in England. And some do, but our cat's very clean.

I am not sure why it is that animals are more diseased in England as it is not an opinion that I have heard expressed before, and Marita was rushing onto the next photograph of her cat. She also had a fish pond and kept fish, so despite her father's disapproval, the British cultural attitude of treating pets as 'part of the family' won out.

One particular story told by Denzu (Anglo/Indian boy, Year 6, Barnlea) shows that location, and the dominant values within it, are also crucial to the way the children view animals. Denzu told me the following story, early in his interview, when he had just told me that he had been on two trips to India:

Suki: Did you enjoy yourself?
Denzu: Yes, its fun and it's hot and we killed a dog.
Suki: You what?
Denzu: We killed a dog.
Suki: You killed a dog?
Denzu: Yes the one that eats ... you see chicken?

Suki: Yes.

Denzu: You see people's chicken, they go hhrrrruumm eat it. So that's why we killed it.

Suki: How did you kill it?

Denzu: We got these massive sticks and all a bit hard and some heavy. And I got my binoculars and looked through this little hole yeah? We saw it, we saw the dog sleeping, and drinking some water yeah? Then after that we quickly quietly went yeah then we saw it and the dog it just looked at us. Then after my friend went woompph in its face, and blood came out and we tied it round its neck, and then we pulled it all the way and then after we tied it up again and then we took it very, very far to a big big when it rains there's a big puddle and you see that puddle? ... There's hole and before school ... and first we untied the rope and it tried to run away and we hit it, then we tied it up again, then we throw it down then we got down, we started hitting it each in turns.

It is of course true that other people in India value animal lives and spirits so highly that they are exclusively vegetarian, and would view the actions of these eleven-year-old boys as would any British pet lover – with some revulsion at the vivid picture. At the time he recounted this story, my own interest was as much centred around Denzu's interpretation of his actions, as in my own horrified reaction to the story and the desire to hide that from him. He said that he did not know whether the dog had suffered but that it had cried. He had not looked at it so it's crying did not bother him. I believe that Denzu's telling of this tale is a classic form of heroic, *Boys' Own* adventure story. He is constructing himself as masculine, brave, heroic and a good citizen in saving his neighbour's chicken. The tale is also very specific to the geography in which in occurred. In Kent, rogue dogs would be the province of farmers and dog catchers, and they would be shot. In this sense it is culturally specific and shows that Denzu is asserting a very strong identification to his Indian heritage. He said that if people asked him where he came from he would say he was 'half Indian and half English' and was more closely identified with his Indian father than his white mother. This narrative told in its generic adventure story form, complete with sound effects, supports and creates such a position.

The more middle-class children in all locations were most likely to have more than one pet. I would suggest that this is due to class values and inferred status, and on a more practical note, due to the cost of pet care, especially feeding and vets' bills. Socio-economic status and location (size of home and/or garden, access to green space, etc.) often mitigate against keeping more than one pet and against larger pets such as ponies. Children often noted that they had to care for their pets themselves – that this was one of the conditions for them having the animal. Pets were often a source of sustained joy and pleasure for the children and not simply a compartmentalised hobby, bounded by interactions in specific times; but they were also a source of great emotional pain. The loss of a pet was felt keenly by the children. In this way the life and death of the pet was linked to training children to cope with everyday life as a social being and offered a taste of the responsibility needed to succeed in the world. The death of pets is often seen as a more gentle preparation to the concept of human mortality, especially the death of loved ones. The children are accorded a considerable amount of power over small pets, literally life and death. Caring for pets was an opportunity for children to practicse using self-discipline and to make a commitment that would need to be upheld over a considerable time.

It was noticeable that girls were more likely than boys to talk in the most effusive tones about the relationships they had with their animals. This is in keeping with typically gendered stereotypes about girls and care and about their fondness for the 'softer', more relational aspects of life. This type of behaviour could be seen to combine three discourses about gender:

1. that girls like the 'softer' sciences and have more interest in subjects like biology and their connection to living things – that they like all things fluffy and pretty. Boys, however, are more interested in the 'harder' subjects and likewise in playing with machines and guns, and so would choose 'harder' pets like lizards;
2. that girls will be more likely to learn to perform gendered patterns of caring even at an early age. 'Caring *for*' pets teaches about responsibility, whilst 'caring *about*' pets begins the training for 'emotional work' that women are expected to do in families and households. Pets are preparation for boys and girls giving love and the ability to 'fall in love', which is still seen as gendered and heterosexualised. Men and women are both required to love, but are expected to do so differently (see Jackson 1993; Duncombe and Marsden 1993; Craib 1993; Delphy and Leonard 1992);
3. that boys cannot speak easily about their emotions. Even when they do, in this case fondness for their pets, they are less likely to express them. In particular, they often find it harder to express loving feelings.

I believe that the most useful way of understanding this phenomenon is looking at the third point, and the more straightforward aspects of communication. Boys showed an equal likelihood to bring in photographs of pets and to be proud of them. It was not that they did not have considerable emotional investment with their pets, they simply did not express it as openly as did the girls.[5] Girls often talked about pets as if they were almost 'romantically' in love with them; they adored them in an all-forgiving 'irrational', 'unconditional' way. Boys showed a far greater disconnectedness in the way they talked about them, even if that was a *method* in showing a particular version of themselves they wished to present; it still showed an *awareness* of 'correct' (normative) gendered behaviour. Boys were also less likely to deal with the messy day-to-day cleaning of pets. For example, Kyle had split the responsibility of caring for his cats with his mother so that he did the feeding and she cleaned out the cat litter trays. This was a typical division of labour when boys could manipulate it. The way in which domestic work and other family practices were gendered will be considered in more detail below.

Family Practices

What children and mothers do within families, and how they are using cultural practices, was another area under consideration in this research. David Morgan (1996) has suggested we should be using the term 'family practices' as a way to convey both 'what it is' and 'how it is' we wish to analyse in families. His use of 'family practices' is based upon these main propositions:

1. this term allows for a lack of congruence between what is understood between the 'observer' and 'observed'.
2. the term implies 'the active' rather than the more static 'family structures'.
3. the term 'practices' implies the everyday. They are '… often little fragments of daily life which are part of the normal taken-for-granted existence of the practitioners'.

He goes on:

- 'Practices' implies not only regularity but also repetition and rehearsal.
- A 'practice' also 'conveys a sense of fluidity'. Not only may they be repetitious, they imply open-endedness. He gives the example of 'feeding the children' which may be seen as 'family practices', 'gendered practices', 'consumption practices', 'ethnic practices', and so on, or may be several of these at once.
- Practices are known to provide us with major links between history and biography. (Morgan 1996: 189–191)

Morgan argues that we must be aware that social actors may have differing views about whether 'family practices' applies to them or their circumstances, but that they are 'to do with those relationships and activities that are constructed as being to do with family matters' (ibid. 192). Morgan's emphasis on *relationships* is of particular use here. Children made clear that the special relationships they had with people were the most important way to identify family. This corresponds with Morgan's notion that the factors outlined above must be *significant* in an emotional, personal or moral dimension (ibid.). He is not clear how economic relationships fit within this framework. However, this framework would seem to be useful to the analysis of what children and parents say they do with their families.

In this research, family practices are imbricated with gendered, ethnicised and classed processes. The fact that they are also inter-generational is also critical to this analysis, as gendered, inter-generational relationships are particularly important in inter-ethnic families, with specific meanings attached to how these inter-racial relationships, over time-space shifts, effect change in ethnic identifications. For example, a mother who describes herself as white and is working class, has a son who shares her class position but is interpellated as a black boy by his school. His mother calls him 'mixed-race', and his white grandfather call him black (Mrs Farmer and her son Tito). The significance of the gender of the parent and the grandparent, and how they articulate with the self-identification of the child across temporal and geographic changes, is complex. The gendered positions are also 'raced'. In order to understand something of Tito's identifications, and how they differ from Talia's (his sister), we cannot miss out one part of the analysis.

We can see that families are constructed through and by relationships and behaviours, as well as by structures. This is a useful way of understanding what is important to the children and parents in this study. In some cases the children had stronger relationships with step-parents or new partners than they did with biological parents, and so they supplanted these people in their affections (see John in Chapter 2). Yet as will be shown, life-histories were often guided by relationships of blood, no matter how distant they may have become (e.g. Jacob). Despite the usefulness of investigating the material everyday practices of families, the concept of 'blood ties' in their stories remained strong, and will be returned to later.

During the interviewing children were asked specifically about the kind of day-to-day activities/practices they carried out in the home. They were also asked about the ways in which they interacted with others in the home; with whom they spent the most time; with whom they got on best, and so on. It was hoped that these often mundane daily activities would show ways in which both cultural and familial work construct each other, through and with constructions of gender.[6]

Mothers and Mundane Cultural Work

Mothers were overwhelmingly still involved in the day-to-day running of the home and were wholly responsible for the mundane domestic tasks that are required in order to maintain the household and those within it. It is these more 'mundane' tasks that may also be seen as a form of cultural production. Although these remain gendered practices, in as much as it is overwhelmingly the mothers who are performing them, the children sought to imply that for the next generation there are less strictly gendered lines of division between tasks.

Boys reported regularly cleaning and cooking and shopping, either with their mothers or on their own. It should be noted, however, that for some of the boys there was an element of exaggeration in their accounts that did not withstand more direct questioning about the actual tasks performed and the frequency with which they carried them out! It is notable that rather than attempt to hide the fact that they were doing housework, which may hold connotations of 'sissiness', the boys claimed that they 'helped out' and had specific responsibilities in ways that suggested that this would elevate their status during the interview. This may have been simply a technique of gaining favour with a (female) interviewer, or a shrewd recognition of the discourses of more thoughtful and helpful masculinities of the 'New Man'.[7] It could also be that they are unaware of the extent to which female members of the family are dealing with day-to-day domestic tasks.

I believe it is more likely that it simply reflects the fact that the mothers in the sample were raising their sons to be more responsible in the domestic sphere, no matter in how limited a form it may take. For many it was a case of having tasks that are associated with males, such as taking out the rubbish, tidying their own rooms or going to the shops for items that had been forgotten in the major shop of the week. This is not to say that no men have ever participated in household chores, rather it suggests that these behaviours are crossing the cultural and class boundaries of the sample in this research. Traditionally, middle-class children have been afforded greater amounts of playtime, because of economic and cultural status (Adkins and Leonard 1996). In this sample of children, the boys responded in remarkably similar ways, with the exception of a few of the Muslim boys who seemed be exempt from the majority of domestic work.

Anthias and Yuval-Davis (1992: 115) suggest that women play a vital and unique role in the re/production of ethnic collectivities:

- as biological reproducers of members of ethnic collectivities;
- as reproducers of the boundaries of ethnic or national groups;
- as participating centrally in the ideological reproduction of the collectivity and as transmitters of its culture;
- as signifiers of ethnic or national differences, as a focus and symbol of ideological discourses used in the construction of ethnic or national categories;
- as participants in national, economic, political and military struggles.

The role that the mothers take within families of inter-ethnic backgrounds is particularly crucial to the development of the cultural/racial/ethnic identities of the children; even more so if fathers are absent from the home. The everyday cultural practices within the house may be overlooked in the desire to note the more obvious markers of cultural and ethnic identity and how they interact with national and racial identities. This is true of the work of Anthias and Yuval-Davis, who focus instead on paid employment rather than domestic work. Like other work on women, ethnicity and families (e.g. Bryan *et al.* 1985; Brah 1996), they foreground families as a source of strength in hostile cultural environments. This kind of approach emphasises that 'The locus of conflict lies outside of the house-hold, as women and their families engage in a collective effort to create and maintain a family life in the face of forces that undermine family integrity' (Hill Collins 1994: 47).

Any analysis of family relations must take account of these exogenous conflicts, but not at the expense of internal cultural analyses. Whilst I asked all the children about their religious affiliations and about the food they eat, both usually connected to ethnic and cultural identity, I also asked about the cooking, cleaning, shopping and how they thought about these jobs. Traditional foods may be cooked and enjoyed on a regular basis within the home, but the children routinely chose 'Western'/North American fast foods as their favourites. Chips, burgers and pizzas were the top choices. These foods represent the most obvious aspects of the neo-colonial cultural globalisation processes at work on a world-wide scale. It is not unlikely that these foods would come out top of the list for the majority of children, regardless of background, in Britain. There were a few notable exceptions of children who chose more 'traditional' dishes or some kind of mixture of contemporary foods.[8] However, this example (food) reveals the ways that 'culture' is neither static nor enclosed, but is in constant development and change.

The majority of mothers were responsible for the everyday cooking, whereas fathers were linked to cooking for a change to 'help out', and perhaps washing up after a meal. In the cases where the fathers are from minority ethnic groups and the mothers are white British, the fathers were responsible for cooking food that has strong cultural and national connections. In a few cases the mothers learned to cook these dishes, and the fathers reverted to occasional helping out. The same is true in reverse. So, for example, Mrs G. Jung cooked 'special' Chinese food for the family as a 'treat' and as a 'connection to their Chinese culture' (mother of Lola at Barnlea).

There was a special role for the fathers of minority ethnic status in families of inter-ethnic backgrounds, as 'authentic' cooks of 'authentic' cultural foods. This circumvented the more usual gendered divisions of food production. The role of the father in these cases was also to provide the special and 'traditional' link to the 'other' culture, and it was this specialness that facilitated cooking by someone who did not usually do it. This is true of families who are not 'interracial', but had particular significance in these instances (see Luke 1994).

Mothers are also responsible for the emotional work within families and as such it is they who are the ones who will maintain family links on behalf of the whole family (see Delphy and Leonard 1992 on emotional work). In this context, this role takes on an added significance as it is these kinds of family links that children cited as ways to develop their family histories, and claim a 'mixed-race' identity. Indeed, as has been mentioned before, this was often the only significant way the children have of 'describing' what their mixed-race status means to them (see Meli on p. 87). Mothers themselves described being the ones who would make the effort to keep in touch with distant relatives, would remember birthdays and make sure invitations were issued to important family members for get-togethers, and so on. This supports findings by Adkins and Leonard (1996) about children's family work commitments, and the gendered forms these took.

My own research shows that where the mother and father of the children had separated, the mother often made a particular effort to maintain cordial relations with the father's family 'for the sake of the children'. In 'interracial' families, this was seen as a way of providing essential information about 'cultural heritage'. It is important to note that at this point in an interview white mothers with black (ex-)partners would talk about the importance of the child spending time with black people generally. Clearly, family relations were not simply categorised as kin who are important to the child in a purely emotional sense; they also provide a familial identification that is 'raced' or ethnicised in some way.

Even absent fathers provided an important source of 'racial' identification for the children. They perceived their racial identifications as predominantly gendered and their emotional identifications were closely tied to their primary carer.

Fathers and Leisure Time

Children routinely described fathers as being especially devoted to leisure time with them. Whether this is true or whether it is just the perception and desire of the child is hard to tell, but it would be supported by other empirical research about fathers' involvement with children, and is of course especially true for fathers who are not living with the child. 'Leisure' may include the everyday practice of watching television as a family or with gendered watching patterns (that is, boys with brothers and fathers), or generational (that is, children watching one television with children and adults watching with adults on another set or later).

Fathers were as likely as mothers to be following stereotypically gendered patterns of interaction with their children. They were more likely to be the parent who took the children to play sport, particularly football for boys, or swimming for both girls and boys. Going to the park to walk and play was a popular weekend activity, but even when families went out together on trips to the park it was less usual for the mothers to engage in playing sport with children. Fathers initiated sporting activities. It was common for the whole family to go to the supermarket at the weekend for a large 'food shop', but the responsibility for choosing and buying clothes was the job of the mother, with some of the children being allowed to help choose their own clothes.

These 'gendered' patterns of family work were the same across racialised and classed families, and irrespective of whether there was one or both parents at home. It was particularly noticeable that the children who saw their fathers rarely were themselves aware that they would have more 'treats' with them and do more of the enjoyable leisure activities than they would with their mothers. But even children who were living in the same house as fathers would claim a different kind of relationship with them:

Suki: Is that what you said? Did you say that she spoils you [your mum]? No you said that you like going with your dad [to the shopping centre].

Marita: Yeah, he ... he buys me loads of stuff 'cos he's a softie.

Suki: Is he?

Marita: Yeah ... but my mum doesn't ... if I said 'mum, please may I have a lolly pop?' and then my dad might say 'no, I'm not buying you anything!' and then I say 'pleeeease' and then he'll do it, but my mum's not like that , if she says 'no' she means 'no'! [laughs]

Marita enjoyed the performance of this little vignette, with her speaking the roles of stern mother and soft father, satirising her own knowing role as persuasive little girl which she reconstructed complete with fluttering eyelashes. There is obviously a particular gendered, sexualised 'daddy's girl' at work here in a very overt way (Walkerdine 1997).

Boys too were engaged in constructing the 'specialness' of time with fathers, as opposed to that with mothers which was 'ordinary':

Suki: [...] You told me that your father lives in London, do you see him often?

Kyle: Um quite often, my mother says I see him more than some kids, than some children do where their dad lives with them. Because before they get up – 'cos when they get up they're at work and when they come in, and when they go to bed, that's when they get in. (Kyle, Fairsham, Year 5)

There is a construction of parents as individuals who have separate roles, which follows a gendered pattern for the majority of children. In a few cases I did hear rather vague references to *both* parents being out at work, rather than fathers, and also that both the mother or father worked nights. This kind of work pattern, which was only told to me by the more economically impoverished 'mixed-race' children, placed a particular strain on family relations. It was also the reason given for me not to interview parents.

Where there was only one parent in the family, the mother in all cases, they were responsible for trying to engage with practices that the children themselves already see as gendered:

Jacob: My mum don't really like sports. Well she would play if she ... well she doesn't like sports but she'd play sport. We go to the park and we go swimming. Sometimes if I am lucky enough I get her to play football with me ... but ...

Even with leisure time as special occasions, there were divisions of gendered labour and responsibility. These were mostly big festivals and holidays, and birthdays in particular. On such occasions it was likely that both parents came together with more extended family members and these became times for defining who is and is not going to be included as 'family'. This is in most cases, as discussed above, the duty of the mother.

Family Traditions – the Culture of Families?

The ways in which families are constructed are both *through* cultural practices and through the telling of stories *about* cultural practices. In this section I will look at the ways in which the two processes are interlinked in predominantly gendered ways.

Christmas Tales

Fathers and other family members who are often absent from the day-to-day household and family activities were still invited to attend special family occasions, such as celebrations – weddings, birthdays, and so on. These occasions seem to provide opportunity for the development of unique family cultures and traditions which exemplify the creolisation of cultural processes, showing as they do the evolutionary progress that comes from the synthesis of the new with the traditional, the broadly shared and the specific organisations of celebrations.

Many of the inter-ethnic[9] families choose to identify Christmas in particular as a time for asserting unique family traditions. Both children and mothers talked of Christmas as being a time for the family, and how celebrating Christmas as a public holiday, even if holding non-Christian religious beliefs, was an important part of family culture and defining family status for the members.

These traditions are reinforced by 'telling' – so Sheila told me about the 'fantastic' gatherings she had at her mother's house (mother of Dinease, Christie in London). With each telling the story becomes stronger and the memories of specifics that may be vague become strengthened (see Kehily 1995). The story-telling is a form of 'Russian doll' with stories within stories as narrators perform the voices of others who were present. When I asked Sheila if she kept any particular family 'traditions', she said at first that there were none. Later when she started talking about her mother and how often she had seen her before her death, she talked about the huge get-togethers at her mother's house at Christmas time. Sheila's memories and the narration of them developed together:

Sheila: I think we used to be more like that before we had our kids, because we all used to congregate at our mum's at Christmas, 'cos that's where the food is that's where you go. [both laugh] Yeah we used to have some brilliant ... and that's where we did get stories like that, 'cos your aunties were down there, your mum was down there and this one or that would drop in. And we used to have some *wicked* Christmases. Or just us kids when we always, 'oh mum you remember when we did that?' 'NOOO!' [she puts on exaggerated storytelling voices and I am laughing and it sounds so warm]. Yes you used to get them kind of, I mean we've had some *brilliant* Christmases like that where, like you'll be saying like, 'you remember when I got beaten for these and you got beaten for that and dadada and you ran off and dadada?' Yeah, we used to do that quite a lot.

This piece of narrative reveals many of the common themes to the establishment of the family culture. Sheila's mother is Montserratian and she herself was born there; they came to England when she was very young. She did not remember telling any particular family stories to her children, but as adults she and her siblings reinforced their identities within the family by reminiscing about their childhood in Montserrat. Simultaneously, they kept alive a national and ethnic identity. In a sense they were working within a particular genre when they discussed these things amongst themselves. We can understand this manner of recounting the tales to each other as a form of dialogue in which each person has a role in negotiating the production: 'Any understanding of live speech, a live utterance, is inherently responsive, although the degree of this activity varies extremely. Any understanding is imbued with response and necessarily elicits it in one form or another: the listener becomes the speaker' (Bakhtin 1986: 68).

In this case the responses are almost ritualised in the production of the narrative from shared memories. However, it is not just the generic form of these exchanges that is of interest, it is also the way in which the discursive contents and their meanings are being used by Sheila in her production of 'family'.

The fact that food also plays a part in the story is extremely relevant to both familial and gendered cultural identity, as it is the mother, taking on the role of head of the family, who prepares the food. In this case, the absence of her father meant that her mother took sole responsibility for this 'special occasion food production' and presentation. The adult children who were living away from home returned for the symbolic nurturing in their mother's home, yet construct it as being common sense and not emotional or traditional – it is simply 'that's where the food is'. Even if that comment was meant to be humorous, it is also the case in real terms. This shows that the discourses of women as providers and nurturers remains salient in the cultural environment. The tradition is interrupted by the arrival of the next generation of children, at which point the provision of food falls to the adult child who has become a parent, in this case Sheila with her own children:

Sheila: But as I said, I suppose when you get a family of your own, like I basi-
         cally stopped going to those so much when, and I think most of us did
         that had our kids because we simply … it's a case of 'well I want *my*
         family this Christmas'. I mean we spend like Christmas day at my
         mum's and Boxing Day at D's [her husband] or something like. And
         next year it would be round the other way or something. And then we
         started drifting away from that 'cos our kids were like growing up a
         bit, and it's a case of you know 'why don't *I* cook my own Christmas
         dinner, if you wanna come down feel free, but I wanna have it in my
         house with my kids', you know? So it has … and now, as I say, my
         mum's died anyway, it has gone a bit like that. I mean over the last few
         Christmases it was a case of all the single ones who didn't have any
         kids would be down at my mum's. They sort of kept that up. But we'd
         like come round after dinner or something like that …

This exchange shows how the family form shifts as the new generation of children 'dictates' the need for change. This is most noticeable with the celebration
of Christmas, which has in more recent times lost its specifically religious overtones and become more a time for families to come together and give and receive
presents without relating this to the original Christian story. The myth of Father
Christmas coming to give toys to the well-behaved children also serves to reinforce this time of year as being 'for the children'. This is why Sheila opted to take
on the role her mother had taken on for her own children, and to start to reinforce
the traditions in her own home. Later she talked about the fact that some of her
family now came to her, and how she cooked the same food as her mother had

done. This is one of the clearest examples of the reproduction of culture through family practices.

Christmas is also a way of embracing a British/European identity, when it is taken up for the first time within a family. Celie's mother is Chinese, and her father white Irish (Jack's mother, Kent). She described going 'completely over the top with Christmas', whilst her British-Indian husband took no part in the preparation yet tacitly approved of her enthusiasm and joined in the celebrations. In one sense this simply fits again with the role of mothers in taking on the mundane preparation for the celebration, whilst the father merely lends his presence to the big day in order to make it 'special'. Another more interesting feature is the way that Celie circumvents an overtly religious upbringing for her children until they are 'old enough to choose', yet incorporates Christmas into the family calendar, and some teaching about the 'stories of Jesus' with their generally moral guidelines for living. This was also true for many of the children interviewed, without particular reference to Jesus. It illustrates the way in which Christmas has lost a fundamentally religious base and has become something associated with being *British* rather than Christian for these families. Whilst many British families may celebrate Christmas from a secular position, it would seem that for those who hold religious and cultural beliefs that form part of a different ethnic and national identity, claiming a part of Christmas is more about a cultural affiliation to England and a commonality, and to a partially British/European identity.

There is a large and growing body of writing that suggests that Britishness is constructed as whiteness, and this is linked with the form of Christianity which underpins the legal and constitutional laws of the land (see e.g. Dyer 1997: 15–18). In this sense the respondents claim part of what they know to be a partially 'white' identity. Of course there are many groups of migrant and settler families who take on aspects of the culture within which they find themselves who would claim that taking part in certain cultural practices did not infer that this meant that they were claiming part of the dominant cultural *identity*. There seems to be more at stake with those who may *already* lay claim to a partially white heritage if they choose to take on these cultural practices. For them, there is a sense in which taking up these cultural practices is about re/asserting a part of an already existent 'ethnic' identity. In Celie's case, this comes from her father's Irish national identity and the fact that she spent most of her childhood in England in Convent boarding schools. Sheila did talk about her mother having an interest in the church, which she maintains. The importance that she ascribes to Christmas is not remarkable, yet she still focuses on it as being an opportunity for a family get-together rather than a religious festival.

Myths and Memories

One of the ways in which the families told their stories was by using specific tales of heroic deeds and humorous events involving family members. These stories often gain an almost mythical status as they become common currency among the family and are repeated over and over and passed down from generation to generation. When first asked, many of the mothers said that they were not aware of any such tales, but during the interview it often emerged that they did, in fact, have stories that had been passed down. Often the grandparents would tell tales of the parent to the child about what they had been like as a child. Kyle told me some stories that his parents and grandparents told him, and these were corroborated by his parents when they were interviewed. In addition new stories were emerging:

Nigel: There are lots of things like that aren't really fam ..., they will become those sort of stories as they get passed down. But there are sort of new generation ones that add to that ...
Suki: Are you creating your own do you think?
Nigel: Yeah, which are ... yeah ...
Suki: It's something that *you* remember?
Nigel: Yeah it's fairly early memories though.
Suki: Would you tell them as stories though, or are they part of a picture that makes up your childhood?
Nigel: You might recount them at that time because certain events trigger those memories probably.
Suki: Would you tell them to Kyle?
Nigel: Yeah yeah ...
Suki: You tell other stories to Kyle?

Kyle was also present at the parental interview and, although he was playing on a computer game across the room, he got drawn into the conversation and came over in order for the family to negotiate between their own individual memories and ideas of who was telling the stories. They did this to find agreement about how important stories were and who said what about whom, with some 'belonging' to particular narrators:

Penny: No that's not my story, that's Grandma's, she needs to tell you that one.

Kyle had too many stories from all family members to think of one for the interview, and noted equal numbers from both parents:

Suki: And do they tell them about them as babies or you as a baby or ...

Kyle: Well me.

Suki: And what about, your grandma you said tells a story ...?

Kyle: Yeah.

Suki: About?

Kyle: Her and her mum and grandad.

Suki: When she was little?

Kyle: Yeah.

Suki: [joking] Oh right, ok so you get hundreds of stories!

Kyle: Yeah, pretty much!

I have quoted this section of the transcript at length because it raises many of the points that were common to the other families, but shows in more detail how the family dynamic works to strengthen the storytelling, and how by sharing the stories they become more important. In this case, Kyle was clear that the telling of tales is a way that both his mother and father give him a sense of his family history and, of course, give him information about his cultural heritage in the broadest sense of the term.

Kyle's father was consciously using the storytelling to give his son a sense of his own childhood, with a clear intention of developing a *shared* family memory with his son through use of his own personal memories. The stories in this case cross four generations and maintain their salience for each. On his mother's side of the family the stories often revolve around his English father meeting his German mother, of their return to England after the Second World War, and of the prejudice they and the children faced living in the North of England. The stories of courtship would function on two levels. One is by introducing interracial relationships and the concept of racism, another is the reinforcement of ethnic identification – in this case of Kyle's grandparents on his mother's side. On his father's side of the family, the stories revolve around his white English grandmother rather than his Trinidadian grandfather who was not present for much of his father's childhood. This lack of storytelling magnifies the absence of his grandfather and his family from his life and his father's.

Just as the status of individuals and their position in the cultural heritage of the children may be diminished by the *lack* of storytelling about them, so they may be built up by the repetition of favourite tales of positive events and actions. In the case of Penny's parents it was courage and determination in the face of opposition to their marriage, based on anti-German feeling; in the case of Darcy, and her child Ella (Fairsham, Year 4), it was an opportunity for her to talk about the favourite uncle's childhood exploits. In the extract below, Ella is still in the process of 'learning' the story and looks to her mother to fill in the parts she is not sure about. The memories and the stories come from her grandmother, but they become transgenerational through Ella's appropriation:

Darcy: [to Suki] Mimi, they call my mum Mimi, Mimi and Grandee – we ran out of names because there were so many left alive.

Ella: And she told me told me a story about Somal who is my uncle he always gets, he always hurts himself and once he climbed up the gutter, and ... He climbed onto the gutter or something to try and get into the house.

Ella: And um and ... he went up to the top and he nearly fell through the glass 'cos they had a glass ...

Darcy: Conservatory.

Ella: Conservatory and he nearly fell through that.

Darcy: But what happened to the gutter?

Ella: The gutter fell down and Mimi and Grandee were angry and Somal.

Darcy: What happened?

Ella: What happened was he said um the wind blew it off.

Darcy: My brother was the most accident-prone child ever, if it was going to break it would break near him. He was so accident prone that he'd constantly be up at the hospital they used to walk in and they'd say 'hello Somal'!

Ella: And they used to say 'what is it now? Er, stitches ...'

Darcy: [to Suki] It was normally stitches.

Ella: '... er stitches or plaster'.

Suki: Stitches or plaster.

The style and the structure of the interaction is very revealing here. The two take turns with the narrative and gradually tell the story. At the end Darcy prompts her daughter to finish off the story and asks her what happened almost like it is a test of whether she is remembering correctly and 'getting it right'. When Ella says 'and they used to say, 'what is it now?', it is as if the memories were her own, first hand, that she was actually there and experienced this for herself. In this case, the 'dialogic overtones' are in place: 'Therefore, the utterance appears to be furrowed with distant and barely audible echoes of changes of speech subjects and dialogic overtones, greatly weakened utterance boundaries that are completely permeable to the author's expression' (Bakhtin 1986: 93).

The telling of this story is almost ritualised and they take turns filling in the blanks and then repeating the sentences in responsive rhythms. These kinds of stories are forms of oral history in as much as they have to be 'learnt'. There is no room for interpretation and development that would alter the meaning of the story, they have to be 'accurate' in order to be passed on. In learning the role of listener as speaker, Ella is obscuring the utterances of others as she claims and 'assimilates' them.

Later when we were talking about something completely different, Ella interrupted as she remembered something else about her favourite uncle – another story from her grandmother. This too was a way of constructing a family history and shared identification between grandmother and granddaughter. In addition it illustrates the role of storytelling as an inter-generational practice which had to be learned. Not only is the story passed down and 'taught' from one generation through to another, but in this particular family the practice is clearly gendered.

The sons in the family take no part in the storytelling, other than being the characters about whom the tale is told. The grandmother has relinquished the major burden, and Darcy now takes on the role of teacher of the family stories. The exchanges above were carried out with a sense of shared comfort and ease, both mother and child slipping into familiar roles and patterns of speech. The fact that these could be shared with a stranger as a way of illustrating family practices lends support to the notion that they are quite crucial to the formation of cultural history in the family and thus a strong sense of familial identity through transference of memories as stories. They are also so strongly ritualised in format as to conform to a generic style, and in this case the learning of the stories quite *literally* positions the listener as speaker (Bakhtin 1986).

Family Secrets

The secrets in families construct them as much as the openly told stories. Scandals, shame and the like which are alluded to without being spoken of publicly, truths that are half known, lies that are half told – all are ways in which families are formed. In the context of the 'confessional' imperative of late modern societies they are also capable of de-forming families or rendering them dysfunctional in the language of 'family therapy'.

The way that the children told the stories of their families was often more guarded and careful than might be expected, given their age. They were often quite discrete about things that mothers had thought that they would have already told me. So Andrea assumed that Sima had told me that she had been raised in Barnardo's children's homes (see also next chapter). Other families told me intimate details about themselves. After spending a lot of time with one child, I went on to discover that the family had suffered a suicide comparatively recently. This was revealed to me by another family member who was very concerned that the school would not find out. Out of respect to the respondent, I will not go into further details. The secret was told me with the understanding that the information might be used in an anonymised form. It was a very powerful example of the ways in which family stories were told with secrets built into them, and that family forms were not always what they appeared to be when first revealed.

The most interesting thing about the secrets was the way in which the children showed a high level of discretion about the things that were subsequently revealed by adults. In the case of Sima and his mother, she assumed that Sima would have told me about her having been raised in residential homes all her life; but he had told me nothing of that. When I talked to him about 'family' he did not mention the fact that his mother was estranged from the bulk of her family. Indeed, Andrea made it clear that she did not want to talk to me about her relationship with her mother, and that she could not even discuss the subject with Sima as it was too painful. She does not discuss this with the majority of people and only gradually told me a little of her story as the interview progressed. Due to issues of confidentiality, I could not give her any indication of what Sima may or may not have said. But he had clearly avoided a very large and important part of his family relations because he felt it was at least extremely private, if not quite secret. None of the parents or children I spoke to made any mention of anything other than heterosexual relationships within the families, and I have to assume that this was also an area in which secrets were to be maintained.

Naming Families

One of the ways in which secrets are well kept in families is through names or titles that are bestowed upon family members. In more than one case the children that I spoke to named their closest family members in conventional terms, only to reveal at a later stage, or for their parents to reveal, that the naming had obscured a more complicated relationship than the chosen name suggested. Most commonly the term 'father' was used, where in quotidian terms 'step-father' would be more usual, or where there was no conventionally recognised 'blood tie' or legal tie to denote 'legitimate' family status. It is not uncommon for close adult family friends to be called 'auntie' or 'uncle', and in recent years, with the numbers of second families increasing, a new partner to a parent may be called 'father' or 'mother' when they are a 'step-parent'. In most cases the term 'new' father would be used to show that there was a 'blood' or 'natural' or 'real' father elsewhere or deceased, and that the 'new' father was now related by marriage. If a parent's partner was referred to by name, it generally inferred that there had as yet been no marriage or formal tie to the child's parent.

Boris is a small, quiet boy from Year 4 in Christie School in London. He told me that he lived at home with his mum and dad, and that they were his family. When I asked him about going to church with his mum, the following exchange occurred:

Boris: Sometimes I stay at home if Geoff's …
Suki: Who's Geoff?
Boris: [Very quietly] My dad.

At the time, I did not prompt him about this relationship any further. When talking about going home to Guyana he said: 'Sometimes [my family] have a chat and we talk about going over to Guyana sometimes … 'cos I stay, we stay separately. I stay at my God-dad's …'

Boris had by now identified at least two 'fathers' in his life, and when he talked about his 'racial' identity it was tied up with painful emotions about racist name-calling and his own father's identity. As with Tito, he simply could not or would not speak about this. He told me that he had been called 'half-caste' and when I asked him why he told me:

Boris: 'Cos, I'm from Guyana. And my mum is black. When I was born … and I was half-caste when I was born.
Suki: I see.
Boris: 'Cos I've got a white dad.
Suki: 'Cos you've got a white dad?
Boris: Mmm.
Suki: Right. And oh sorry is that the same dad as you've still got in your house now?
Boris: I don't think I can tell you that.

In response to Boris completely closing off the conversation and clearly feeling uncomfortable, I spent the next couple of minutes reassuring him that he did not have to tell me anything that he didn't want to; that there were many different ways of thinking about family, and if Geoff was important to him 'like a dad' that was fine. He responded with a correction that Geoff was his step-dad. On the tape I sound desperate to reassure him that I do not want to pry or drag up any difficult issues for him.

Boris chose to name his variously positioned male adult influences in his life as some kind of father figure. He did this strategically to both protect his privacy and to throw me off the trail. When I discovered that there were variations in his use of the term 'dad', he simply shut down. He talked about something that seemed to be both secret and shameful in some way. It could simply be that the difficulty lay with the fact that he was being positioned as 'half-caste', or it may have been connected to other deeper family concerns about his biological father and his relationship with Boris's mother. From other things that were said I would suspect the latter. Calling Geoff his dad for much of the interview was also, more simply, reflection of the important role he was taking in Boris's life and the fact that Boris clearly had strong emotional ties to him.

By contrast, other children chose to reveal rather than conceal their relationships by using very particular language to name people they thought of as family. Kilde (Barnlea, Year 4) came to be interviewed with her photographs of 'home' which showed her with her mother, her 'Guardian' and her 'Guardian Auntie'. I had never heard any of the other children use this term in the school, but she was very confident in using it. When I questioned it she told me that she was not her 'real' auntie, but was her guardian's sister. The expression 'Guardian Auntie' seemed a bit cumbersome to her but she persevered with it for some time. I then asked her what her guardian's name was, and she told me both his name and his sister's, and it sounded almost formal and certainly quite cold and distant. Suddenly she described a photo that included her guardian, referring to him as her 'dad'. I did not question this at the time and waited to see if she would return to the theme of explaining their relationship when I asked about whom she thought of as family. I did ask her directly what she called her Guardian Auntie when they were together, and she said she just called her 'Susan'. From then on that is how she referred to her in the interview.

The importance of generic forms of 'speech acts' are revealed by Kilde here (see Bakhtin 1986). The first is guided by the generic form of the interview context. She came prepared with this title in order to facilitate my understanding of the formal role this man played in her life, privileging that over the emotional and 'incorrect' title of 'dad'. She believed that she was making my task easier by using this specially prepared name, because it made the legal relationship clear, and I as interviewer/researcher was after information about her 'family'.

The second generic context produces different kinds of naming processes – what she *actually* calls these people when she is with them. At home she calls her Guardian 'Paul' *and* 'Dad'. She is also in touch with the person she called her '*real*' dad, another commonly used phrase. Her 'real' dad was revealed to me in the interview when the form of our interaction became more relaxed and informal and we were beginning to communicate as research friends. The confusions of having two dads became easier to manage, as I had a more complete picture of her relationships. This again shows the ways in which generic forms are not discreet and are learnt. Kilde had 'practised' or 'rehearsed' for the interview, with myself as the imagined dialogic partner/listener. It also confirms further Morgan's idea (1996) that families are practices and relationships, as Kilde's new dad is someone who performs the caring role of father.

Creating Family through Narratives

Several more important insights can be gained from these investigations into the way in which children and mothers (and two fathers) construct families. It would seem that the *visual* representations of family follow generic codes which both children and adults know and operationalise. The 'family snap' facilitates memory re/production, which provides the impetus for the lengthy verbal responses which establish kinship. In many instances, visual images powerfully circumvent the inadequacies of language as pictures of faces and places tell the story of multi-locational selves. However, their absence can still be used in the memory work of research (Kuhn 1995). Through remembering and the telling of stories of families, new aspects are constructed diachronically and then become as important as the actual experience of events. Ella appropriated stories for her own sense of family history, and Kyle did the same in a style more in keeping with stereotypical masculine verbal reticence.

The ways in which children talked about their families showed a great investment in keeping secrets, often, I believe, trying to protect their parents from my intrusions. Through the naming processes, Kilde was trying to make things *easier* for me. In using 'Guardian' she was not only helping me with my understanding of her family but was being creative. This seems to be constructed in opposition to 'keeping a secret' because Pares (her mother) said that she had *never* heard Paul call her guardian, or Susan her guardian auntie: she was actually facilitating dialogue.

I would like to conclude this chapter by asking some rhetorical questions:

- What is the meaning of this kind of naming process for a child with two sets of 'parents' who have differing racial identities?
- Is it more or less important if the child identifies with the old or new parent?
- What if the new parent is not of the same racial identity as the old one do they have to hold on to these names in order to keep these strands of their identity separate?
- How does this fit with John, who has 'become half-caste' because of his new dad? (see Chapter 2).
- How does Geoff identify 'racially'?

I suspected that Geoff was also 'white' at first, but the way that Boris refers to being half-caste *at birth* makes me feel that he is now with a black dad. I think that Boris was trying to become/stay black. His 'origins' were a secret, so how is it that people call him 'half-caste' as he is a dark-skinned boy without any of the phenotypical signs that 'usually' connote half-caste.

These questions are a few that are unanswerable at the present time. Others are a little more straightforward. I would suggest that children were much more comfortable and flexible in the way they manipulated discourses of 'race' in the public domain. There is a paradox evident in the way in which this occurs at 'home'. They seem both constrained and liberated by discourses of family. They are being creative (Boris, John, Kilde), and, as will be shown in Chapter 7, this provides them with a way to make discourses of 'race' in educational contexts at least partially meaningful. But they are also being constrained by the idea of continuity, so that families must be 'spoken' into being and visually represented in traditional and generic ways. In the next chapter the ways in which 'home' constituted, and was constituted, by 'family' will be detailed.

Notes

1. From now on I will refer to 'mothers' rather than 'parents', as their accounts make up the bulk of the data and will make specific reference to the two fathers who took part where appropriate.

2. Kehily uses this term in conjunction with stories of 'self' in the process of 'self-narration'. I am using it to refer to stories of 'families' and how they are also ways of narrating selves.

3. Adkins and Leonard (1996) use the term ' a sense of family', which I also use later. Using 'family-like status' I hope implies that it is created and structured so that it is recognised both within and outside the families. It reminds us that families 'we choose' are often non-traditional and difficult to identify (Weston 1997).

4. I am using 'ethnicised' here to denote the non-biologically grounded basis for 'othering' that ethnicity implies and the material practices that construct groups.

5. See Mac an Ghaill (1994: 90-102) for the ways in which heterosexual masculinites are constructed through sex-talk, but concomitantly with an absence of talk about feelings.

6. I am using the model of kinship/family work that Lisa Adkins and Diana Leonard (1996) developed in their study of children's family work and its effects on educational choices, which utilised aspects of research by di Leonardo (1987).

7. Richard Collier (1999: 52) suggests that masculinity and fatherhood are produced relationally and discursively in the rhetoric of the 'New Man'.

8. Most children claimed pizzas as favourites. Some were proud of 'traditional' food, which they said I would not understand. In a few cases, with children of both genders but middle class, they chose pasta dishes.

9. I am using the differing terms 'interracial', and 'inter-ethnic' families to denote a difference in the area under particular scrutiny at the time. For example, issues of appearance which for children are often about colour would be referred to as 'interracial'. When talking about different cultural, religious and national traditions held within families, where 'race' is secondary, 'inter-ethnic' will be used. In some cases, 'inter-cultural', or 'international' may be more appropriate. The use of different terms is not denoting an elision of one with the other or that they are being used inter-changeably; on the contrary they are being used to denote different emphases of focus. The same may be said of referring to 'mixed-race' children at one moment and multiheritage, multiethnic or inter-cultural at another.

–6–

Moving Homes: Gender, Diaspora, Ethnicity

When does a location become a home? What is the difference between
'feeling at home' and staking claim to a place as one's own?

> A. Brah *Cartographies of Diaspora:*
> *Contesting Identities*

Introduction

In the previous chapter I showed how the *concept* of home was closely intertwined with the concept of family in ways that are both complex and unpredictable. Families are usually found within a place called 'home', but they could
also be dispersed throughout many different locations. It is possible for families
to be created by, and to create, the domestic space that is known as home. The
relationship between the two is dynamic and flows both ways. The families of the
children in this study had all had some experience of migration at some time in
their history – either on the mothers' or fathers' side, or both. There were a range
of reasons for this, and it may even have been that the current generation of children had personally experienced some form of national or regional relocation.
For this reason the overwhelming majority of respondents had simultaneously
multi-locational notions of 'home' as both a place and as an emotional centre to
their 'racial' or national identity. 'Homes' are constructed within a matrix of
psychic and geographic spaces – they are conceived of as both real and imagined,
and are lived through domestic and (inter)national locations. It is these complex
ties between home, nationality and family that help to inform the central area of
inquiry, the negotiation of 'mixed-race' identity.

Diachronic readings of 'home' made by parents are mediated through a sense
of belonging and dis/placement. They are not necessarily imbued with a 'homing
desire', even when they add meaning and value to the sense of national and
ethnic identifications parents make. For children, the synchronic understanding
of home as the place where they currently live is held in parallel with notions of
'where they come from' as discourses of space and place, articulated with
discourses of nationality and ethnicity. The families in this study were engaged
in constructing their own understandings of nations through narrative processes

in ways that were in keeping with those suggested by Bhabha (1990b). In addition mothers were undertaking family practices of cultural production and domestic work which created 'safe homes' for children (see Morgan 1996). The necessity to 'belong' is one that informs the ways in which both children and parents are making sense of multiethnic positionalities.

Homes and Diasporas

The concept of diaspora is one that has been usefully employed in writing about migrant and translocated peoples. Historically it has been used by those who have been forcibly exiled from countries of origin. Avtar Brah uses the concept of diaspora in connection with 'home' but simultaneously critiques the notion of fixed origins (Brah 1996: 193). In the case of multiethnic/national positionings across family and individual identities, notions of diaspora retain salience in the ways in which 'home' is spoken about, but may not have the same meaning for those with (seemingly) 'monoracial' and multicultural histories, and may not always be incorporated in a *consciously strategic* way into family narratives. It was not a phrase that was used in the everyday language of those who were interviewed. This may be because for the majority their relocation was through 'choice', either for economic reasons such as the search for labour or because of familial responsibilities. Elaine Unterhalter (2000) argues that the concept of diaspora should hold to its political origins by being used by those who belong to groups who have been forced into exile and retain a sense of denied return, and in this formulation the term would be inappropriate to those who were interviewed. The choices that fuelled the movements of the families in the project were certainly informed by Western post/colonial relations, but were not always forced in the sense of war or some other oppressive and genocidal project on the part of another ethnic group living in the 'homeland'.

I would agree that the de-politicising of 'diaspora' is problematic; neither is it necessarily an appropriate term for those of multiethnic heritage, unless they retain connections with, for example, 'the' African diaspora. It is a term that needs to be used with sensitivity. However, there are other aspects to Brah's work that are relevant to the respondents in this study, even if we do not agree with her choice of terminology or its origins. One of these aspects is the theoretical framework she calls 'diaspora space'. I believe that the use of 'diaspora' with the word 'space' substantively alters the emphasis, and that the sum of the two words has a different meaning than the parts. For Brah, the concept of diaspora space is 'the intersectionality of disaspora, border, and dis/location as a point of confluence of economic, political, cultural, and psychic processes ... The concept of diaspora space references the global condition of "culture as a site of travel" Clifford (1992) which seriously problematises the subject position of the "native"' (Brah 1996: 208).

This space is inhabited by both those who migrated and those who are considered to be indigenous, as their genealogies are entwined. This multi-locational positionality is relevant to those who are from multiethnic/racial families. The most useful part of such a theoretical framework is the way it allows for complex subject positions to be interrogated from the perspective of transboundaried narratives which are historically specific, politically informed and mediated through hegemonic discourses in everyday social relations. But it also suggests that the hegemonic cultural processes need not totally overwhelm those of the minority: 'There is traffic within cultural formations of the subordinated groups, and ... these journeys are not *always* mediated through the dominant culture(s)' (ibid. 209).

This plurality in cultural constructions at the level of the group and the individual is essential when looking at the stories of those of 'mixed-race' and the way they talk of 'home'. Brah is looking to debunk the notion of a 'pure' indigenous 'native', and to suggest a potent way to reduce the power of the (ethnic) dominant over the dominated, a binary which she eschews. This is to be commended in a multiethnic, multicultural society that continues to reify notions of 'race' and nation. What she does not consider (in any depth) is how the 'psychic' axis to which she refers is mediated by family narratives, and stories of 'blood and bone' – those to whom we belong in a familial sense. Individuals' social circumstances, their social geographies, as well as histories, will work through individual psycho-subjective positions but will have their resonances in the body in very immediate ways (see Chapters 3 and 4). The physicality of the children is the site of border crossings of the 'racial'; and the physical body mediates the psychic meanings of the children's emotional responses to family narratives (see Chapter 4).

Many of the stories of family construct notions of home that are more conventionally connected to the discourse of diaspora. Further, the domestic space of the home, at the level of the household, is the site for the contestation of global vs. local understandings of histories. In order to understand the way that the children frame 'home' within their identifications we must consider the crucial impact family narratives, as well as family structures, have on these ideas. As was shown in the previous chapter, it is often these narratives that mediate the disjunctures of time and space in national and 'racial' histories for the children.

One of the interesting findings was how clearly children understood parents' views about home, and how these ideas differed with the new generation's understandings of the local and the global. At this stage of their lives children often talked of their families and homes in synchronic fashion, whereas for adults the diachronic themes ran through the narratives and constituted current understandings.

The way that mothers (and through them, other family members) expressed the 'homing desire' played a strong part in how the children understood their own diaspora connections. Home is social, spatial and spiritual and is constructed through family practices, stories and imaginings. It is a complex and important part of the *identifications* that the children made, and was just one aspect of their sense of multi-locational being. Again, the influence of personal biographies, and different movements and settlements among respondents, produced different responses to a globalised sense of belonging.

Places in the Heart: Geographic Locations

Penny: Home ... the concept of home is important, but I've never been too bothered about my surroundings. But I think that that will change when we
get into a house of our own.

Parents – mothers – often made a separation between home as concept and place *before* that had been asked of them, as Penny's comment shows. As the research progressed, many of the children revealed a feeling of belonging to another place. For Meli, it was New Zealand; for Boris, Guyana, and so on. But they only made sense of this distant belonging through the discourses of heritage and family. For most of the children, however, home was always first thought of as the place in which they currently live.

Show Homes
The children in the study were asked about what they thought about 'home' before the mothers were contacted. I had hoped that the photographs the children had taken would represent things that they thought meant 'home' or 'family'; things that were important to them in constructing these concepts. As noted earlier, there was a very interesting gendered divide in the way the children did this. With one notable exception, it was boys who chose to represent their homes in terms of the building itself, often from the outside.[1] Zendu only took pictures of his front door with its number, and of the various rooms in his house, although when I talked to him he offered to bring in some other family photos which showed some of his relatives. There were girls who took pictures of their rooms which contained their favourite doll collections, but they always included pictures of people and of course pets! Several of the boys took pictures of their rooms and their computers and football trophies. They were more likely to do this without other people in the pictures, apart from in just one or two of the images. There were many possible reasons for this, one of which was, predictably, terminology.

  Children overwhelmingly thought of 'home' as a geographic location that was easily represented as the place in which they lived with their (immediate) families. They had a less sophisticated way of thinking about the idea of home as a concept, rather than at the level of the immediate. They could relate easily to the idea of family as being people who were important and 'blood relations', but could also readily relocate family to other places. Many of them spontaneously offered to bring in pictures of family in other locations and in other 'homes'. But they referred to these as family photographs. The children not only thought of their homes as the places they lived, but could separate that out from another place which was where they 'come from', which may not have been the same as their birthplace. This links national/familial identities and shows how as Gilroy (1993b, 1993c) suggests, concepts of diaspora are inscribed with and through roots and routes.

Going Home

The children all talked of the place they currently lived as home. However, many could identify the fact that their *parents* had *different* ideas about this. When first asked in a literal way about what their parents talked of as 'home', the children chose the current household or domestic space. But if they were asked specifically if their parents ever talked about 'Going home' (to another place where they had been born or still had family), they understood the question better, and could relate it to conversations within the family. The children could also identify with the question 'where do you come from?' in a way that they could not for 'what is home?' They could reformulate where they came from to include another more distant 'home' – such as in John's case, Nigeria, or in Jacob's and Tito's case, Jamaica. The idea that their racial and national identifications were intertwined with multi-locational 'homes' will be explored later in this chapter.

Many of the parents in the study were originally from other areas of Britain or from other countries. The parents who were interviewed were also asked about where they thought of as home. Although, like the children, many responded that their current location was their home, it often emerged soon after, through the dialogic process of the interview, that they simultaneously felt that other places were home as well. This supports Denzin's analysis: 'Any specific representation is part of a larger process that dialectically builds upon itself and elaborates itself as it unfolds over time … This historical, narrative logic must be unravelled and connected to specific textual representations' (Denzin 1997: 248).

The need for continued discussion about the meanings of such multi-layered constructions such as 'home' is essential. Again, using narratives, mothers created positionings that could encompass multifaceted and nuanced concepts of home.

When Sheila talks of home she is clearly maintaining two geographic locations at once: 'So really as far as I'm concerned this [London] is my home. This is where I live. I, you know, I contribute, I give out and I take back and whatever else, but that's [Montserrat] where my parents are from, my gran ...' For Sheila, Montserrat is still important as a place with meaning for both herself and her children who have an Irish father. When news of the volcanic eruption on the island came through the television media in 1998 she was very shocked and upset: 'and it like really like made me sad 'cos I thought "Oh my kids will never see that". And it's a nice little ... it's only a little island but it's nice you know. I remember it ... what I can remember it was a lovely place and stuff like that ...' This is not just about a home at the level of concept, it is about a physical place and how it differs from the current family location which is a flat in London. Sheila's memories of the place are strong enough to inform some of the family stories that are passed down, such as her running away from school one day and hiding in the mango trees at the end of the garden.

Not all of the parents had such a different location to inform their stories of home. Those who were born and raised in Britain were more concerned with the construction of the current family home, and only refer to other family homes peripherally, even if their family histories were linked to international locations. This may be because having their own children confers greater importance on their current surroundings, or may be because they have not had the emotional upheaval that comes with national relocation.

Darcy has a very rich family history. Her mother is English, with one of her great-grandparents Italian-Jewish. Her father's family is 'Ceylonese'-Tamil, [2] but he was born in Singapore. He still has siblings in Singapore, but now lives in England. Despite this, Darcy has a very uncomplicated view of home:

Suki: So where do you think of as home?
Darcy: I suppose I think of Brighton as my home.

This is where she was born and raised until she went to college. She maintains strong ties with friends in Brighton and still goes to see friends and family there regularly. In Darcy's case her personal history, her own birthplace and subsequent schooling and social networks in England, overrode links to her father's place of birth. In his case, however, she reported that although he had been born in Singapore his links with Ceylon were extremely strong and that he still thought of it as 'home'. He wanted to return to Ceylon and was following the civil unrest with great anxiety. Although this affected Darcy as well it was at a distance mediated across space and generation. It also points to a complex notion of cultural and ethnic history, which seems to have even less salience with her children. Her partner, the children's father, is white ethnic English.

Other mothers reported much more complex ideas about home, which have changed over time:

Celie: Home. Now home is a bit more of a problem because … home for me was always Singapore if I had to look to a geographical place. I was there from the age of 5 until I went away to boarding school, but then my parents didn't leave Singapore until I was 19, and I would go out, when my parents could afford the fare I'd go out and that kind of stuff …

The area in which she lived in Singapore has changed enormously over time, and the house where she was born had been pulled down. She continued:

Celie: … Home now is really, I very strongly feel it is this small little plot. It has to be this because the other thing is actually gone, and my parents' home has all kinds of has all sorts of mixed feelings about that particular place. I don't feel it to be my home, funnily enough I've never felt that house that they bought 20 years ago to be my home at all. It's *their* home.

In this case, the parents' home, which was, coincidentally, Singapore, was, by her own choice of words, a geographical place. When the physical place of her birth disappeared (her old house) she lost the connection to the country, despite the fact that her parents continued to live there. It seems that it was, as with Darcy, the 'Britishness' of her life that then overtook the original emotional and geographic ties to Singapore; she then looked to creating her own home. She talked again of the physical space by describing 'this small little plot' as her present home. These discussions about places are always linked with emotions and are merely being separated in order to analyse them. These concepts will be shown to be inextricable from each other in the way the respondents themselves talked of them.

Places in the Heart: Emotional Locatedness

As mentioned above, the emotions associated with the concepts of home were often profound and were by no means constant throughout the lives of the parents in the study. For some the responses were about a sense of belonging that transcended the 'rational'. In others, the feeling of security and safety within a home was of paramount importance. It is also true to say that children were less able to express their emotions about their homes in such direct ways as their parents, and their emotional responses were often hidden within what they reported. In many cases the ways in which home was multi-locational even surprised the respondents themselves.

Despite the fact that she had had a very difficult time in her teenage years, which resulted in her running away from home, Mrs Farmer (Margaret) still had emotional connections to the place she was born:

> Funnily enough it always felt like going back to where I grew up as a child. Um then when I came to London, [it was like] 'I'm going back home'. Because I've lived away for such a long time ... and the way people live down there [Yorkshire], and in comparison to here ... I often feel like a fish out of water.

Even though she still had mixed feelings about her visits to Yorkshire over the years, and she feels very uncomfortable there, she holds the emotional connection to her birthplace but simultaneously feels 'at home' in London.

Spiritual Homes

Talk about 'spiritual homes', and the use of that phrase, was unexpected. Emotional connectedness to place was important and was expressed in many ways. I believe that this phrase was used to indicate something that was not 'real', although it was *felt*. It was, however, a 'real' link with a 'real' place, so it was often spoken of at the same time as geography.

One of the mothers interviewed spontaneously used the term 'spiritual home' in a very early stage of the interview. Andrea was one of the most openly politically informed parents, and she is the mother and the primary carer of her child, a ten-year-old boy named Sima. She presented in the interviews as very articulate, and was thoughtful and reflexive throughout the whole process. Andrea describes herself as black and is also emphatic that her son is black too. She told me she was born and raised in Britain, but home meant more than one place:

Suki: So actually one of my questions is about how important home is to you.

Andrea: Home. Ah! Yeah! Jamaica's home. I mean it's home in a spiritual sense, I couldn't live there, but I could certainly go there and spend long periods ...

Interestingly this response came to the question of how *important* home was, not *where* it was. The answer is unequivocal at the level of the metaphysical. This idea of a spiritual home is very powerful to her, and is not simply a sentimental and romantic yearning for a place beyond reach. She has no illusions about the impact of the material upon her position in relation to her kin on the island, nor about differing lifestyles and levels of economic power:

Andrea: But the difficulty about going home it's that people want things from you, and umm. You know that there's an expectation that you'll take things over there and that people do ask you for money. I think the assumption is that you must be reasonably well off to be able to travel to Jamaica …

Andrea managed to maintain a closeness with her spiritual home despite the sometimes painful distancing effects of location, culture and material wealth. She spent her childhood in a Barnardo's Children's Home and has a very painful relationship with her family, other than her sister and those with whom she has made contact in Jamaica over the last ten years. It is no wonder that the spiritual is evoked by her. This endorses the position that 'The homing desire is not the same as a desire for a homeland. Contrary to general belief, not all diasporas sustain an ideology of return' (Brah 1996: 197).

Others talked of similar feelings without using the word 'spiritual', and this was also related to the concept of roots, genealogies and of one's ancestry or heritage. Sheila had already talked of Montserrat as a place – an island with warm weather and white houses – but she also explained the important emotional tie in an almost physical way. When asked directly if there was an emotional connection with Montserrat as an important part of her history, she said that it was, but that she thought that it also helped to shape her children's identities:

Sheila: That's where I was *born,* and that's where I'd like my kids to see it one day if possible.
        […]
Sheila: Er um oh important? Mmmm … [musing pause] I think it's important that they know that that's where I'm *from*. Because I mean they *know*. You know Dinease especially; 'My mum's from Montserrat!' [in a proud voice] you know?

Dinease did indeed know of her mother's heritage, and it played a part in her identity as she chose to describe herself in her own words. She had accepted the fact that her mother used the term 'mixed-race', but was herself very strongly identified with black culture. Her friendship networks were mostly with black girls both in school and outside. She shared her mother's view that she was English, and that her home was where she lived in the flat in London with her family. She did not identify herself as 'half Montserratian' as some of the other children might have, but did identify her *mother* as being 'from Montserrat'. Again the ways in which geography and nationality form emotional strands that run through the discourses of 'identity' and 'history' is clear, as is the way that it is only partially transmitted across generations who do not share the immediate closeness to the locations.

Safe Houses

The way in which new locations took on the true title of home was by acquiring a degree of permanency that allowed for a sense of security to develop. This was expressed at the level of the household, the city and the nation.

For one of the single white mothers, Mrs. Farmer, the subject of home came up spontaneously when she was talking about her family and the death of her father the previous year. She said: 'It's still a little bit sore actually, I won't get into it too much. I think I want the children to … and my family live in Yorkshire, I've got five brothers and one sister. But I've lived in London now twenty-five years, so this is home to me.' She had moved to London from a troubled family life at the age of 16. The distance from her family still bothered her, but it seemed that this concept of home was in part acquired purely through the length of time that she had spent in London. It was also related to the fact that it was a place that she had created independently, thus acquiring stability for herself and, subsequently, her family.

Family practices played an important part in Mrs. Farmer's narratives of home and family. The processes of cultural production and caring for her family in Yorkshire and then her children in London formed a major part in her identification of herself as a mother. Her own mother had died when she was fourteen years old, and as the eldest daughter a great many family responsibilities had fallen to her. These included all of the domestic work in the home, caring for herself, her father and her brothers. She had been in and out of reform schools and children's homes before she had run away to London. Obviously safety and security for her children were of paramount importance to her, and she admitted to being overprotective of them. She did not really talk much about the flat that she lived in other than to say that it was a great improvement on their previous home, and to talk with a sense of pride of the decor. The place that was home for her was a city where she was allowed to be herself, where she fitted in and felt comfortable, where she had been accepted by people and where she could be 'who she was' with no sense of shame. This included her 'multicultural' approach to life and the desire to be free to associate with whom she wanted. *Cultural environment* was the major consideration after the family home, as was the case with Celie.

When Celie was talking about her changing sense of home she referred to the need to create a home when she felt that she had none, in order to create a safe space for herself and her family. Her husband's job had required a move to Bahrain where she had stayed for ten years and where her three children were born, but it was never 'home'. She explained it in the following way:

Celie: Um it's really odd, so this is really my home now and it's obviously to do with Jack and the children …

Suki: So you've created your own?

Celie: Yes I felt I had to, I really strongly felt that I have had to.

Suki: So that the concept is important and finding kind of a root …

Celie: Yes.

Suki: For it?

Celie: Yes it was very, very important and in fact a big bone of contention between us, coming back. Because for me I always felt that I had created this home, because I always felt like I was living in a borrowed home in Bahrain, um … and um … So coming here I knew we were coming, for Jack it was coming, for Jack it was coming home for Jack. I mean it's not India at all. I mean he wanted to, 'cos he grew up and spent all his life in north London …

In this revealing piece of text the underlying anxieties of having children in a place that felt unsafe are obvious, as is the fact that her husband did not necessarily share that view. It is also implied that Celie had considered living in Singapore again, whereas for her English-born Indian husband there was no place other than England, and, more specifically, his own home town of London – that was home. Celie described the fact that he was completely Anglicised, as his parents (who still live in London) had wished. Their eldest son, Josh, who was at Fairsham school in Year 5, also showed none of the anxieties of his mother and remembered Bahrain fondly as a place with brilliant weather and unlimited access to a swimming pool! He said he would still rather live there because of those things.

These divergent views are all held within the same family group and it is interesting that the mother feels the need to 'create' the place of safety, a word she used twice, in an emotional sense. Her links with her Singaporean 'roots' are also more important to her than her husband's roots, and she is the prime mover in talking to her children about their 'racial'/ethnic/cultural roots, despite the fact that she herself has found a compromise 'Eurasian' identity that developed at boarding school, and continued to be useful into university and beyond.

One of the two fathers who were interviewed introduced a dimension to home that was touched upon by the mothers, though not as early in response to the question and not so directly:

Nigel: Um it's not been important in the past, but it sort of is now but I suppose it's a concept of security.

Suki: Do you mean financial or emotional?

Nigel: Both really, yeah it is more important than it was in the past … Trappings are fairly important to me as well.

Suki: Trappings?

Nigel: The trappings of a home.
Suki: Things? Home comforts that sort of thing?
Nigel: Yeah.

Here Nigel is putting emotion and material acquisitions on an equal level of importance. He shared care of his son (Kyle) with his ex-partner who lived in Woodvale. Some of the mothers made reference to 'comforts' and wanting to make homes comfortable for families, but they did not usually mention that as part of what home actually *meant,* and none talked overtly about financial security as being crucial, even though financial difficulty may have been alluded to. This seems to be a rather stereotypically gendered view, although in this case the child's mother was also working, so the 'breadwinner' role or 'head of household' was not applicable to Nigel. One way of looking at Nigel's response is to consider that security can be expressed in many different ways and that the material is merely one of them that he still felt to be important. He mentioned having been aware of financial difficulties when he was a child, and it could be that this informs his own ideas about parenting and providing security in a way that defies gendered interpretations.

Two Home Families
A few of the children talked of having two homes when their parents were separated and they had regular access to time with both parents. These were the exception however, with the majority, who all lived with their mothers, talking about their fathers having 'another house' which they went to even if they had new families in these homes. The children seemed to prioritise one place over another even if they spent a lot of time at both. One of the exceptions was Kyle who said: 'Well I've got two homes actually, one in Woodvale and one in London.' He said this with a smile and was quick to point out that this was because his father (Nigel, mentioned in the previous section) lived in London and that he often went to see him. When Kyle later brought in his photographs he began by showing his mother drawing up to school in her car to collect him, and the images followed through their evening together, with Kyle narrating this chronology with snippets of information about their life together. However, suddenly the location changed: 'And here we have my dad at another house, his big old car garage house.' He then began to show his father's house and tell his stories of all the objects in the house. He explained how he had saved some of the exposures on his camera until the weekend so that he could take pictures of his father and his home in London. Clearly, despite the rather odd terminology of 'another house', rather than 'his house', he felt that these two homes were of equal importance for the representation of his life 'at home'.

This was a very rare occurrence, even though many of the children interviewed talked of having good relationships with the parents who were absent – overwhelmingly fathers. There is a way in which Kyle has similar ways of narrating home to the parents, using diachronic and multi-locational versions of home because he also related that he used to live in London before he moved to Woodvale. In this sense 'home' was also connected to his birthplace. This would seem to be the main reason why the children have more simple ideas of home. Most of the children of mixed-parentage had lived the majority of their short lives in one place. They were at this time less likely to be connected to a place of birth unless it was another country; their identifications were much more immediate even if their heritage indicated affiliations to other places. They could say that they 'came from', for example, Nigeria, but talked of home as being England or more likely the place, literally the house or flat, in which they currently lived.

Collectivities: Homes Away from Home

The children in this research had many ways of utilising the concept of 'home' for themselves, not all of them coherent to the researcher at the time of the research. One of the ways in which the concept was interrogated at the analytical level was in questioning the links between concepts of 'home', diaspora and belonging. In the preceding sections the links have been made directly by children and parents themselves. In this section I will look at how belonging (and not belonging) to collectivities plays a role in producing understandings of 'homes'. I then show how this informs the process of identification. In a sense, 'families' are micro-collectivities that take on additional (ethnic) significance to those of 'mixed-race'. Also, as outlined in Chapters 1 and 2, for sociologists the concept of ethnicity rests heavily upon a notion of a collective process and belonging to a group. For the children of 'mixed-race' the family was one such group, and the idea of a nation-state to which they could claim allegiance was another. Paul Gilroy has suggested that:

> In the Americocentric alternative [to cultural integrity], a postnationalist essence of blackness has been constructed through the dubious appeal to the family as the connective tissue of black experience and history. Family has come to stand for community, for race and for nation. It is a short–cut to solidarity. The discourse of family and the discourse of nation are very closely connected. (Gilroy 1993d: 203)

In this research I do not see respondents engaged in a 'post-nationalist' project, rather they are mediating narratives of selves through nation, family, home and belonging. I am not suggesting that 'trope of the family' is here being 'wheeled out to do the job of re-centring things every time the debates [in this conference] on black popular culture have promised to threaten spurious integrity of ideal, essential racial cultures' (ibid: 194). On the contrary, I would argue that it is the very partiality and constructedness of 'black' or 'raced' positions that must be interrogated within families. Interracial and multiethnic families in particular imbue this particular deconstructive process with even more urgency.

National Identities

From the extracts in the preceding sections we can see that parents and children often use a nation or country as a way to talk about a part of their identity and that this usually connected with a family history that has its origins in that country. The national identity of the children can often be entwined with very complicated identifications with 'race', culture and ethnicity. The use of a framework of diaspora was not invoked by the respondents in this research.

When asked to describe themselves in the first instance during the group work with the videos, the majority of children included some notion of a 'national' heritage, which was often contradictory to the rest of their identifications. These contradictions are more easily exposed within children who claim a monoracial identity. For example:

> I'm Sita and I come from England. My mother is Indian and she was born in Bolton, and my father is Indian and he was born in London. (Sita, Year 4, Barnlea School, 1998)

The child is holding several national identities: child of parents who are both British in terms of birthplace, but Indian here is being used not only to describe a familial heritage but, I believe, her ethnic and 'racial' identity. For Sita, in this context, 'Indian' was used to explain that she was brown-skinned and had partic-ular language, dress, food and religious affiliations that were connected to a national identity. Here, Sita claims a link to an 'imagined community' which is both a 'national collectivity' and 'ethnic collectivity' (Anthias and Yuval-Davis 1993). This is an active resistance to a simple identification with Englishness, and shows the way in which affiliations to the 'myth of common origin' continue to be transmitted across generations through ethnic markers (ibid.). I suggest that while Anthias and Yuval-Davis are right to question the desirability of the racialisation of nation, ethnicity and culture, that is often, in very simple terms, what the children do. For example, I was told that one child 'looked Somali', and when I asked about it found that it was his physicality that had earned him this description.

The children were extremely revealing of the way in which nation, ethnicity, culture and race are linked in everyday discourses of identity, and in the constructions of categories for self and others. The following extract comes from an interview with Kyle (Year 5, Fairsham), and shows the ways in which these processes are both present and yet invisible to the children:

Suki: Do people ever say to you Kyle where do you come from?

Kyle: Yes! A lot!

Suki: Can you tell me ..., what kind of people, when ...?

Kyle: Well only when well well friends tend to, or when I'm moving to a new school I normally get that question.

Suki: And what would you say?

Kyle: I'd say England.

Suki: Why do you think they ask you?

Kyle: Because of my skin colour.

Suki: Ok. Do they ever speak to you about your skin colour?

Kyle: No.

Suki: Why do you think it is about your skin colour?

Kyle: What do you mean 'why do you think it is about your skin colour?'?

Suki: Well you said 'I think they ask me because of my skin colour' ...

Kyle: [interrupting] Because it's dark.

I think that Kyle knew all along where this conversation was going and was trying to avoid it because it made him feel uncomfortable. He clearly knew that when people ask him about his genealogy they ask because he is 'dark' in a mainly white area and school. The dialogic interview continues with Kyle's evasiveness being rather heartlessly ignored because of my own prior knowledge of his 'mixed-race' heritage:

[...]

Suki: Ok, I'd like to know how you'd describe yourself as in skin colour?

Kyle: I don't know er ... it's not black and it's not white, so I'd ... brown I'd call it.

Suki: Have you ever heard the expression 'mixed-race'?

Kyle: Yes.

Suki: Who's used it?

Kyle: I don't know. I've just heard it before, not to me, I just think I have heard other people saying it.

Suki: Do you know what it means?

Kyle: Yes it's from when like somebody's half English, half German something like that.

Suki: Umm. Now when I spoke to you said that your parents are both from England and that's how you would describe yourself, your parents are both from England.

Kyle: Well my mother's half German, or quarter German.
Suki: Ah and what about your dad?
Kyle: I think he might be, be quarter Ind ... half Indian or quarter Indian.
Suki: Your dad?
Kyle: I think he is, is he? You know ...
Suki: I do actually.
Kyle: What is he?
Suki: He's half Indian but you could say 'Indian' but his parents from there they were from the Caribbean, they were Caribbean Indian.
Kyle: Lucky! Caribbean.
Suki: Yeah? Why's that lucky?
Kyle: 'Cos you get to grow up in the Caribbean.

In this section of the transcript, I, as interviewer, make the connection between skin colour and 'race' and then 'mixed-race'. Again, at first, Kyle de-raced it, in hegemonic terms.[3] He used 'German' and it then transpires that his mother is white and 'half German'. This slippage shows the ways in which he evades dealing with the issues, but they are present in his utterances.

He knew that I was aware of his father's heritage, and he was happy with my explanation. Being brought up in the Caribbean would be a good thing because, I believe, Kyle sees himself in terms of the 'brown' person, privileged and materially wealthy, living one extended holiday in the Caribbean. This imaginary life is completely based within his localised understandings of the global, and filtered through a 'white middle-class' lens. He does not deny he is brown, but he is *English brown*. However, he uses national identities to describe *why* he is brown, moving from 'raced' to 'de-raced' understandings of nation and 'home'. He said that he had never encountered racism from the other children, and that his family and the school had never talked about such things because they had never come up. In fact, his mother Penny told me that they had specifically talked about him being 'mixed-race' when a child at school had said that his skin was the colour of 'dog poo'.[4]

This extract highlights the ways in which nations become 'homes', but that they are not experienced by the children in the same way as the adults. The children used 'nations' in more complex and strategic ways than the adults did. I do not believe that the children or parents are essentialising their 'race' by doing this as Gilroy suggests. This would only be (potentially) true for a family which claimed a 'monoracial' identification, which none of the families in this research did. Rather, children and adults are trying to operationalise discourses that constrain them, in ways that help to explain some of their lived multiplicities.

The ability to inhabit multiple positions is particularly useful in a school context that is multiethnic, but is not so visible in the mainly white school. The white children in Farisham were very keen to claim international heritages, which I believe they did from the position of security in which they were interpellated as white. For those who were not, the need to be neutral, brown or beige, overrode pride in multinational family. However, differences could be subsumed in the need for a collective school identity at particular moments.

Locations of Homeliness

Home is central to identity. Being at home, feeling at home, knowing 'where you come from' and where your spiritual roots are, all are crucial for ('mixed-race') identities. In this chapter I have shown how home has multiple meanings and locations, which may at times be in conflict for those who have multiple positions. However, through speech acts, narratives of 'home' and 'belonging' are reconciled, even though there is a level of ambivalence for most who took part in the study.

Narratives of nation, belonging, home and identity have been shown to be used in the absence of any other meaningful way of talking about self, and also as a positive assertion of identification with family members. Bhabha sees the margins of modern nation-states as productive and useful in destabilising the post-imperialist national imperative:

> The marginal or 'minority' is not the space of a celebratory, or utopian, self-marginalisation. It is a much more substantial intervention into those justifications of modernity – progress, homogeneity, cultural organisism, the deep nation, the long past – that rationalise the authoritarian normalising tendencies within cultures in the name of the national interest or ethnic prerogative. In this sense, then, the ambivalent, antagonistic perspective of nation as narration will establish the cultural boundaries of the nation so that they may be acknowledged as 'containing' thresholds of meaning that must be crossed, erased, and translated in the process of cultural production. (Bhaba 1990b: 4)

It is also clear that children in particular can be extremely fluid about their identifications with communities and collectivities. These shifts are directly linked to context, so that in the case of football, the 1998 World Cup, all the usual divisions fell away as the children assumed that they would all support England. In other contexts, the children showed their differing readings of nations, such as Sita's choice of positioning of herself as English and her parents as Indian. They did this as they all now lived in England and so it was now home for them. This supported the way the majority of children spoke of home as the place in which they currently lived, whereas parents had greater connections to places lived in the past and to places of birth.

These conversations actively subvert the notion of Englishness as whiteness.

For many of these children, Englishness (and in some cases, Britishness) is now defined by those who *claim to be* English. Being English is determined by what they do, and how they take part in communal and common popular cultural activities. This finding reinforces the rather romantic 'melting pot' image of a New Britain under New Labour, in which we are all judged by what we do and how we behave as citizens. We may have a variety of cultural heritages but in reality we share a common ideal of what it is to be English, if not 'British'. There is a shared sense of belonging amongst the children in the educational contexts at least.

I suspect that this will not remain so for the children as they get older, even as they reach secondary school. As the experience of racism grows, as political understanding grows, it is likely that children will increasingly feel a need to explore their 'roots' also. That is not to say that they will lose a sense of their Britishness or Englishness even if they remain in this country. Sheila, Celie and Darcy all show this; despite being born in different locations their English upbringing remains a major influence in the way they identify. Yet in this research these allegiances are mediated by the level of acceptance the respondents have felt that they have had in Britain, and I believe that this is also linked to their appearance, as a great deal of 'racism' is still linked to skin colour.

For now, the children were content to embrace a form of belonging to both school and nation in a strategic and pragmatic fashion. I have talked about children who come from a variety of heritages as one in this last section, but I believe the children of 'mixed-race' show this pragmatic ability from a much more emotional base. Those who feel tied by 'blood' to particular countries of parents' origin can argue for their inclusion of this part of their hyphenated identity. Yet they may shift this to become British when 'needed' or, indeed, wanted. Recent migrants, and 'monoracial' children who are second or third generation settlers, also show this ability, and in many ways it is more marked with them, as illustrated by the description Sita gave above – being English but Indian. Her use of nationality gives a very clear example of the need for detailed stories of heritage when directly questioned, and yet these are discarded in the realms of collective national sporting identity.

Avtar Brah has called for an analysis of 'how and why originary absolutes are imagined' (1996: 197). I believe that those of 'mixed-race', in common with many migrant and translocated individuals, do so because they *have* to *trace* and *imagine* absolutes in many cases in order to speak themselves into place, and they have the *desire* to do so in most cases.

In Chapter 7 I will interrogate the ways in which the discourses of families and home are utilised in schools, and the ways in which the children and teachers develop and implement their ideas of what race and 'antiracism' mean. The understandings that children have of 'nation' and belonging, and of 'race' and 'racism' are supplemented by their own narratives and genealogies when the discourses available in schools are unworkable or inadequate to their own positionings. It will be shown that children are actively creating spaces in which to explore their own multiethnic positions, even though they have limited understandings of these processes. It also reveals the failings of the existing policies and practices as they are currently being implemented at the three schools in the study.

Notes

1. The girl in this case was a young Japanese girl who was in Year 4 at Fairsham. She had not been at the school long and was extremely shy and nervous and repeatedly picked on by the other children. She gave me pictures of the outside of her house, her car and her empty garden. Her family were completely absent from the images.
2. Darcy did not use the name 'Sri Lanka' in her interview and continued to talk about 'Ceylon', the preferred name used by her father. For this reason I have continued to use it throughout the text.
3. In this example I believe that Kyle chooses two 'same race' positions as he understands them as both 'white', and in this sense, to him, as non-racial. The rest of the transcript would support this.
4. It is interesting that another of the boys at Fairsham, Jake, said that he had not encountered racism, and his mother, Celie, told me that he had. It seemed to be a gendered response of stoicism in a place in which reporting it would reinscribe and verify it to the detriment of the children's 'neutral' identifications.

–7–

Discourses of Race and Racism in the Schools

[My teacher] said that it doesn't matter what colour you are, that you're all equal and all the same, in different ways. That you're different in different ways, that if you were to cut someone in half, um if you were to cut two people in half they'd be exactly the same.

Interview with Marita: May 1998

Introduction

This chapter considers the way in which schools provided discourses of 'race' and racism which impact on children's racialisation processes. In the first section I discuss some of the influential themes within educational discourses of 'race'. I will then introduce the children's readings of teachers' discourses of antiracism and multiculturalism.[1] Thirdly, I will use interviews with staff to show how schools relate policy to practice and consider the commonalities and differences between school/teacher approaches to discourses of antiracism and multiculturalism.

My own observations and discussions with both staff and pupils showed that in all cases there was little consensus as to what the current approaches were, whether they were effective and how they might best be improved. The second most striking thing was the lack of faith that the children had in the school system to deal with bullying in general, and racism in particular. That is not to say that there was complete chaos with regard to these issues, neither was there any evidence of apathy. What there was, however, was a lack of *coherence* in the attitudes of the staff, and thus in the place they found for such matters in their classrooms and in their responses to incidents in their respective schools. The third finding of the research in schools shows that the complexities of readings of mothers and children about issues of 'race', ethnicity, culture, nationality and 'home' are not being addressed by current 'multicultural' education.

Children interviewed show that they *are* aware of a respect for 'difference' as an 'antiracist' ideal, but while some of the children in London were familiar with the terms such as racism, those in Kent were not. The ('mixed-race') children were not able to express ideas about nationalism, ethnicity or culture in meaningful ways and so they resorted to the creative use of their own biographical details to make sense of these terms. More importantly, the findings show that whilst the academy is increasingly concerned with reinstating class into agendas of educational research, and introducing critical approaches to whiteness and masculinity, teachers in these classrooms were not as yet confident in doing so. To this end the teachers I spoke to were also drawing upon autobiographical narratives to deal with the ways in which multi-positionalities challenge existing discourses.

Educational Discourses of 'Race'

The changes in the types of language used and methods of combating discrimination and prejudice in education cannot hide the 'unpalatable truth' that Homi Bhabha describes as follows:

> [C]ultural diversity becomes a bedrock of multicultural education policy in [England]. There are two problems with it; one is the very obvious one, that although there is always entertainment and encouragement of cultural diversity, there is also a corresponding containment of it ... which says that 'these other cultures are fine, but we must be able to locate them in our own grid' ... The second problem is, ... that in some societies where multiculturalism is encouraged racism is still rampant in various forms. (Bhabha 1990: 28)

Rattansi argues that the there have been two main strands to educational, teaching and activist approaches to 'race' in Britain throughout the 1980s and into the 1990s. He conceptualises them both as essentialist. Firstly, he identifies 'multiculturalism', which is an 'additive model'. From this position one can see that there are many cultures within society and one should learn about them and respect them all. The focus here is on 'culture' not 'race', which he calls a form of ethnic essentialism (Rattansi 1992: 39) Secondly, he cites 'antiracist' approaches which disallow heterogeneity amongst groups and try to maintain a 'black community' struggle, a 'reification of community'. This latter position tends to marginalise groups that do not fit into such a category easily; he mentions Greeks, Turks, Jews and Irish (ibid.: 40). Rattansi does not mention those who are inter-ethnic or 'mixed-race'; he also chooses to focus on known 'groups'.

Rattansi separates 'racism' from 'racial discrimination'; 'racism' is used to define groups who are allocated as such on the basis of some kind of biological signifier. He continues to include nationalism which may be based upon 'racialised' discourse, and ethnocentrism which, he suggests, is unavoidable at the level of the individual who centralises their language and cultural practices of origin. Rattansi is one of the few writers who not only mentions class and gender but argues for the need to centralise sexuality in analyses of racism and, thus, 'the operations of the unconscious and the dynamics of psychic reality' (1992: 37). These include the sexual and the processes of pleasure and desire.[2] He suggests a recognition that there are many ambiguities and contradictions in the process of 'Othering'. This may not *necessarily* be something that is *only* a white phenomenon. I will show how 'mixed-race' identifications may, in some cases, highlight these kinds of social and psychic contradictions and show the pragmatic ways they may be handled.

In previous chapters I have shown how ethnicity is often mobilised to define differences. Anthias and Yuval-Davis (1993) highlight how concerns about Muslim fundamentalism played out in schools reflects the 'new racism' (Barker 1981) that cites *cultural* difference as the basis for conflict. The racialisation of Muslims is on the increase, and one of the main areas of cultural conflict in schools is religion (Anthias and Yuval-Davis 1993: 154). 'Islamophobia' is a term that has been developed to name this phenomenon (Mac an Ghaill 1999). More generally, 'ethnocentrism' in schools, and elsewhere, is a form of prejudice that can be far more complicated than that based on 'race' and the visual signi-fier skin, and that this is always gendered. But many of the incidents that inform such debates include highly gendered facets. Mac an Ghaill reports on the fact that schools are in the process of constructing 'hierarchies of masculinities' in which Muslim boys are constructed as 'folk devils' (ibid.). One can only assume that these will complement the stereotypical femininities that already constrain Muslim girls. Of course, in order for discourses to be gendered, they are inevitably sexualised. These concerns were evident in the discussions held both with children and teachers, as below.

Children's Perceptions of School Policy and Practice: 'The Teachers Don't Do Anything'

From what the teachers said, I was expecting the children to have very clear ideas about what racism was and how the school dealt with it. I also thought that they would be able to discuss what they thought the terms meant to them. In practice, of course, things were a little more complicated! The children had numerous ways of bringing in other subjects and subsuming them under the heading of racism. They also tended to shift their positions slightly as the interviews progressed, and they began to trust me and to talk more freely. They did this in particular when talking about the way the school dealt with these issues.

Racism or Bullying?
There was a wide variation in the levels of understanding that children had about the term 'race'. In fact, this was often completely separated conceptually from

the term 'racism'. When I first asked the children whether they knew about 'race' and what it meant, they often didn't know or, like Larry at Fairsham (see p. 50) thought it was something to do with running. Yet if I asked them about 'racism', children in multiethnic schools knew that they had heard of the term, and had some idea of how it was applied. It was commonly described as someone 'cussing you' about your 'colour', your country or your religion. But they would often digress straight away into talking about more general bullying and name-calling, and it would be very hard to tell if they felt that there was a difference or whether it was in fact because they considered it to be a part of the same problem.

Troyna and Hatcher (1992) did some work in mainly white primary schools about the meaning of racist name-calling. They found that there were occasions when children claimed to use the names as means of wounding that were not necessarily intended to be racist. In my own research, I asked the children about the name-calling and found that they often did it when they lost their tempers, and that it was something that they knew would hurt. These 'hot situations' were when the children used the names in both what the authors would call a 'strategic fashion' (ibid.; see also Chapter 5), knowing it would hurt a child, and in a 'non-strategic fashion', when they may regret the fact that it just 'slipped out' in anger (ibid.) However, I would question why it was that the children chose these forms of abuse over others.

Just as Troyna amd Hatcher found in their study, all children would also use other forms of name calling like 'skinny b-i-t-c-h' (Meli). However, in nearly all cases, the white children did not suffer from as much 'racist' name calling as children from minority ethnic groups with dark skin. More importantly, black, South Asian and Pacific Asian children who may have worn glasses or had weight 'problems' were never *solely* identified by these aspects of their appearance; it was always to do with skin colour, or culture or ethnicity as represented by clothing or speech, etc. The black, South Asian and Pacific Asian children were also able to situate themselves in their wider communities by talking about racism that they and/or family members had experienced. There was never any confusion as to whether *this* was racism; it was always accurately and horribly relayed to me. The white children never relayed similar stories, which is not to suggest that they had never noted interracial conflict out of school time, but they certainly did not feel that it was important enough to tell me about it in these discussions.

Mohamed (Year 4 teacher) at Christie School in London noted that the ways in which children swore at each other were not constant but changed over time. One of the most common forms of abuse at that time was to 'cuss your mum'. One child told me they say, 'You've got so many dogs in your house you don't know which one is your mother.' Another became embroiled in trying to explain a particularly 'naughty' form of abuse without saying anything 'bad', and managed: 'Your colour is so dumb that you get into bed with a girl and you do horrid thing with your mum.' These kinds of insults often got abbreviated to being simply 'Your mum'. Many other insults were specifically gendered, such as the use of 'bitch' or 'tart'. In conjunction with a racial element these insults were the most likely to result in incidents turning into physical conflicts.

Another disturbing and unexpected finding was the *level* of interracial abuse. Beatrice, a white girl in Year 4 in Christie, said that 'coloured people called white people rubbish'. Later, others in her group identified a black boy who would call the Turkish children 'Turkish delight', and said that black, white and Turkish children would use the term 'Paki' to describe anyone of South Asian descent, and that some children are 'mean to Muslims'. One white boy in Year 4 of a London school told me he got called names about his name. When I asked whether that was racism he said, 'No'. Another white boy, also in Year 4 (Barnlea), said a South Asian boy was name-calling:

Suki: He calls you racist things?
Jay: Yeah, he says that my mum is a bitch and all that.
Suki: Is that racism?
Jay: He cusses the colour of my skin and all that.
Suki: Does he?
Jay: He says that whites are idiots and poofs.

There are a number of possible separate and interconnected reasons for these behaviours, and I would argue that one of them is the need for the children who are perceived to be 'racially other' to try and respond to conflict in the language of the playground. In this way they assert their own identities as non-white, but do it by devaluing 'whiteness'. This extract above also reveals the way in which white masculinities were more likely to be positioned as homosexual than any other racialised group.

The conversation below took place between a group of Year 4 children in Barnlea, the most racially and ethnically diverse school in the study. The group contained James (white boy), Dumesh (Bengali boy), Judd (white boy), Dasta (black African girl) and Aron (black African/Caribbean boy):

Suki: Have you heard of racism?
James: Yes.
Suki: What does it mean?
James: When people cuss your family or your blood.
Suki: Your blood?
James: Yeah or your skin colour [points to his cheek].

Aron: Long time ago people got racism to the blacks and they called them rude name, but I forgot.

Dumesh: I know, 'nigger'
            [They talk about the nursery rhyme that contains the line 'catch a nigger by his toe']

Dumesh: And sometimes because I'm a Muslim they think ...

Judd: They call you a Paki.

Dumesh: They call me a Paki.

Dasta: What are Pakis?

Dumesh: People who come from Pakistan, I'm Bengali.

Aron: They think it's a funny name.

Dumesh: [wrinkles up his nose in disgust] Pakis ... uuggghhh!

This shows the same kind of need to assert 'racial' and national and ethnic clarity in one's identity as Meli explained (see Chapter 4, p. 87). James pointed to the fact that it is to do with family and 'blood', as Meli did, and also Dumesh who was born in England. Dumesh also placed a premium upon being Bengali as opposed to the ultimate insult – being 'Paki'. It is clear that the children in this study did understand that racial abuse was significantly more wounding than any other type. The white children may not have held generally racist beliefs, but in choosing this kind of abuse over any other possible, I believe they were repeating and understanding the hegemonic discourses of racial superiority as Troyna and Hatcher (1992) suggested. They did so by asserting the centrality of whiteness as a 'racial' identity from which some children were excluded.

Appearance and Acceptability

Some of the main themes of the research came to the forefront very early on in these discussions, and can be seen in the extracts in the previous section with reference to family, homosexuality, skin colour, religion and nationality and what are appropriate heterosexual relationships. As the previous chapters have shown, these form the basis of the discursive register children use to speak themselves.

The children in this study:

* intersperse their talk about 'race' with that of 'culture' and 'religion' and nationality;
* use these discourses to construct themselves and others within their school relationships;
* are acutely aware of themselves as gendered beings;
* are beginning to manipulate discourses about gender and how that is sexualised;

- suggest that much of their understanding of 'race' is about appearance, and it is upon that basis that they make discriminatory choices.

Making derogatory remarks about appearance was one of the main things that children used in name-calling. Even if the name was not directly about appearance it would have been connected to it, as in the example given above. Being called a 'Paki' is a derogatory remark that is applied to anyone of an indeterminate 'racial type'. Therefore the young boy with brown skin was called a 'Paki', regardless of whether that was accurate or not. It is a generic term of racial abuse for someone who is 'non-white'. For children of 'mixed-race' it is often used in the absence of being able to place them into a singular 'correct' racial category. In most cases children were ascribed membership to a recognised group that was referred to in a derogatory fashion. In the case of the black and South Asian children referring to the white children as 'paper' and 'ghosts', the tables cannot be neatly turned.

As Troyna and Hatcher (1992) found, the white children did not feel as badly about those comments as did the black children. The use of that kind of abuse served only to show that these were acknowledged and everyday ways of 'cussing out'. It also showed a greater degree of 'racial' pride on the part of the black children, who are also asserting a collective social identity through the use of exclusive forms of colour coding. Turkish and Roma children were usually identified by name or language, and by religion in the case of those who were Muslim. In order for insults to be levelled at them the abusers required knowledge of their background and could not solely rely on appearance. In most cases the abuse did contain an element of 'racism' as the children understood it, although it was in fact often a form of xenophobia; that is, it was a fear or disapproval of another national identity, or 'foreigner'. On these occasions it was *not* appearance that guided the choices of insults.

Telling Tales

The children all started by saying that the school did nothing about racism, with the exception of Barnlea which had a concerted campaign against bullying going on at the time I was there. Even so, the first port of call when reporting incidents were the playground supervisors, who were often content to separate children. The children in that school did confirm that the head teacher, Gina, talked to them about racism in assemblies and some of the children recalled one or two class teachers, one a black Caribbean woman, the other a Greek Cypriot woman talking in class.

In Christie, the children were on the whole convinced that the teachers did not really 'care' about bullying, yet they too knew that the subject of 'racism' came up in assemblies. They seemed to be able to separate the two areas, which at other times they could not. I have many examples of interviews in which children start by talking about 'cussing your skin' and move on to include other non-racialised forms of abuse. They were also aware across the years that the Year 6 teacher, Evi, would be tough on the subject, as would the head, but they thought things would have to be really bad to go through to them. Again they could name the playground attendants who they thought were the least likely to deal with incidents which the children may have thought were quite serious.

At Fairsham, there was a similar story; key individuals amongst members of staff who the children felt they could trust to take both sides of a story and look into incidents and take them further. The children at this school said that when they reported incidents they were often told to 'stop telling tales' or 'just stop playing together' until they could 'be nice to each other'. I thought that this showed a shocking disregard for the concerns of the children until I caught myself telling two children in one of the groups I was interviewing to stop talking to each other if all they were going to do was argue!

However, the criticism of the telling of tales and the separation of quarrelling children were reported in all of the schools. On this basis the children felt that they could not go to teachers for help, with the exception of the named one or two in each school. They felt particularly aggrieved by this when the incidents involved repeat offenders. They could all name particular culprits in their respective schools.

The differences between the schools arose from location. At Fairsham, the children did not seem to ever report racism directly to staff. Children could recall racist name-calling, but claimed it had never been reported. It seemed that as the children who were picked on were in such a minority they did not take the matters further. One child at Fairsham, who was a boy in Year 5 of mixed-race (Jake; mother Celie), had a classmate inform staff who then informed his parents when he was being racially abused. Most of the children talked about particular individuals being picked on because of what I would describe as class differences. They may also have been white and British, but they came from lower-class families than the majority of the children and had less money, poorer housing and clothes, and in one case had a mother who 'looked nasty' and 'talked loudly and not very nicely'.

Most of the children wanted to be able to report incidents and talk about them. They had some faith in the individual members of staff but on the whole felt that the school was lacking in support for their concerns. The race of the member of staff who they perceived as supportive did not matter, but did feature in accounts of teacher racism (see also Mirza 1992: 125).

'Mixed-Race' Positions in Schools

During the first discussions and group interviews with children they began to reveal their own ideas about their racial identities. I was also observing children in the classroom and playground. These interviews were explored in detail in Chapters 3 and 4. In this section I will outline my observation of the interplay between the different groups of children, some of whom had already been identified by the teachers as being of 'mixed-race'. It was also true that as the teachers had suggested, general discussions on the meanings of 'race' and racism allowed children to informally bring up their own family and personal circumstances where they had multiethnic backgrounds.

In this extract from an interview with Marita (Year 4, Barnlea, white English/black Trinidadian), her own reading of the racial abuse that she has received is that it is 'incorrect' – that she cannot be insulted by the name 'nigger' as it does not fit with her own positioning:

Suki:	They've called you horrible names? Like what?
Marita:	Nigger.
Suki:	Where do they call you that?
Marita:	Called me out in the playground.
Suki:	At school?
Marita:	Mmhm.
Suki:	What do you say to that?
Marita:	I just walk away.
Suki:	Umm what do you think when they say that?
Marita:	That they don't know anything.
Suki:	Yeah?
Marita:	Firstly, I'm not fully black, and … there's nothing, there's no reason to be racist, 'cos we're all the same, but we've just got different colour skin.
Suki:	And how *would* you describe yourself, you say you're not fully black so how would you describe yourself?
Marita:	'Mixed-race'.

Marita knew what racism was, and that she should 'ignore it' despite the fact that she said it made her really angry. She managed to diffuse her anger by making the racism 'wrong' for two interconnected reasons. Firstly, 'niggers' are black, and she is not 'fully black'. Secondly, we're all the same under the skin – blackness doesn't mean anything anyway. This second position is one I heard many times from teachers and parents, who passed it on to children. What it does, of course, is leave intact the notion of (authentic) 'blackness'.

I never heard the children use racism in any of their informal talk. I did observe at Christie, that as Mohamed the Year 4 teacher, and Dave A., the Year 5 teacher had said, the children tended to play within their own 'racial and ethnic groupings'. The children who were 'mixed-race' clearly had to make their friendship choices based upon a variety of things that included the need to make an alliance to a group which would have a predominance of one ethnic type. Both the boys and the girls in Years 5 and 6 chose to identify with the black children, with one exception. Hannah was of white British/black Caribbean heritage and she was always on the edge of the friendship groups. She had a best friend called Marina, who was Portuguese, and the two of them tended to be off on their own. Thomas was called 'gay' because he was 'vain'. But this particular form of abuse was usually reserved for 'white' people. He was, however, characterised as black by the majority of the school including the teachers. At Christie, as with Fairsham, children were overwhelmingly separated by gender in their choice of friends to play with in the playground.

It was reported to me at later stages of the research that the 'mixed-race' children would bear the brunt of the same kinds of insults that were levelled at the other black children. However, they were also likely to be discriminated against by the black children and South Asian children. So Jenny was often called 'yellow face' because her ancestry was black Caribbean, Indian and Chinese. Dinease's mother told me that her daughter had had an argument with some of her friends who would not let her be a member of the gang which they were setting up because she was too white.

At Barnlea similar stories were reported. Just as Meli had been called a 'white b-i-t-c-h' by her black peers, so her white peers had at times shunned her. Meli was part of a group of black girls who were a loosely formed network that was often realigning. Yet her *best* friend was a white girl called Maisie. At Barnlea, in the lower years, the friendship groups were more likely to be formed by mixtures of children, both in terms of gender and 'racial' identity. Yet the same type of insults were used during arguments. Kilde (Year 4, Barnlea) was both black *and* Turkish Delight.[3] What characterises these forms of racialised abuse is their basis in skin colour.

The children's acceptance into certain friendship groups is based upon shared cultural currency, yet their exclusion was often based upon their appearance. So the girls such as Dinease and Jenny (Christie) were part of the group of African–Caribbean girls who organised the dance group and talked about their relationships, and Thomas (Christie) was a member of the most powerful gang of 'bad boys' who were mostly black (Connolly 1998).

At Fairsham the children from minority ethnic groups were so few that they had no choice but to join in with the dominant cultural and ethnic group who were white and middle class. Those children who had suffered racist abuse were loath to tell me, yet they all had. It was their friends and classmates who told me about the name-calling, which again was based on appearance facial features, skin colour, and so on.

In each of the schools, the racist name-calling appeared to be coupled with an attempt to exclude a child from a particular social group, sometimes friendship groups and at other times from the hegemonic cultural group, white or black. The basis for doing this is to assert difference and gain social status and power over the child. In doing so children are forging particular identities, and the children of 'mixed-race' are most likely to be subtly shifting position in relation to the groups they are attached to and in opposition or relation to.

Discussing 'Race' with Teachers

As the teachers knew about the purpose of the research project they seemed to assume that they did not have to talk about the position and experiences of staff themselves, or about how policies were applied to issues such as staff development and promotion. In both London schools the heads made reference to the difficulty in staffing generally, and recruiting staff from minority ethnic groups. In particular, several (white) teachers refuted the idea that black teachers automatically helped as role models for pupils or that simply by being black they would automatically be politicised. Indeed, black teachers were acutely aware of the limiting role models for students, but were equally sure they could not be 'representatives' of the heterogeneity of blackness, or themselves 'tied to a narrow definition of blackness' (Osler 1997: 83-84). Members of staff in the London schools appeared to segregate along racial lines in the staff room, something that was only referred to by three women teachers. I believe there was an underlying racial tension amongst staff in the London schools that was absent from the interviews, but I cannot speculate on how that played out in their interactions or in school policy and practice.

In all of the schools there were different ways of relating to the terms that I introduced in the questions, and these will be explored below. Both teachers and children used 'racism' to cover a range of interracial conflicts, but also to describe prejudice and abuse based on language, ethnicity or culture. When talking about interaction amongst children Troyna and Hatcher suggest (in line with the Swann Report) that there are different ways of understanding whether incidents are 'racist', 'racialised' or 'interracial' (Troyna and Hatcher 1992: 15). They believe that it is the society-wide belief in the superiority of 'whiteness' available to children that confers upon white children the power to impose racial 'Other' status upon children from minority ethnic groups within schools. My own research has shown that this racialisation is not just the prerogative of white childrem. However, they go on to suggest that in mainly white primary schools

'The concept of *contradictory common-sense* is central to our understanding of what race means in the cultures of children' (ibid.: 46 emphasis added).

In this research, that would also appear to be the case. Children often held views about 'racial egalitarianism' yet would make racist remarks, as was detailed in chapters 4 and 5. Some of these ideas are returned to below, and similarities and differences explored between views held in the mainly white and multiethnic primary schools.

Behaviour and Practice: Teachers' Approaches to Racism

Some very obvious themes emerged early in the research:

- All of the school heads and deputy heads had an awareness of and commitment to development of good 'antiracist' and multicultural practice within their schools, utilising a whole school approach;
- within the schools there were differing opinions amongst members of staff as to whether the current policies were effective or not;
- all of the staff members had differing ideas about what 'good practice' might include and how to go about achieving it;
- within each school there were perceived to be 'pockets of good practice' and 'areas for concern';
- teachers felt that children understood what racism was, and that they knew it was not acceptable.

The way in which these points were discussed seemed to centre upon two factors:

1. The behaviour and opinions of the children and how to deal with them.
2. The curriculum, resources and materials, and pedagogic practices.

For reasons of simplicity they will be referred to as the personal sphere and the pedagogic sphere. This is not intended to suggest that the two areas are mutually exclusive; rather, these two areas are perceived as requiring different if not separate methods for integrating 'racial awareness' issues. The personal sphere is seen as the relationships that the children have with each other within the school environment, especially in the informal space of the playground. The school policies and teachers' inputs may not *directly* inform it at those moments of interaction. It also refers to the attitudes and beliefs children hold and express in informal ways in the classroom. The pedagogic refers to the educational environment of the classroom, assembly, school clubs and so on where formal education is delivered. It highlights the way in which it is delivered, how and with what tools and skills, and the policies that inform its delivery. Obviously there is personal interaction involved in this sphere, but for analysis this will refer mostly to teacher/pupil interaction.

From these points it is clear that in developing a whole-school awareness, and in implementing practice and policy, ongoing and complicated negotiations between differing levels of staff and management are necessary. It is also clear that, with one or two notable exceptions, there is some confusion amongst the teaching staff themselves as to the best ways of doing this, as well as an awareness that despite their own good intentions they may not be doing things the way they feel they ought to or would like to.

There is a clear shift in discursive language between the two spheres highlighted above. The behaviour and language of children is still discussed in terms of 'antiracism', even when there may be elements of ethnic or cultural superiority, in the kinds of incidents reported. The pedagogic, however, is now being talked about in terms of 'multiculturalism'. This is in line with the kind of 'deracialization' within school policy that Gillborn (1995) describes. He cites Troyna when he suggests that 'notions of history, culture, religion, nationality /nationhood, language and "way of life" have come to act as "proxy concepts" allowing policies to adopt a superficially deracialised format while directly addressing issues of relevance to existing and future racial inequalities' (Gillborn 1995). So whilst there is an effort to talk about 'other people and other countries/religions etc.' it may be kept within very specific areas of the curriculum. It was also clear that there is little or no discussion of complex ethnic positions within the schools. Neither is there any *systematic* interrogation of 'whiteness' or nationality in terms of Britishness when the subject of race and racism come up, although a small minority of women teachers did include this. It is these issues that will be discussed in greater detail below.

Avoidance

At Fairsham school in Kent, Pat, one of the young women teachers whom I interviewed, was quite clear that antiracism did not need to be 'pressed' in a predominantly white school.

> I have a few children in my class who are overweight, now we could put an issue in the school policy on tackling *that*, but I don't think that we *need* to take every aspect, every sort of thing that could be picked on and put a different policy. It all comes under one umbrella policy of respect for them really.

She did think that there should be some kind of multicultural policy and for her that meant that 'other cultures' were included in schemes of work in Geography and History. She noted, however, that the children found it very difficult to understand that people may live differently from the way that they did now 'even in History', and that kind of discussion would be better suited to secondary school. Religion provided another opportunity to discuss 'difference' but she found it became a 'paper pushing exercise': 'I have touched on a few of them [religions] with the children and it just throws them ... then when you start talking about Judaism and you get the idea that some people are Jews as well as their religion as Jews ... and its just *way* above them.' She feels that when issues come up 'naturally', such as 'race' or 'mixed-race', they are dealt with. She also felt that the materials in the school were adequate yet often stereotypical, and that the children reflected stereotypical ideas about cultures.

In her interview, Pat shows some of the contradictory positions that were prevalent in some of the staff in Fairsham; an awareness that some of the children held views that may be perceived as racist, but a reluctance to tackle them through discussion. She thought that it would require changes to schemes of work to fully implement multiculturalism within the curriculum, which she dismissed as a ridiculous idea. Her main reservations were the ability of the children to deal with issues as 'complicated' as these at an early age. However, we may also read Pat's concern with multiple changes as anxiety about her own role as an educator and the limitations placed upon her in terms of time and resources. Teachers have to manage such factors (resources, time, policy), etc. to best advantage (Grugeon and Woods 1990: 123). Implicit in Pat's statement is the increasing bureaucratic pressure teachers find themselves under. Teachers now experience increased regulation of their work in relation to the curriculum, and even teaching methods, and this places them under a constant 'performance pressure'. Despite or perhaps because the school is a high achiever these pressures may be multiplied further. Pat implies a sense of isolation in trying to deal with such conundrums, which may not be the way other teachers in the school perceive it.

In fact, the head at Fairsham had stated that it was *more* important for them to talk about race and culture, yet he still felt that there was 'no problem here'; that there may have been in the past but that it had been ironed out (Gaine 1987, 1995). He was not 'one hundred percent' convinced about the materials the school was using but said that the materials had been improving steadily and that older books should still be used until new ones were in place. How this fits in with other schools is evident from similar conversations about seeing pupils as individuals and also only dealing with things as they come up. Such positions tended to go along with the idea that the materials were adequate.

Dave A. at Christie School in London also felt that it was 'sometimes made too much of an issue really'. He saw the need for a good antiracist policy, and for curriculum and pedagogy to provide equality of opportunity for children, but was clear that the best way to deal with it was to wait until issues came up and to make sure that he treated the children equally. In saying this he talked about treating the children the same, just as had the head teacher in the mainly white Fairsham School, as well as the more 'conservative' white, male, Fred, at Barnlea. He called this being 'colour blind'.

In both of the London schools, as well as Fairsham, many of the teachers showed similar ideas about respecting individuals regardless of their 'racial' and 'ethnic origin' rather than embracing that as a part of a positive part of the identity of the individual. This is consistent with findings in other research such as Ghazala Bhatti's ethnographic work with 'Asian' children. She says that 'The immediate response, the most common one, about children's ethnicity was that the school did not differentiate between people because of their ethnic backgrounds' (Bhatti 1999: 70). The difference I found was that this was *school* policy at Fairsham, but not so in the two London schools. Nonetheless it was a view held, at least partially, by some London teachers.

In Christie the Year 4 (Mohamed) and Year 5 (Dave A.) class teachers, both male, in their forties and both with multiethnic origins had a view that things were dealt with on a day-to-day basis when they arose as particular incidents of bad behaviour. Dave A., the Year 5 teacher, said that he thought that he treated all the children equally and that they all knew that he felt it important to teach children without thinking of their race, focusing on their ability. He went on to say that he also chose materials on the basis of whether they were good teaching aids, not if they had a pictures of minority ethnic people in them:

> I think people just teach. I don't think that people are too aware when they are planning lessons for instance, 'How can I make sure that the Asian girls get the same attention as whatever. I think that people tend to take the class as individuals as if someone's quiet you draw more out of them. But certainly for me, I don't sit here and think 'I'll have to make sure that the black boys or the black girls get equal treatment to the white kids.' It's very much an individual thing, so you take everyone as an individual. So I suppose it's a sort of colour blind policy, well as I apply it.

In this extract it is clear that there are two levels of awareness of the existence and meaning of 'race' – that of the group and that of the individual – and that this is what the teacher is separating in his understanding of classroom relations. He rejected the idea that an antiracist teaching style should treat all black children as the same and in need of the same kinds of 'special' or 'preferential' treatment. This is clearly not what an antiracism policy is likely to have suggested, yet he used that interpretation as a means of dismissing it. He was concerned that the whole class was treated as individuals, and in order to do this he eradicated 'race' from the equation, becoming 'colour blind'. As a result he inadvertently reinforced the original problems identified with not being aware of specific difficulties that may arise from the 'race' of the child.

This was similar to a view held by Gwen, the Special Educational Needs Co-ordinator at Fairsham, when she stated that 'we always treat everybody differently anyway' and because of that there was no need for an antiracist or multicultural policy within the school. Later in the interview she said:

> I wouldn't think it was part of my remit at all really, I have taught in Birmingham and there I mean you've got much more of a balance where you have to redress ... everybody here ... to be honest I wouldn't notice anybody being different here, at all, I would never sort of, it would be the last thing that you would notice, sort of consider ... sort of ... what children look like, and there has never been a need to redress it, address it.

Again she simultaneously called for both treating the children the same way and treating them all differently as individuals, and for her this meant de-racialising them. It is clear that this is particularly true as the school is mainly white and therefore there was no need to '*redress*' any imbalances because there were no issues that needed dealing with. As with the example of Dave A. she saw antiracism as something remedial.

At Barnlea, the deputy head, Elena, said that she was aware that she sometimes slipped into seeing the children 'for what they present, rather than their ethnic background. And maybe I should be more aware, you know, that there is a hell of a lot of other stuff from home, you know their cultures and their traditions.' She was concerned that she should perhaps be 'doing something else'. Her view neatly encapsulates the difficulties with situating 'race' or ethnicity within the picture of the 'whole' child. She reveals anxieties about the multiple ways in which we are forced to identify and categorise children, including not only a 'racial' identity but also gender, dis/ability, behaviour, personality, friendship groups, and so on. Here, Elena chose culture and tradition as the most likely sources of potential 'difference' and, therefore, source of problems.

Action

Elena's dilemma with how to deal with individuals, and whether or not she always deals with the 'whole child' and not just the 'problem' or behaviour they present to her in school, is common. This kind of uncertainty underlies the differing beliefs in the best ways to deal with antiracism and multiculturalism. Across the three schools there were a surprising number of commonalities, but there were quite distinct ideas about the best ways of tackling the two areas mentioned above. In short, teachers seemed to be disposed to being either proactive or reactive depending on how central they thought these issues were to school life overall.

Being reactive – dealing with incidents as they arose – was a very common approach to dealing with the concept of 'racism' within the schools. Many of the teachers felt that this was the most appropriate way to deal with children of this age, and that there were more important things to think about when teaching the children. In some cases this was an extension to a position that the subject should not be made a priority because drawing attention to it could make things worse. Pat (Fairsham), Dave A. (Christie) and Fred (Barnlea) all showed this reactive behaviour. They saw no need to do anything other than deal with single incidents. For Fred, a Year 4 teacher, this sometimes meant that 'it might sound on the surface like racism, but when you get to the bottom of it, it isn't' (June 1998).

Many of the more 'conservative' members of staff at all the schools suggested that children used racist language as a form of abuse without intending to 'be racist'. However, for many teachers 'firefighting' was recognised as an inadequate form of crisis management. They talked in much more proactive ways about needing to take strong action against individual incidents but also saw them as part of a more organised approach to eradicating problems within the school.

Gina, the head of Barnlea, was very clear that she dealt with all racist incidents very severely. All incidents of bullying, sexism, and racism were recorded in a book and every child involved would have to see her personally after the play-ground supervisor or teacher had dealt with them. But she was also aware that this was just the tip of the iceberg: 'I think dealing with the overt racism is fairly effective, ... because as soon as it is overt we can deal with it. My main concern is the covert racism.' She suggested that in order to tackle this, the school and staff needed to create an environment in which children felt able to talk about things and to try to minimise the fear of placing their trust in the teachers and retribution from their peers. She felt that the school needed 'systems and struc-tures' in place to deal with the subjects of antiracism and multiculturalism within the school.

This theme of communication was also important to those with positive and proactive views in both of the other schools. For them, although 'firefighting' had to be done occasionally, and required firm treatment when incidents arose, it also encouraged children to talk about such issues. Both Barnlea and Christie had adapted 'Circle Time' to manage these kinds of discussions.

Robin, the acting head at Christie, was particularly positive about this as a way to develop good communication between the children. He described an incident that happened in a Year 2 class:

Basically there were some children being invited to a party, and um, one girl who was white wasn't invited and she said to the girl whose party it was 'Well, I don't want to go to your black party anyway.' Um, other children heard and became very upset um, and there were accusations of racism on both sides. Number one, um that the black girls had organised this party and not asked white children, and on the other side you know, the white girl saying 'I don't want to come to your black party', and sort of labelling it that rather than them seeing themselves as students and things, um all together. Um so those are the issues that I particularly want to deal with for Year 2 children at that level.

He felt that this had to be dealt with in an open and direct fashion: 'I've actually suggested a series of Circle Times which actually start with on Friday and they are going to carry on to the end of term, to deal with issues of race specifically, but with the children talking together not about a specific incident ... but with maybe some role-play and things like that.'

At Barnlea, the time set aside for Personal, Health and Social Education was used to discuss a broad range of issues with those in Year 6, which included racism, while in the lower years the subjects were sometimes decided on a more *ad hoc* basis and would be a more spontaneous way of dealing with incidents as they arose.

For those who had a more proactive view about racism, a key strategy was to develop good relations with parents. All the head teachers mentioned parents spontaneously at various times during interviews. One of the perceived difficulties in all the schools was about reaching parents and making sure that they were involved in the processes of eradicating racism and were understanding and supportive of such projects. In most cases this involved opening dialogue with parents and setting up parent groups for consultation about policy-making in these areas. Teachers did not speak extensively about this as these initiatives were quite new in the schools.

Representing Multicultural Values

The most popular response to questions about multiculturalism was to prioritise teaching materials in the development of multicultural awareness. In particular, the need for greater representation of minority ethnic groups across the range of materials was seen as being the main way in which the apparent deficiencies of previous years could be remedied. Again there were differing levels of criticism of current positions on resources across all three schools. Some teachers were less concerned about representations rather than, as Dave A. a Year 5 teacher at Christie put it, 'how good the teaching material is, and how good a teaching aid it's going to be'. He went on to say that he would look for this above all else. He would consider whether it represented 'all the different races so that kid does not feel alienated by them when they do it. I don't think they do personally, unless the book is really dreadful.'

It is interesting that he is able to separate out whether the book will be a good teaching aid from whether it conforms to his idea of what multiculturalism is about. Elizabeth Grugeon writes poignantly of an eight-year-old South Asian boy 'struggling with a story where understanding of the narrative depended on the reader knowing about canals'. She concludes that 'At 8 he was rapidly becoming a non-reader. The idea that reading might be for pleasure had not occurred to him' (Grugeon and Woods 1990: 63). Dave A. knew that there are concerns about 'alienation' from texts, but did not seem to be willing to link that to even greater conceptual and cognitive difficulties in the way some children may be able to approach the work in the book. His reluctance to do this was coupled with his concern for individualism, and that the idea that saying these images may be 'representative' is universalising and therefore stereotypical. However, he *was* typical in immediately suggesting representation in materials to be one of the first considerations in bringing multiculturalism into the school.

Kara, a Year 6 teacher and home/school liaison at Barnlea in London, had a more sophisticated view that was shared by the more proactive members of staff in all the schools. She believed that resources needed monitoring and she explained that the newly created Equal Opportunities officer would be responsible for this: 'For example, we have actually been looking at our resources and chucking things. There's actually been a debate on for example, geography. Do we keep some stereotypical pictures to actually explore stereotypes or do we chuck them?' She acknowledged that there was not just a problem with the absence of certain groups of people, but that where that were some kinds of representations that were negative, and needed challenging.

The problem of negative images in books was also raised at Fairsham by the head, Perry:

> I think obviously when you are looking at teaching materials you're looking for what you think is the best you can get … We have looked at stuff as it's come in and said, 'Look this really isn't suitable', or 'This is somewhat sexist or racist or whatever.' Obviously there are books in the school which have been here for a number of years which obviously don't … don't cater for that, and I think you know, we can't wholesale throw everything out.

What was common to the teachers in these schools was some recognition that representation has an effect on the child's learning, and is also the first consideration for multicultural education. This was not what I originally expected from asking about multicultural policies. The question was intended to prompt a much more general answer about the way in which multicultural life in Britain was central to the whole curriculum, as well as to ask whether the school acknowledged a need to discuss and learn about a variety of cultural and ethnic positions globally and which recognises the post-colonial, hi-tech age in which we live. A few members of staff did take a broader view.

Evi at Christie said that you could not talk about the Second World War without including discussions on fascism, which meant tackling issues such as 'whiteness' and national and racial superiority. Another Section 11 teacher at Barnlea, Beth, also said that she talked to the children about whiteness – that is, 'white South African-ness' – in discussion with individuals or small groups about racism, and in comparative terms with the education system in this country. At Fairsham, only the head teacher made direct reference to multiracial/multicultural Britain and how it was important for a mainly white primary school to be aware of the fact that multiplicity was outside the children's experience and thus needed *more* work within the school environment.

The second most frequently talked about methods to introduce multiculturalism were through three subjects – religion, and history and geography. Most discussions I had with teachers mentioned all three, but centralised religion. In London schools the children were used to being introduced to various different festivals and to talking about the religions from which they came. This was seen as standard practice in schools that have such a large ethnic mixture. In both of the schools there was a separate assembly for the Muslim children, and at Christie there had been discussions with parents about not having a member of staff take the assembly, but having a community religious leader coming in. At Barnlea, Gina, the head teacher, said that the assemblies she held once a week contained 'about fifty one per cent Christian ethos and then I would deal with other religions and so on'. Her assemblies were always themed and always 'linked with value and respecting cultural diversity'.

Pat had made it clear that this level of 'religious tolerance' was not found at Fairsham. The head teacher, Perry, did recall an occasion when an attempt to diversify had provoked an angry response from parents. From his description it sounded like it was the same occasion which Pat herself had described as a failure:

> We had a group last year who were dealing with one aspect of religious education, I can't remember what it was now. I think it was one of the Jewish festivals or whatever, and they came in and talked to the children about it, and I had a letter from one of the parents saying they didn't feel it was appropriate, and this was a Christian family who wrote in saying 'Children shouldn't be taught this at school.' And I said 'Well, actually it is part of the national curriculum, and it's a religious festival which is upon us now, and we felt it was important the children, other children hear about it in the news, they see it on the television, it's important that they have experience of what it's about. And erm … we deal with Christian festivals, and we deal with other festivals as well, and its just part of what goes on in schools now.'

Perry was very open to the idea that this was something that children had to 'experience' because it was not something that came up in their lives usually. He had two letters about it, and he felt surprised by this. Despite this he intended to continue to develop this aspect of the curriculum. His comments also make it clear that the parents and wider community need to be central to developments of antiracist practice and policy.

Making Sense of Multiculturalism

From the discussions with teachers and children it became clear that there is as much juxtaposition of terms and their meanings in the everyday school environment as there is in the academic environment. The way the teachers responded to my questions shows this extremely clearly.

'Antiracism' and racism are most often used to describe the verbal exchanges between children; or to describe negative or stereotypical images in books; or behaviour of teachers that are perceived as prejudiced. However, when incidents are described in detail it may reveal an exchange in which a child has, for example, ridiculed another's appearance, such as wearing a turban. In interaction with teachers and children, and between children, it may be their gender and nationality or religion that are perceived as 'racial' markers and are then described as incidents of 'racism'.

For example, Dave A. talked about stereotyping the 'Asian girls', and Mohamed mentioned that the children said to him, 'Oh, you were picking on the Muslims for a certain thing.'[4] In that context it was the children themselves who chose membership to a religious group as a way of identifying a group of children they felt were being 'racially discriminated' against, and Mohamed reported it as alleged 'racism'. He was one of the few teachers who commented on needing to pay close attention to the way he spoke about 'race' because children may not understand the terms and what he was trying to discuss. He said they were likely to report inaccurately to their parents and it would result in 'all sorts of problems'. He did not do this from the position that they were too young to understand, rather that it was his responsibility to lead discussions in such a way as to avoid confusion.

The images in school books may have been limited, but not one of the teachers described them as ethnocentric, Eurocentric or monocultural. Only two women teachers in the London schools took an active part in deconstructing 'whiteness' and nationalism in the classroom. This may be part of the fear of difficulty with the terms that both Pat at Fairsham and Mohamed at Christie have talked about (above), and how it places them as teachers in vulnerable positions with parents. It will be shown in the next section that the wariness over terms is as salient in discussion with children, and the caution on the part of some teachers to tackle issues head on is seen as complacency by the children.

Rethinking Multiculturalism and Antiracism

The schools in the study could be seen to be very different in terms of their location and the 'racial' and ethnic make-up of the children attending. The differences in locations did not however reflect a neat split in ideas and policies held by staff within the schools. There were both similarities and differences in the ways in which teachers talked about their feelings about dealing with antiracist and multicultural issues in the school. Despite differing levels of engagement with the subject, in all cases there was recognition of its importance and the need for a 'whole school approach'. Teachers seemed to favour either reactive or more proactive methods of dealing with 'race' and in talking about this used different terms for different spheres of school experience. The terms 'racism' and 'antiracism' were used to describe interaction within interpersonal relationships between children and to a lesser extent children and teachers. 'Multiculturalism' was more usually used to refer to a more abstract concept of social harmony that is aspired to and that is reflected in schemes of work and curriculum materials, representation and ideas.

The London schools had such a large variety of students that as Millie, the Section 11 teacher leader, suggested 'the white children are the minority really'. Nonetheless, they are aware that in the broader social context they are the majority, and understand the social power dynamics of that privilege within the school context. Children were aware of 'racism' as a concept at the level of 'cussing out' each other, and some of the white children felt that they had also been the recipients of 'racist' abuse. Troyna and Hatcher (1992) differentiate between 'racist' and 'racial' abuse and I believe this may be a useful way of characterising some interactions, whilst being cautious about how they may reinforce or obscure power relationships.

The children of Fairsham School were in a mainly white demographic context and had access to a slightly different set of discourses about the meaning of racism. It was the only school in which the discourse of 'sending them back to their own country' came up. In the London schools the children had a much more sophisticated awareness of potential for multiple identifications to home and country. Such a phrase was not mentioned as a form of abuse. In all of the schools, racist abuse was seen as being the thing that hurt the most. During interviews the children who admitted to using racist language were *aware of its power*, and racist or interracial name-calling would often lead to fighting amongst the boys. This would support the notion of 'strategic' use of these terms (Troyna and Hatcher 1992); children are aware that using 'racism' causes pain and results in fights. The fact that children chose this form of name-calling over others implies that there is indeed a special awareness of 'race' as a major factor in day-to-day life, although not *all* relationships are based around this, and it does not exclude other types of arguing and abuse.

Children *are* learning about 'race' in school, but multiple positionalities such as 'mixed-race' are missing from common discourses of 'race', ethnicity and culture in school policies (limited as they are), curricula, activities and practices. The subject of 'mixed-race' arises in classes in an informal way if it is spoken of at all. Inter-ethnic/inter-cultural and international positions are usually discussed as a method of understanding abstract concepts about 'race', or possibly religion. They are also used when religious, historical and geographical materials fail to recognise multiplicity. Personal histories are ways of making the ideas more relevant or real. Several of the staff (mostly women) had either volunteered or had been asked to reveal personal biographical details, and children then began talking about themselves and their families. Children are being given *informal* information about how to talk about these positions, and it takes the usual form of listing one's national affiliations. Again this shows the lack of available language and the importance of using family histories when trying to form partial identifications.

In the next chapter I will revisit some of the existing theoretical positions and empirical studies that were first outlined in earlier chapters. The failing school policy in the area of multiculturalism in the schools visited is only one such area of concern. I believe that this research has implications for family studies, 'race', ethnicity and cultural studies, as well as ongoing concerns within feminism about the continued hegemony of the acquisition of normative gendered positions.

Notes

1. Interviews with teachers and the school policy documents, general school information, attendance at after-school clubs, and so on, were meant primarily to show the ways in which the school intended to approach 'race' and racism, and multiculturalism. These provided a *context* for the voices of the children. This research is not meant as an exhaustive piece of research into the schools themselves.
2. Rattansi does this using psychoanalytic theory which I have not used in my own analyses.
3. Although the latter is often based upon nationality it is also, Kilde suggested, alluding to what she called her 'olive skin'.
4. Mohamed was himself 'mixed-race' and was born in the North of England. He told me something of his history but did not mention whether he was a practising Muslim. It is hard to know whether the children 'read' him as ethnicised in any way, but I believe that he is showing here a de-raced position as a teacher.

–8–

'Mixed-Race' Futures

I'd say, if anyone asked me about me or my ancestors – if they said, 'write it down', I'd say 'My mum's ancestors were "whities", my dad's ancestors were African slaves, and my gran's ancestors were Jewish.'

Thomas (Year 6, Christie School, 1998)

Introduction

In this chapter I will review the findings from the research and show how they raise further questions for writings on ethnicity, culture and 'mixed-race' and for future work in the area. In order to investigate gendered, 'mixed-race' identities I analysed the ways in which current academic and political terms and accounts of 'race' and racism were being understood by children. I also explored how such discourses were being mediated through school and familial contexts; I was particularly interested in the ways in which discourses of 'home' and 'family' were being used in identifications, and how children were reading 'race' in images from popular culture.

This book, utilising a feminist theoretical framework, was conceived as a critical project, if not quite an emancipatory piece of research. These are rather grand labels for a small piece of work; none the less, I believe that in some ways they are appropriate. In using auto/biographical accounts of children's own identifications I have shown that the children are often quite consciously engaged in such liberatory projects for themselves. The children's critical reading of 'race' within popular culture, and the verbal and visual narratives provided by children and adults in families and schools, has provided unique insights into the ways in which the children in this study are beginning to construct their 'own' versions of selves, that I believe can be termed 'political', even though that is not a term they would use themselves. In this descriptive form the book shows the ways in which children are actively negotiating their complex, incomplete and dynamic subjective positions in educational and familial locations. At an analytical level, it reinforces a commitment to critical empirical research in this area.

In the first section, I discuss terms and phrases used in cultural and poststructuralist theory and their limitations for the 'ordinary' lived experiences of those who took part in the research. Using popular culture with children provided a way to explore such meanings, and revealed the confusions surrounding the terms and their appropriateness to their situations. In the second section, I will outline the ways in which using popular culture revealed another significant and unexpected finding: children were reading and re-reading (in peer groups), classed, 'raced' and hetero/sexualised positions in popular culture. They did this in ways that are, for the most part, free of an adult 'visual politics'. They are working with images to produce meanings that reconcile difference and, at times, conflict within their lives.

The research with families showed that patterns of parenting and child-care continue to be the gendered responsibility of mothers, but that there is no clear indication that the gender and 'race' of the mother has *specific meaning* for the racialisation of the child in any *inevitable* fashion. More importantly, the *classed identifications* of the family seem to have a major impact on the way in which culture and racialisation are perceived within families, and are thus represented to children.

As shown in Chapter 7, teachers in schools are showing commitment to discourses of multiculturalism and, to a lesser extent, antiracism, but such discourses are currently inadequate for the task of including the complex subject positions held by pupils. Much of what the children understand from their teachers is limited to static and confining notions of monocultural and ethnic positions. The fourth section of this chapter contains a consideration of how the antiracist project in the schools should progress.

Finally, then, I will suggest some of the ways in which imagined futures of children and families may help us in our attempts to dismantle hegemonic discourses of racialisation and a 'racial' politics of singularity in societies. They are using creative approaches to belonging in ways that, although trapped within contemporary linguistic and conceptual frameworks, can offer important insights for post-race possibilities.

Meanings of 'Race', Ethnicity and Culture: Spaces for Mixedness?

One of the intentions of this research was to explore the ways in which the termi-nologies of the academy were being received in the schools and homes of those of 'mixed-race'. I particularly wanted to explore the ways in which children and parents were making sense of the three main terms that describe 'racialised difference': 'race', ethnicity and culture. This aspect of the research provided common findings across locations.

The first and most obvious is that whatever the rhetoric of inclusive education (although that is mostly aimed at 'special educational needs'), it is not being translated into school practice and policy. Teachers were not happy using language that incorporated critiques of hegemonic whiteness, nor that which challenged the Eurocentric and ethnocentric materials they had in schools. Understanding of multiculturalism was still imbued with a very simplistic ideal of 'tolerance' of 'other' cultures, which inadvertently reinforced very static and hierarchical notions of what culture meant. None of the staff at the schools were using the term 'inter-cultural education' (Gundara 2000) – not even in Barnlea where the staff were more aware of changing practices and policies. The term 'ethnicity' was used with some hesitation by a few teachers, and for many of parents it had negative connotations because of its connection with the term 'minority', and therefore with subordinate status in society.

What this shows is that there is a gap between the ways in which academics are attempting to push theories forward and the ways in which new language and its meanings are being used in schools and homes. This is most graphically shown in the way that children still routinely use the term 'half-caste', and that they are not always aware of its pejorative nature. The language of the academy is often bound by finite notions of 'groups', but when it moves into the realms of the decon-structive becomes meaningless to many. We need to find a way to move through this double bind in order to make post-race thinking a possibility for practice. At a paper Ann Phoenix (1996) gave about her work with Barbara Tizard, I vividly remember an angry woman asking why she had to give up the term 'mixed-race' and use 'mixed-parentage', 'just because academics said so'. This was of course one particular interpretation of the work presented that was not shared by all present, but nonetheless it was a powerful exchange which revealed the difficul-ties of finding new language that can be meaningful in ordinary contexts.

I am reminded of this incident when I see syncretism, creolisation, hybridity, *mestizaje, metis/se, griot/te* and so on used in academic texts and think of how children are speaking in playgrounds, and writing and performing their own bodily texts. How can such terms be useful analytically or theoretically when they are so culturally specific, and the realities to which they refer infinitely diverse? Children have often resorted to visual signs that are contained within their speech acts; that is, the 'image' of others that they are interested in and talk about. This happens when the language they need is absent, or simply does not exist *for them.*

Children negotiate complexity with images and bodies in ways that circum-vent the need for specialist language. As I said in Chapter 1, all these (racialised) terms are problematic from a theoretical perspective. Children revealed the gaps in the *concepts* that are needed to inform language production, and also the failure of the *language* to inform the concepts. The children negotiate and live with these unlivable positions, whilst exploring the discursive limits placed upon them. My respondents and informal contacts all share the concern with naming, but will use 'mixed' *because* of its vagueness.

In the British context, specialist language such as *metis/se* and *mestizaje*, and so on, is linked to specific intellectual and cultural positions and most often connected with binaried black/white, brown/white mixing. I believe that for different racial/ethnic groupings the phrases would sit less easily. These terms often require a sure knowledge of a connection to, for example, an African or Latin diaspora, which some in my research simply do not feel. At present I think it would be difficult to open these terms out to include *all* individuals with some kind of 'mixed' heritage.

An umbrella term 'mixed-race' *could* result in a 'tripartite system' within a black/white paradigm (Ifekwunigwe 2000: 180), but there are so many other variations of multiplicity that challenge these ideas in differing temporal and spatial locations. I believe that we should be attempting further deconstruction of 'mixed-race' *alongside, through and by* deconstruction of existing (binaried) racialisations, to begin to move away from talking 'race' and to interrogate the specifics of inequities through post-race thinking.

Processing Mixedness

In his outline of the case-study approach to narrative, Polkinghorne describes the 'epiphanic moment' as a key feature of self-definition (Polkinghorne 1995: 20–21). An epiphany as reworked from Denzin (1989) is: 'a major transactional moment that disrupts the flow of ordinary life and makes problematic the usual definitions given to the facets of one's world' (Barone 1995: 71).

Epiphanic moments can be seen in writing on mixedness which identify moments of 'becoming black.'[1] Such *negrisence*, or 'coming to terms with one's blackness', is dependent on a starting point that is not just not-blackness but, rather, is *whiteness*. Although the parents I interviewed have noted changes in children's perceptions they did not claim 'epiphanic moments' of recognition. Neither have any of the adults that I have spoken too. There *were* other moments that were similar, and involve racialisation, but they were not conceptualised as a '*moment of recognition*'. Taken together the accounts both of children and adults show that although there may be moments that are influential, that these are ongoing processes of racialisation that are changing and not constant, and are often open to significant reinterpretation.

There is in the language of identification an implication that blackness is cultural and learnt, it endorses a form of cognitive ebonisation (Katz 1996). The argument about deconstructing 'race', refuting colourism, and developing differing levels of 'mixed-raceness' is now destabilised through recognition of a *learnt identification* with 'black culture' that can *only be taught* by a 'black' person. I believe that this occludes the possibilities arising from multiethnic environments and cultural translation in urban spaces where cultural processes are cosmopolitan and dynamic.

In this research I have confirmed that 'mixed-race' individuals do not neces-sarily inhabit spaces of in-between-ness as suggested by Bhabha (1990b). They (we?) occupy multi-layered, multi-faceted positionalities. This means that the children manage a range of different aspects to what they call 'self' in ways that are not easily mapped onto a notion of a 'third space' and are heavily influenced by embodiment and embodied practices. Poststructuralist theories of materiali-sation of bodies provide possibilities for understanding this 'mixedness' in process. Sarah Ahmed suggests that:

> Significantly, with the shifts in form of racism towards a fetishising of the cultural rather than biological difference (Balibar 1991: 22), passing for black becomes an increasingly powerful individual and national phantasy. Passing for black is enabled by adopting the elements of black culture, a process of adoption which then fixes and freezes those elements as indicators of what it means to be black. (Ahmed 1999: 100)

However 'real' a situation this may be for many of the children – white, Chinese, 'mixed' – it has not touched the lives of those in Fairsham.

For the children in this study, presenting differing racialised faces and bodies was an on-going and skilled process. It required a form of 'self-regulation' that revealed the influence of both agency and constraint. The children are involved in developing the technologies of the self in ways that deploy aspects of racialisation, heterosexuality, class and gender through discourses of attractiveness, aspirations and ability. Throughout all of this, their use of (popular) culture was central.

Racialisation, Hetero/sexuality, Popular Culture and Peer Relations

Children's readings of popular culture provided extremely rich accounts of their daily interactions and concerns. Through these practices, children confirmed the importance of the work of theorists such as Hall ([1974] 1993), Johnson (1983) and van Zoonen (1994). Meaning is produced in and by negotiation with an array of psychic and social activities. Children of this age are reading the popular in groups and using images of others to mediate their understandings of sex and sexuality. 'Race' was less salient in children's 'readings' of attractiveness and desirability than their perceived ideas about *sexual* attractiveness. This is not to say that 'race' was not operating at some liminal level, but this was not the way the children *chose* to make sense of their readings.

In both same and mixed, sex friendship groups at all three schools in all the years, learning to 'do' girl and boy and acting appropriately for those labels were the basis upon which other discourses of 'race', class and ability were worked through. Foucault has argued that sexuality lies at the heart of the modern project of regulation and disciplining of subjects:

[Sex] was at the pivot of the two axes along which developed the entire political technology of life. On the one hand it was tied to the disciplines of the body: the harnessing, intensification and distribution of forces, the adjustment and economy of energies. On the other hand, it was applied to the regulation of populations through all the far-reaching effects of its activity. (Foucault 1998: 145)

Foucault does not discuss how populations of Europe were formed at the expense of the Others, but the technologies that he talks about were central to the racial economies of sex. Children showed that they were engaged in these processes of self-regulation in their discussions of gender and heterosexuality. Gender could be understood in many different ways, and appropriate and therefore attractive (in both moral and physical terms) gendered behaviour could encompass a range of styles in both the personal and technology-mediated national and 'global' spheres.

The methodologies incorporating use of narrative, genre and discourse, and use of visual methods, provided tools for investigating the lived realities, perceptions and reported experiences of the children in the study. However, it was obvious from the beginning of the research that the children were limited by the discourses they encountered that forced them to think through who they are, where they come from, and, importantly, 'what they are becoming', in the language of 'race' and 'ethnicity'. Using images, bodies and music helped them to form shared social spaces in which such difficulties could be resolved (see also de Block 2000). The children used verbal and visual dexterity in order to do this, showing how they used generic forms of speech to both explore and transgress discursive boundaries.

Bakhtin has suggested that 'Our repertoire of oral (and written) genres is rich. We use them confidently and skilfully *in practice*, and it is quite possible for us not to even suspect their existence *in theory*' (Bakhtin 1986: 78). Children did not express frustration at a lack of expertise in language use, and challenged generic forms of learning using their genealogies in skilled ways. They were often aware of the ways in which they did this. However, it was in their visual 'speech acts' that they did this most unselfconsciously, using visual signs in media to examine 'raced' heterosexuality through discourses of attractiveness.

By utilising shared un-raced, rather than de-raced, readings the children were engaged in developing dynamic forms of cultural production. These retained elements of their own particular cultural heritages, but increasingly, as a way of utilising an omnicultural social space that facilitated acquisition of a new form of social capital in the school. These forms are also undoubtedly filtering back into homes and, in negotiation with 'tradition', continue to evolve. Peer relationships were an essential part of these processes, with both likes and dislikes – the love/loathe discourse – facilitating dynamic relationships.

Children in all the schools rejected hegemonic ideals that privilege whiteness in discourses of beauty and attractiveness. The *fear* of interracial liaisons is less evident amongst these children than writers such as Young (1996) suggest is present in adults, and this requires us to rethink the ways in which Othering processes stress both desire *and fear* that *inevitably* result in 'racist' psychologies (Young 1996; Rattansi 1992). Such theories do not allow us room for developing de-racialised, or rather, post-race positions, as racist antagonisms are the only possible outcome of 'normal' psychic development. 'Interracial' families who took part in this research showed that they were attempting to circumvent such inevitabilities.

Families and Identifications: Gender, Ethnicity and Class

In contrast to the work of Jayne Ifekwunigwe who centralises the role of mothers, Ilan Katz (1996) has suggested that the 'race' of the *father* is most significant to 'racial identity' in children with 'mixed-parentage'. My own research suggests a far more complex relationship between gender and 'race' in the identification processes of young children, and supports initial findings by Tizard and Phoenix (1993). My findings show that the most important aspects of the day-to-day care of young children continue to fall to mothers, supporting the bulk of feminist sociological analyses (see Delphy and Leonard 1992). In consequence, the everyday cultural practices that produce *dynamic and evolving cultural forms* in late modern homes are overwhelmingly the responsibility of the *mother in nego-tiation with the child*. Creating families through invitations to 'special occa-sions', which may or may not have a specific ethnic origin, is also the domain of mothers. Fathers are more involved in the pleasurable aspects of child-rearing, the 'treats', games and special occasions, this being reflected in the ways children talk about fathers.

However, as children are heavily invested in developing *gendered* identities at this age, visual gender identifications with parents came to the fore in their conversations. I believe that this plays a part in the development of 'racial' iden-tifications in families, even when for boys, fathers are absent. Mothers making a particular contribution to children's racialisation awareness *can* circumvent this 'lack of a father' (see Ifekwunigwe 2000). Children at this age may *first* think through gendering processes, but they are also aware of the importance of 'racial' identities. In short, there was no simple relationship between proximity to a parent and 'racial' identity. Children imagined themselves to be 'like' a parent of the same gender. But they also read 'race' as 'colour'. If children perceived them-selves as visually 'of colour', they could claim to 'look like' the parent they perceived as 'racially Other', regardless of gender. So Lola was not 'Chinese-looking' enough to make her 'look like' and 'racially identify' with her mother.

Children of both black and white mothers, in all locations and across classes, identified themselves as 'mixed-race'. Children of both black and white mothers also identified as black. None of the children from Malaysian, Polynesian, Chinese or Turkish backgrounds identified *solely* with that part of their heritage. All of these factors raise questions for those who have argued against transracial adoption, by simplistically suggesting that if a child 'is' 'mixed-race' they should be referred to as 'black' (see discussions in Gaber and Aldridge 1994; Kirton 2000). What seems to be most important is the way in which parents (mothers) communicate with children about their identities. In this process, location and parental history, and parental connections to 'diaspora' or an imagined 'home', play a crucial part for the negotiation of ethnic identification. One of the most interesting findings, and one that I had not anticipated to see so clearly, was the role that social class played in ethnicised discourses of families. It is this area that for me is the most pressing for future research in this area.

In Fairsham, all the parents interviewed had relatively privileged backgrounds, and were to all intents and purposes 'middle class'. The form that this took was ostensibly a 'white' English middle-class position, or at least it did not involve a specifically 'non-white' element at the level of the everyday. Special occasions were more likely to be the time for connecting to diverse cultural practices. Three of the four parents at Fairsham were themselves 'mixed-race' but had very Anglicised upbringings, which no doubt influenced the way they raised their children. In successful jobs and comfortable houses, it struck me that they had been accepted into the 'white' middle classes and they strove to maintain that for their children. This was seen as strategically necessary for them in a racist society in which they (and in some cases, their parents) had suffered racism. For children of 'mixed-race' in these households, class seems to act as a kind of 'buffer' against racism. This does not mean that there is an unproblematic acceptance and entry into 'white middle classness' as 'race' never fully disappears from the picture. Darcy and Celie both said that they felt limits to their belonging that arose from their 'race'.

These mothers and one father (at Fairsham) had not completely lost touch with their own particular versions of belonging to a 'diaspora', but for at least three of them it did not play a significant part in their day-to-day negotiations of life as 'ethnicised' beings. For those who had monoracial, migrant parents there were feelings of conflict over past and future identifications for themselves and for successive generations; a need to keep in touch with 'roots' but to look to the future in an adopted homeland. For these families, social and spatial geography continued to work with these processes as the children were brought up in a 'white, middle-class' environment.

None of the parents or teachers used the term 'diaspora', but I believe that what many are describing is something close to Brah's 'diaspora space'.

However, I continue to question the politics of using the term. Brah argues that 'the *concept* of diaspora – *as distinct from the trajectory of specific or historical or contemporary diasporas such as African, Jewish or Asian* – should be understood as an ensemble of investigate technologies for genealogical analysis of the relationality within and between different diasporic formations' (Brah 1996: 241; emphasis added). Here she attempts to show the separation of 'concept' from 'history', which I find problematic. However, as a framework for analysis it is useful for understanding the parents' narratives. Through the use of an analytical matrix consisting of a *concept* of ' "*diaspora*", "*border*", *and* "*the politics of location*" ' (Brah 1996: 242; original emphasis), parents revealed highly individualised 'diasporic formations'. Using the term 'diasporic formations' seems a less controversial way of expressing the same kinds of concerns with the multifaceted nature of identifications than even that of 'diaspora space'.

For mothers of children in the London schools there were also varying degrees of separation from their own parents and 'homes'. These were negotiated in differing ways depending on life experience. Again it is not possible to generalise. For the working-class mothers, the immediate concern for their children was that they were accepted for who they were. Some black, working-class mothers recognised 'mixed blood'. Sheila (black, working class) was one such case. She said that she was a black woman, but her children were mixed. Sheila did not care what 'colour' people were; it did not matter. What mattered was whether they were good people. As colour 'did not matter', her children could be 'mixed-race' because they did not *need* to be black. But for Andrea (black, middle class), who had suffered a lot of discrimination in her own upbringing, there was no room for her son (Sima) to think of himself as 'mixed', and he did describe himself as black. Either way the discourses of colour had to be managed in a society that recognises them as important.

Mrs Farmer (Margaret) claimed the same discourse as Sheila from a *white* working-class position. She also called upon the discourses of self-improvement, achievement and aspirations for her children. So Tito and Talia also had to be 'proud of who they are', and she wanted them to 'do well' and 'be happy'. This echoed middle-class aspirations of the type expressed by parents in Fairsham. However, middle-class, white Lesley, who had 'improved' herself from her Scottish working-class roots, had, through her job as a public sector worker in a multicultural borough of London, received the 'politics of singularity' and taught her son that he should be black (Jacob see Chapter 4, p. 88).

The ways in which mothers invested in their children's futures was guided by interpretations of their own social and cultural capital and their life-histories. Reay suggests that 'For most of the middle-class mothers, parental involvement [with schooling] was much more an issue of continuity with the past than disjuncture. It was a question of doing what one's mother did rather than, for most of the working-class mothers, doing something different' (Reay 1998: 58). In my own research, the ethnic and geographic history meant that the intergenerational change was more profound for the middle-class mothers. Celie, Darcy, Jung G. and Andrea did not have a straightforward connection to a middle-class history. They were the first generation of women to become middle class in their families and they had done so despite their position as 'racial outsiders' in the educational stakes. They were not all migrants, but even for those born here, racialisation meant that they had 'the wrong cultural capital' (ibid.). They wanted to maintain this newly found and fragile respectability, without losing sight of the fact that the low-status attached to racialisation would make this harder for their children. They invested in cultural practices which were in fact contrary to this project and balanced 'tradition' with 'respectability' (Skeggs 1997) by using cultural translation in dynamic ways.

The working-class mothers, who all classified themselves as 'white' or 'black', were invested in bettering and changing their children's possibilities through education. In this way they differed from the mothers in Reay's sample, of whom she said: 'Most of the middle-class mothers were working with a very different form of maternal intervention [from the working-class mothers] which prioritised academic achievement over individual volition' (ibid.: 93). My own work suggests that the working-class mothers were equally invested in academic achievement and saw it as the best way for children to escape working-classness. I believe this is because of the intricacies of lives that had such diverse cultural and ethnic inputs, as well as classed positions. Their readings of acceptability are mediated not through allegiance to one particular social or cultural position, e.g. black African diaspora, but through the understanding of their children both belonging *and* not belonging to a *singular* position. There is personal politics in these accounts that suggest a form of *dis*-identification with the working-classness that Skeggs (1997) reports. Paradoxically these are tied to strong *identifications* with cultural and ethnic positions that are often automatically positioned as working class, simply by being *outside* of the boundaries of the acceptable face of white middle-classness (Mirza 1992; Reynolds 2000).

The parents have all shown that they place a high premium on educational achievement as a way of their children earning social acceptability and an unspoken classed mobility. In the next section I will consider the ways in which ethnicity and 'racism', as discourses of inclusion and exclusion to social acceptability, were negotiated by teachers and children in the schools.

Teaching and Learning 'Race' in Schools

The children were all invested in exploring their racialised positioning within school contexts. Here, children encounter 'official' versions of what it means to be a 'racialised' being. Not all the children were racialised in those discourses; however, the ones who were white remained centralised and unspoken – 'unraced', with their whiteness the norm against which 'coloured' others were constructed in opposition and in subordination. In countering these hegemonic texts, the children of colour and minority ethnic status (in multiethnic schools) were actively constructing 'whiteness' in similar ways to their own understandings of blackness and other Othernesses. In conflict, they use terms of abuse which construct themselves and their peers within the same imaginary racialised frameworks. These were attempts to eradicate the hierarchies of 'race' in the schools and simultaneously a way of claiming status. This was not happening in the mainly white school in this study, which would support the argument that 'white superiority' is hegemonic. It forms a discourse that operates at macro- and micro-political levels and is not negotiated in an environment in which it is not challenged by the presence of (enough) disruptive 'Others'. The children of minority status in the mainly white school were engaged in living out overtly 'de-raced' identities within the school context. It was hard to judge whether this was a strategic decision or whether it was simply a consequence of the dominance of the white, middle-class English codes through which the school operated.

Children felt that the schools provided them with a very limited form of understanding of what 'racism' was and, through that, what 'race' meant. However, interestingly, though they may have understood the concept of 'racism', the majority did not know that it came from the word 'race' and that it implied ways of categorising people. Larry, in Chapter 3, was just one of many children who struggled with the term. This suggests that teachers were so worried about using direct language about these subjects, and the potential for attempts to do so bringing accusations of racism upon themselves or further confusion, that they rarely discussed the origins of terms in ways that were meaningful for the children. Both teachers and children recognised that children routinely used a variety of different ethnic and cultural differences as forms of abuse. Teachers remained engaged with eradicating 'racism' in the schools from a variety of positions, and Barnlea appeared to be the most successful at tackling it across the whole school.

These comments about the teachers and schools are, as I stated at the beginning of Chapter 7, not intended to provide an analysis of the *schools* as such. They do, however, provide us with an idea of how teachers received ideas about multiculturalism and passed them on to the children. Across all the schools the ways in which discussions of 'race' and racism went hand in hand served to limit the ways in which children could explore such issues by reinvoking static and singular views of ethnicity and culture. Teachers were also aware that there are failings with these sanctioned views of a multicultural Shangri-La. The reality of the pressures under which the teachers teach compelled them to look somewhat superficially at the ways in which multiculturalism was experienced by those in their classes. Despite these constraints, in all cases children with multiethnic backgrounds would disrupt the available discursive spaces and create opportunities for multiplicity and fluidity in expression. The way they did this was by incorporating their own biographical details and narratives of 'home' and 'family' into the educational contexts.

I cannot make a detailed comment upon the policies in the schools, but suggest that many of the findings support the excellent contribution to this area made by David Gillborn (1995). The London schools show how the demographic profile of pupils is important but not the main factor in dealing with issues of 'race'. What is more important is the 'sensitive management' of issues that involve 'core groups' of staff 'working on' and 'working in' other staff members to facilitate change (ibid.: 180). The head at Barnlea was not positioned as 'sensitive' by the staff, but she had successfully begun the process of whole-school change by mobilising groups of staff who were beginning to work with parents and children on the issues. For reasons of managerial instability, such a move had been slower to happen at Christie, but seemed to be beginning. Fairsham teachers showed a different dynamic in action, with some pockets of active resistance to any concept of change which used 'antiracism' rather than the discourse of 'equal opportunities'. I would suggest that this school would need a great deal of preliminary work introducing antiracist teaching principles before it could be effectively worked through policies and practices.

My work has shown the urgent need for antiracist teaching to involve recognition of multiplicity; Alibhai-Brown (2001) also makes this point. Not multiple, singular models of 'race' and ethnicity, but perhaps, and I use the term with reluctance, some notion of 'hybridity'. By deconstructing whiteness as well as minority racialised positions we may begin to dismantle the hierarchies of 'race'. It is hard to imagine how this may be achieved without *beginning* the 'racialisation' of whiteness which I believe would simply reinforce the same erroneous values. In attempts to tackle 'racism', Gillborn details the way in which involving 'white' students helps to allay their fears that antiracism is automatically biased against them as a 'racial group' (ibid.: 167–175). However, he also reminds us that intra-racial and racialised forms abuse need to be included in this process. In order to be effective, these processes need to centralise the links between micro- and macro-political processes.

Black children in this study were using 'hybrid' forms of modern culture to claim cultural superiority over white, Turkish, Cypriot and South Asian children. They used 'racial' insults against those groups as a way of using the power relations they know to be in existence, and a partial understanding of racism for their own ends, in order to assert a cultural and racialised identity that accrued status. The cultural hegemony in multiethnic primary schools is black British, and it is fed by African-American, global and local influences. Such complexities in cultural forms, coupled with the children's cultural expertise in readings and performances in these areas, will require skilled navigation on the part of teachers. The need to consider more reflexive models of new ethnicities is essential for this process.

Imagined Futures: The Possibilities of Post-race

The rhetoric of 'racism' has moved into the realms of the ethnic and the cultural, and these terms, while not in common use with children, remain potent at a most fundamental level. 'Ethnic cleansing' is nothing short of genocide; 'tradition' and 'cultural integrity' linked to fundamentalism, nationalism and a form of 'cultural imperialism'. Despite these developments, there have still been few attempts at untangling what it means to be a person who occupies a multi- or inter-ethnic/'racial' position. As I have shown above, the sheer complexity of post-race analyses of ethnicity, 'race' and culture as they are constituted within and by discourses of family, nation, gender, generation, class, dis/ability and sexuality makes it an extremely daunting task.

   The children who took part in this research are at a point of change in their lives. They are in the process of recognising the meaning of the 'politics of race' as a discourse to which they have access. In some cases they are deploying this discourse to construct positionalities with which they are happy. In other cases they are operationalising discourses of 'family' and 'home' to form connections with the spiritual or spatial; with kin and with places. These are also political practices that challenge the constraints to their own identities imposed by hegemonic whiteness. The children all managed to work with the fact that their identities were in process and contextualising and contingent. In conversation with me, they all revealed that racism had played a part in their lives and had to some extent constructed their understanding of their own positions. This is not to imply that the children were simply reactive. They deployed any number of re/sources in order to develop satisfactory positions. In doing so they explored genealogies of belonging.

   The ways in which children may retain or relinquish some of the positions they currently hold can only be imagined. If other social perspectives on identity development apply, they will be under a new set of stresses when they move to secondary school and then again as they reach a more mature adolescence. These, and many other possible and probable life changes, will undoubtedly have profound effects on all aspects of their lives. These major changes are more likely to include generic (epiphanic) narratives of change. As Denzin suggests: '[epiphanies] leave their marks on people's lives ... [they alter and shape] the meanings persons give to themselves and their life projects. Having had these experiences, the person is never quite the same' (Denzin 1989: 15).

These need not be explicitly raced, as mentioned above, but will undoubtedly have an effect on that aspect of their identifications. At the time of the interviews children still seemed resistant to the dominant discourses of 'race' that forced them to choose singular positions. For those who develop an increasing awareness of the need for collective organising, they may feel obligated to move into a position of singularity, at least for 'political' purposes. Until we broaden our language and conceptualisations I can see no way in which they can avoid this, and in doing so the circuit of cultural re/production will continue.

Racialisation is an active process that currently rests in the hands of the most powerful in society. The 'naturalness' of whiteness as both 'race' and ethnicity is still hegemonic, despite the impact of 'black culture'. I also believe that the naturalness of 'blackness' is hidden within many academic texts and policies which purport to talk about 'culture'. I started this research with a recognition of the power of the politics of 'race' and the need for 'strategic essentialism' on occasion. I am ending (this stage of it) with a much more uncertain grasp on the reason for this. Like Paul Gilroy (2000: 34), who talks of the fear of 'being "out" about [his] own radically racial deconstructive aspirations', I too wonder how such moves will be received; but I feel myself moving inexorably closer to that position. This research has shown that for many young children 'race' is not always the most salient factor in their lives. It has shown that there are multiple meanings to the word 'racism' and that what they really are concerned about is 'colourism', culturism and nationalism. How children look matters, how they talk, dress, pray, eat and make music matters, and 'where they come from' matters. Most importantly the sex/gender matrix matters. The absolutely over-riding need to develop appropriate heterosexualised behaviours runs through all of the above. In the future the children will probably 'learn' the 'correct' ways of being social beings and use 'race' more often. They will be/come increasingly racialised. The challenge for the ('mixed-race') children is whether they can use post-race thinking to provide new spaces for identity within societies for which the idea of 'race' still has real and profound effects.

Note

1. I am loathe to return to the black/white binary for examples, but they dominate this kind of literature.

Appendix

Numbers of Children, by School

CHRISTIE SCHOOL	No. of Groups	No. of Children	Individual Interviews Mixed-race	Inter-ethnic
Year 6	6	25	4	1
Year 5	5	20	3	
Year 4	5	21	3	
Mixed/Year 3	3	8	1	
TOTAL	19	74	11	1

BARNLEA SCHOOL	No. of Groups	No. of Children	Individual Interviews Mixed-race	Multi-ethnic
Year 6	5	24	2	1
Year 5	5	27	6	3
Year 4	5	26	4	
Mixed/ Other	1 (yr 4) 1 (yr 5)	8	3	
TOTAL	17	85	15	4

FAIRSHAM SCHOOL	No. of Groups	No. of Children	Individual Interviews Mixed-race	Inter-ethnic
Year 6	7	29	1	
Year 5	7 +1	31	3	6
Year 4	8	31	2	2
Mixed/Year 3	2 (yr 5)	13		
TOTAL	25	104	6	8

Total 'Mixed-race' children = 33
Total 'multi-ethnic' (inter-ethnic) = 13

Parents of children interviewed

Christie
Sheila (mother of Dinease)
Kate (mother of Hannah)
Mrs O (mother of Kallie) (short informal)

Barnlea
Parse (mother of Kilde)
Lena (mother of Alice)
Lesley (mother of Jacob)
Mr Jung G. and Mrs Jung G. (parents of Lola)
Andrea (mother of Sima)
MN (in her role as SENCo mother of Marita)
Mrs Farmer (Margaret) (mother of Tito and Talia)
Mala (mother of Meli)

Fairsham
Ceile (mother of Jake)
Darcy (mother of Ella and Kieran)
Penny and Nigel (parents of Kyle)

All mothers apart from Mr G and Nigel

Total = 12 full interviews with 14 parents, one with parent talking as SENCo and parent, and one short informal chat.

Teachers Interviewed

Christie
Acting Head
SENCo
Section 11 Teacher Leader
Class Teachers × 4
Head of Afterschool Clubs   Total = 8

Barnlea
Head
Deputy
SENCo
Home School Liaison
Equal Opportunities Co-ordinator
Class Teachers × 6
Section 11 support for Years 4 and 5   Total = 12

Fairsham
Head
Deputy Head
SENCo
Class Teachers × 4   Total = 7

Bibliography

Adkins, L. and Leonard, D. (1996) *Young People and Kin Work: The Gendered Constitution of Ethnicity*. Report: Economic and Social Research Council Grant No. R000221179.

Ahmed, S. (1997) '"It's a Sun-tan Isn't it?": Autobiography as Identificatory Practice', in H. S. Mirza, (ed.) *Black British Feminisms: A Reader*. London and New York: Routledge.

Ahmed, S. (1999) 'She'll Wake Up One of these Days and Find She's Turned Into a Nigger: Passing Through Hybridity', in V. Bell, (ed.) *Performativity and Belonging*. New York and London: Sage.

Ahmed, S. (2000) *Strange Encounters: Embodied Others in Post-Coloniality*. London and New York: Routledge.

Alcoff, L. (1997) 'Cultural Feminism versus Post-Structuralism: The Identity Crisis in Feminist Theory', in L. Nicholson (ed.) *The Second Wave: A Reader in Feminist Theory*. London: Routledge.

Alderson, P. (1995) *Listening to Children: Children Ethics and Social Research*. Ilford: Barnados.

Alexander, C. (2000) *The Asian Gang: Ethnicity, Identity, Masculinity*. Oxford and New York: Berg.

Alldred, P. (1998) 'Ethnography and Discourse Analysis: Dilemmas in Representing the Voices of Children', in J. Ribbens and R. Edwards (eds) *Feminist Dilemmas in Qualitative Research: Public Knowledges and Private Lives*. London: Sage.

Allund, A. and Granqvist, R. (eds) (1995) *Negotiating Identities: Essays on Immigration and Culture in Present Day Europe*. Amsterdam: Rodopi.

Ali, S. (1999) 'How Scary? Using Popular Culture to Research "Race"', Conference Paper presented at University of North London, 'Researching Culture' Conference.

Ali, S. (2000) 'Who Knows Best?: 'Politics and Ethics in Feminist Research into "Race"' in S. Ali, K. Coate and W. wa Goro (eds) *Global Feminist Politics: Identities in a Changing World*. London: Routledge.

Ali, S. (2002) 'Friendship and Fandom: Ethnicity, Power and Gendering Readings of the Popular', *Discourse: Studies in the Cultural Politics of*

Education, 23 (2).

Ali, S. (2003a) 'Reading Racialised Bodies: Learning to See Difference', in H. Thomas and J. Ahmed *Cultural Bodies: Ethnography and Theory*. London and New York: Blackwell.

Ali, S. (2003b) 'To Be A Girl: Culture and Class in Schools', in *Gender and Education. Special Edition 'Diverse Femininities in Education'* Vol. 15, No. 3 pp. 269–283. Oxford: Carfax Publishers.

Ali, S., Hillman, S. with Davies, H. (1998) 'Youth Talk: Language and Popular Culture', Unpublished research commissioned by BBC Television.

Alibhai-Brown, Y. (2001) *Mixed Feelings: The Complex Lives of Mixed-Race Britons*. London: The Women's Press.

Alibhai-Brown, Y. and Montague, A. (1992) *The Colour of Love: Mixed Race Relationships*. London: Virago.

Ang-Lygate, M. (1995) 'Shades of Meaning', *Trouble and Strife*, no. 31 Summer.

Anthias, F. and Yuval-Davis, N. (1993) *Racialized Boundaries: Race, Nation, Gender, Colour and Class, and the Anti-racist Struggle*. London: Routledge.

Back, L. (1996) *New Ethnicities and Urban Culture: Racism and Multiculture in Young Lives*. London: UCL Press.

Back, L. (2002) 'Wagner and Power Chords: Skinheadism, White Power Music and the Internet', in V. Ware and L. Back *Out of Whiteness: Color, Politics and Culture*. Chicago: University of Chicago Press.

Bakhtin, M.M. (1981) *The Dialogic Imagination: Four essays by M. M. Bakhtin* (edited by Michael Holquist; translated by Caryl Emerson and Michael Holquist). Austin, University of Texas Press.

Bakhtin, M.M. (1986) *Speech Genres and Other Essays* (edited by Caryl Emerson and Michael Holquist; Translated by Vern W. McGee). Austin: University of Texas Press.

Balibar, E. (1991) 'Its There a Neo-racism?" in E. Balibar and I. Wallerstein (eds) *Race, Nation and Class: Ambiguous Identities*. London: Verso.

Ballhatchet, H. (1980) *Race, Sex and Class Under the Raj: Imperial Attitudes and Policies and their Critics, 1793–1905*. London: Weidenfeld and Nicolson.

Banks, M. (2001) *Using Visual Methods*. London and New York: Sage.

Barker, M. (1981) *The New Racism*. London: Junction Books.

Barone, T. (1995) 'Persuasive Writings, Vigilant Readings, and Reconstructed Characters: the Paradox of Trust in Educational Story-sharing', in J.A. Hatch and R. Wisniewski (eds) *Life History and Narrative*. London: Falmer Press.

Benson, S. (1981) *Ambiguous Ethnicity: Interracial Families in London*. Cambridge: Cambridge University Press.

Berger, A.A. (1997) *Narratives in Popular Culture, Media and Everyday Life*. London and New York: Sage.

Berry, G. and Asamen J.K. (1993) *Children and Television: Images in a*

Changing Sociocultural World. Newbury, Calif. and London: Sage.

Bhahba, H.K. (1990a) 'The Third Space: Interview with Homi Babha', in J. Rutherford (ed.) *Identity: Community, Culture Difference*. London: Lawrence and Wishart.

Bhabha, H.K. (1990b) 'Nation and Narration: Introduction', in H.K. Bhabha (ed.) *Nation and Narration*. London and New York: Routledge.

Bhatti, G. (1999) *Asian Children at Home and at School: An Ethnographic Study*. London: Routledge.

Bhavnani, K. and Phoenix, A. (eds) (1996) *Shifting Identities: Shifting Racisms. A Feminism and Psychology Reader*. London: Sage.

Block, L. de (2000) 'Television, Friendship and Social Connections', Paper Presented at Education for Social Democracies, CCS Conference, Institute of Education, London.

Block, L. de (1997) Unpublished essay for MA Module 'Gender, Culture and Identity', Institute of Education.

Boushel, M. (1996) 'Vulnerable Multiracial Families and Early Year Service', *Children and Society*, 10: 1–20.

Bradshaw, C.K. (1992) 'Beauty and the Beast: On Racial Ambiguity', in Maria P. Root (ed.) *Racially Mixed People in America*. New York: Sage Publications.

Brah, A. (1992) 'Difference, Diversity or Differentiation', in Avtar Brah (1993). 'Re-framing Europe: Engendered Racisms, Ethnicities and Nationalisms in Contemporary Western Europe', in *Feminist Review*, no. 45 Autumn.

Brah, A. (1996) *Cartographies of Diaspora: Contesting Identities*. London: Routledge.

Brah, A., Hickman, M. and Mac an Ghaill, M. (eds) (1999) *Thinking Identities: Ethnicity, Racism and Culture*. Basingstoke: Macmillan.

Brannen, J. (1999) 'Children's Family Networks and Significant Others', Paper presented at ESRC Seminar Group 5 'Postmodern' Kinship: Changing Families/Changing Childhoods, University of Leeds, December.

Breger, R. and Hill, R. (eds) (1998) *Cross Cultural Marriage*. Berg: Oxford and New York.

British Agencies for Adoption and Fostering (BAAF) (1987) *The Placement Needs of Black Children*. Practice Note 13.

Brown, J.D. and Schultze, L. (1990) 'The Effects of Race, Gender and Fandom on Audience Interpretations of Madonna's Music Videos', in Dines and Humez (eds) (1995) *Gender, Race and Class: A Text Reader*. Thousand Oaks, Calif.: Sage.

Bruner, J. (1985) *Actual Minds, Possible Worlds*. Cambridge, Mass.: Harvard University Press.

Bryan, B., Dadzie, S. and Scafe, S. (1985) *The Heart of the Race: Black Women's Lives in Britain*. London: Virago Press.

Buckingham, D. (2000) *After the Death of Childhood: Growing Up in the Age of Television*. Buckingham: Open University Press.

Buckingham, D. and Sefton-Green, J. (1994) *Cultural Studies Goes to School: Reading and Teaching Popular Media*. London and New York: Taylor and Francis.

Butler, J. (1990) *Gender Trouble: Feminism and the Subversion of Identity*. London: Routledge.

Butler, J. (1993) *Bodies that Matter: On the Discursive Limits to Sex*. London: Routledge.

Camper, C. (ed.) (1994) *Miscegenation Blues: Voices of Mixed Race Women*. Toronto: Sister Vision Black Women and Women of Colour Press.

Carby, H. (1982) 'White Women Listen! Feminism and the Boundaries of Sisterhood', in Centre for Contemporary Cultural Studies, *The Empire Strikes Back: Race and Racism in '70s Britain*. London: Hutchinson/CCCS, University of Birmingham.

Cauce, A.M. *et al*. (1992) 'Between a Rock and Hard Place: Social Adjustment in Biracial Youth', in M.P.P. Root (ed.) (1992) *Racially Mixed People in America*. New York: Sage.

Cealey-Harrison, W. and Hood-Williams, J. (1998) 'More Varieties than Heinz: Social Categories and Sociality in Humphries, Hammersley and Beyond', *Sociological Research Online*, 3 (1).

(charles) H. (1992) 'Whiteness: The Relevance of Politically Colouring the "non"', in H. Hinds, A. Phoenix and J. Stacey (eds) *Working Out New Directions for Women's Studies*. London: Falmer Press.

Chiong, J.A. (1998) *Racial Categorisation of Multiracial Children in Schools*. Westport Conn.: Bergin and Garvey.

Code, L. (1991) *What Can She Know? Feminist Theory and the Construction of Knowledge*. Ithaca, N.Y. and London: Cornell University Press.

Cohen, P. (1979) *Subcultural Conflict and Working Class Community*. Working Papers in Cultural Studies 2. CCCS, University of Birmingham.

Cohen, P. (1987) *Racism and Popular Culture: A Cultural Studies Approach*. Working Paper No. 9. London: Centre for Multicultural Education, Institute of Education.

Cohen, P. (1988) 'The Perversions of Inheritance: Studies in the Making of Multi-racist Britain', in P. Cohen and H. Bains (eds) *Multiracist Britain*. London: Macmillan.

Cohen, P. (1992) '"It's Racism What Done It!": Hidden Narratives in Theories of Racism', in J. Donald and A. Rattansi (eds) *'Race', Culture, Difference*. Buckingham; Open University Press.

Cohen, P. and Bains, H. (eds) (1988) *Multiracist Britain*. London: Macmillan.

Collier, R. (1999) 'Men, Heterosexuality and the Changing Family: (re)constructing

Fatherhood in the Law and Social Policy', in G. Jagger and C. Wright (eds) *Changing Family Values: Feminist Perspectives*. London : Routledge.

Connell, R.W. (1995) *Masculinities*. Cambridge: Polity Press.

Connolly, P. (1998) *Racism, Gender Identity and Young Children: Social Relations in a Multi-Ethnic Inner City Primary School*. London: Routledge.

Cosslett, T., Lury, C. and Summerfield, P. (eds) (2001) *Feminism and Autobiography*. London and New York: Routledge.

Craib, I. (1993) 'Some Comments on the Sociology of Emotion', *Sociology*, 29 (1): 151–158.

Curran, J., Morley, D. and Walkerdine, V. (eds) (1996) *Cultural Studies and Communications*. London: Arnold.

Daniel, G. Reginald (1992) 'Passers and Pluralists: Subverting the Racial Divide', in M.P.P. Root (ed.) (1992) *Racially Mixed People in America*. New York: Sage.

Davis, A. (1982) *Women, Race and Class*. London: Women's Press.

Davis, A. (1990) 'We Do Not Consent: Violence Against Women in a Racist Society', in A. Davis *Women, Culture and Politics*. London: The Women's Press.

Deleuze, G. ([1988] 1999) *Foucault* (translated by Sean Hand). London and New York: Continuum Books.

Delphy, C. and Leonard, D. (1992) *Familiar Exploitation: A New Analysis of Marriage In Contemporary Western Societies*. Cambridge: Polity Press.

Denzin, N.K. (1989) *Interpretive Interactionism*. Newbury Park, Calif.: Sage.

Denzin, N.K. (1997) *Interpretive Ethnography: Ethnographic Practices for the 21st Century*. London: Sage.

Dines, G. and Humez, J.M. (1995) *Gender, Race and Class: A Text Reader*. Thousand Oaks, Calif.: Sage.

Donald, J. and Rattansi, A. (eds) (1992) *'Race', Culture, Difference*. London: Sage/Oxford University Press.

Dove, N. (1998) *Afrikan Mothers: Bearers of Culture, Makers of Social Change*. New York: State University of New York Press.

Driver, E. and Droisen, A. (eds) (1989) *Child Sexual Abuse: Feminist Perspectives*. London: Macmillan.

Duncombe, J. and Marsden, D. (1993) 'Love and Intimacy: The Gender Divisions of Emotion and "Emotion Work": A Neglected Aspect of Sociological Discussion of Heterosexual Relationships', *Sociology*, 27 (2): 221–42.

Dyer, R. (1997) *White*. London and New York: Routledge.

Ehrenreich, B. and English, D. (1979) *For Her Own Good: 150 Years of the Experts' Advice To Women*. London: Pluto.

Elliot, F.R. (1996) *Gender, Family and Society*. Basingstoke and London: Macmillan.

Epstein, D. (1993) *Changing Classroom Cultures: Anti-racism Politics and Schools.* Stoke-on-Trent: Trentham Books.

Epstein, D. (ed.) (1994) *Challenging Lesbian and Gay Inequalities in Education.* Buckingham: Open University Press.

Epstein, D. (1998) 'Are You a Teacher or Are You a Girl?', in G. Walford (ed.) *Doing Research in Education.* London: Falmer Press.

Epstein, D. and Johnson, R. (1994) 'On the Straight and Narrow: The Heterosexual Presumption, Homophobias and Schools', in D. Epstein and R. Johnson *Schooling Sexualities.* Buckingham: Open University Press.

Epstein, D. and Johnson, R. (1998) *Schooling Sexualities.* Buckingham: Open University Press.

Epstein, D., Elwood, J., Maw, J. and Hey, V. (1998) *Failing boys?: Issues In Gender And Achievement.* On behalf of the Centre for Research and Education on Gender, Institute of Education, University of London. Buckingham: Open University Press.

Erben, M. (ed.) (1998) *Biography and Education: A Reader.* London: Falmer Press.

Evans, J. (1995) *Feminist Theory Today: An Introduction to Second Wave Feminism.* London: Sage.

Fanon, F. (1970) *Black Skin, White Masks.* London: Paladin.

Fetherston, E. (ed.) (1994) *Skin Deep: Women Writing on Color, Culture and Identity.* The Crossing Press Inc. USA.

Ferri, E. (1976) *Growing Up in a One Parent Family: A Long Term Study of Child Development.* Windsor NFER.

Finch, J. (1984) '"It's Great to Have Someone to Talk To": The Ethics of Interviewing Women', in C. Bell and H. Roberts (eds) *Social Researching: Politics, Problems, Practice.* London: Routledge and Kegan Paul.

Fine, M., Weiss, L., Powell, L. and Mun Wong, L. (eds) (1997) *Off White: Readings on Race, Power and Society.* New York and London: Routledge.

Fiske, J. (1992) 'The Political Economy of Fandom', in L.A. Lewis (ed.) *The Adoring Audience: Fan Culture and Popular Media.* London: Routledge.

Foucault, M. (1978) *The History of Sexuality. Volume One: An Introduction* (translated from the French by Robert Hurley). London: Allen Lane.

Foucault, M. (1980) 'Power and Strategies', in C. Gordon (ed.) *Power/Knowledge: Selected Interviews and Other Writings 1972–1977 by Michel Foucault* (translated by Colin Gordon, Leo Marshall, John Mepham and Kate Soper). Brighton: Harvester Wheatsheaf.

Foucault, M. (1991) 'Nietzsche, Genealogy, History', in P. Rabinow (ed.) *The Foucault Reader: An Introduction to Foucault's Thought.* Harmondsworth: Penguin.

Foucault, M. (1998) *The Will to Knowledge: The History of Sexuality Volume 1* (translated from the French by Robert Hurley). London: Penquin.

Fox Keller, E. and Longino, H. E. (eds) (1996) *Feminism and Science*. Oxford: Oxford University Press.

Frankenberg, R. (1993) *The Social Construction of Whiteness: White Women, Race Matters*. New York and London: Routledge.

Frith, S. (1996) 'Music and Identity', in S. Hall and P. Du Gay (eds) *Questions of Cultural Identity*. London and New York: Sage.

Fryer, P. (1984) *Staying Power: The History of Black People in Britain*. London: Pluto.

Gaber, I. and Aldridge, J. (eds) (1994) *In the Best Interests of the Child: Culture, Identity and Transracial Adoption*. London: Free Association Books.

Gaine, C. (1987) *No Problem Here: A Practical Approach to Education and 'Race' in White Schools*. London: Hutchinson.

Gaine, C. (1995) *Still No Problem Here*. Stoke on Trent: Trentham Books.

Gamman, L. and Marshment, M. (eds) (1988) *The Female Gaze: Women as Viewers of Popular Culture*. London: The Women's Press.

Giddens, A. (1993) *The Giddens Reader* (edited by Philip Cassell). London: Macmillan.

Gillborn, D. (1990) *'Race', Ethnicity and Education: Teaching and Learning in Multiethnic Schools*. London: Unwin Hymann.

Gillborn, D. (1995) *Racism and Antiracism in Real Schools: Theory, Policy and Practice*. Buckingham: Open University Press.

Gilman, S. (1992) 'Black Bodies, White Bodies', in J. Donald and A. Rattansi (eds) *'Race', Culture, Difference*. London: Routledge.

Gilroy, P. (1987) *There Ain't No Black in the Union Jack*. London: Hutchinson.

Gilroy, P. (1993a) *Small Acts: Thoughts on the Politics of Black Cultures*. London: Serpent's Tail.

Gilroy, P. (1993b) *The Black Atlantic: Modernity and Double Consciousness*. London: Verso.

Gilroy, P. (1993c) 'One Nation Under a Groove', in P. Gilroy (1993) *Small Acts: Thoughts on the Politics of Black Cultures*. London: Serpent's Tail.

Gilroy, P. (1993d) 'It's a Family Affair: Black Culture and the Trope of Kinship', in P. Gilroy, *Small Acts: Thoughts on the Politics of Black Cultures*. London: Serpent's Tail.

Gilroy, P. (1993e) 'Frank Bruno or Salman Rushdie', in P. Gilroy *Small Acts: Thoughts on the Politics of Black Cultures*. London: Serpent's Tail.

Gilroy, P. (2000) *Between Camps: Nations, Culture and the Allure of Race*. London: Penguin.

Glaser, B. and Strauss, A. (1967) *The Discovery Of Grounded Theory: Strategies for Qualitative Research*. New York: Aldine.

Glenn, E.N. (1994) 'Social Constructions of Mothering: A Thematic Overview', in E.N. Glenn, G. Chang and L.R. Forcey, *Mothering, Ideology, Experience and Agency.* New York and London: Routledge.

Glenn, E.N., Chang, G. and Forcey, L.R. (1994*) Mothering, Ideology, Experience and Agency.* New York and London: Routledge.

Goldberg, D. (ed.) (1990) *Anatomy of Racism.* Minneapolis and London: University of Minnesota Press.

Gray, A. (1997) 'Learning from Experience: Cultural Studies and Feminism', in T. McGuigan (ed.) *Cultural Methodologies.* London: Sage.

Gray, A. and McGuigan, J. (eds) (1993) *Studying Culture: An Introductory Reader.* London and New York: Edward Arnold.

Grearson, J.C. and Smith, L.B. (1995) *Swaying: Essays on Intercultural Love.* Iowa City: University of Iowa Press.

Grugeon, E. and Woods, P. (1990*) Educating All: Multicultural Perspectives in the Primary School.* London: Routledge.

Gundara, J. (2000) *Interculturalism, Education and Inclusion.* London: Paul Chapman Publishing.

Hall, C. (1992) *White, Male and Middle Class: Explorations in Feminism and History.* London: Polity Press.

Hall, S. ([1974] 1993) 'The Television Discourse – encoding and decoding', in A. Gray and J. McGuigan (eds) (1993) *Studying Culture: An Introductory Reader.* London: Edward Arnold.

Hall, S. (1992) 'New Ethnicities', in J. Donald and A. Rattansi (eds) *'Race', Culture, Difference.* London: Routledge.

Hall, S. (1996) 'Introduction: Who Needs "Identity"'?, in S. Hall and P. Du Gay (eds) *Questions of Cultural Identity.* London: Sage.

Hall, S. (ed.) (1997) *Representation: Cultural Representations and Signifying Practices.* London: Sage, in association with the Open University.

Hammersley, M. and Atkinson, P. (1983) *Ethnography: Principles in Practice.* London: Tavistock Publications Ltd.

Hanmer, J. and Maynard, M. (eds) (1987) *Women, Violence and Social Control*, Explorations in Sociology, British Sociological Association Conference Volume Series. London: Palgrave Macmillan.

Haraway, D. (1988) 'Situated Knowledges: The Science Question in Feminism and the Privilege of the Partial Perspective', *Feminist Studies.* (14) 3: 573–599.

Haraway, D. (1997) *Modest Witness @ Second Millennium Female Man © Meets OncoMonse™.* London and New York: Routledge.

Harding, S. (1987) *Feminism and Methodology.* Milton Keynes: Open University Press.

Harding, S. (1991) *Whose Science? Whose Knowledge? Thinking from Women's Lives.* Milton Keynes: Open University Press.

Harris, C. (1996) 'The Unbearable Whiteness of Being', Unpublished seminar paper presented at University of Greenwich, School of Social Sciences.

Hartley, R. (ed.) (1995) *Families and Cultural Diversity in Australia*. St Leonards: Allen and Unwin.

Hatch, J.A. and Wisniewski, R. (eds) (1995) *Life History and Narrative*. London: Falmer Press.

Haug, F. *et al*. (1987) *Female Sexualization: A Collective Work of Memory* (translated from the German by Erica Carter). London: Verso.

Hewitt, R. (1986) *White Talk/Black Talk: Interracial Friendship and Communication Amongst Adolescents*. Cambridge: Cambridge University Press.

Hewitt, R. (1996) *Routes of Racism: The Social Basis Of Racist Action*. International Centre for Intercultural Studies, Institute of Education, University of London, with the London Borough of Greenwich Central Race Equality Unit and the Greenwich Youth Service. Stoke-on-Trent: Trentham Books.

Hey, V. (1997) *The Company She Keeps: An Ethnography of Girls' Friendships*. Buckingam: Open University Press.

Hill Collins, P. (1990) *Black Feminist Thought: Knowledge, Consciousness and the Politics of Empowerment*. London: HarperCollins Academic.

Hill Collins, P. (1994) 'Shifting the Centre: Race, Class and Feminist Theorising About Motherhood', in E.N. Glenn, G. Chang and L.R. Forcey, *Mothering, Ideology, Experience and Agency*. New York and London: Routledge.

Holland, P. (1991) 'Introduction: History, Memory and the Family Album', in P. Holland and J. Spence (1991) *Family Snaps: The Meanings of Domestic Photography*. London: Virago.

Holland, P. and Spence, J. (eds) (1991) *Family Snaps: The Meanings of Domestic Photography*. London: Virago.

hooks, b. (1984) *Feminist Theory: From Margin to Centre*. Boston, Mass.: South End Press.

hooks, b. (1991) 'Stylish Nihilism: Race, Sex and Class at the Movies' in b. hooks, *Yearning: Race, Gender and Cultural Politics*. London: Turnaround.

hooks, b. (1992a) *Black Looks: Race and Representation*. Boston, Mass.: South End Press.

hooks, b. (1992b) 'Madonna: Plantation Mistress or Soul Sister?', in G. Dines J.M. Humez (1995) *Gender, Race and Class: A Text Reader*. Thousand Oaks, Calif.: Sage.

Hull, G.T., Scott, P.B. and Smith, B. (eds) (1982) *All The Women Are White, All The Blacks Are Men, But Some Of Us Are Brave: Black Women's Studies*. Old Westbury, N.Y.: Feminist Press.

Humm, M. (ed.) (1992) *Feminisms: A Reader*. New York and London: Harvester Wheatsheaf.

Ifekwunigwe, J. (1997) 'Diaspora's Daughters: On Lineage Authenticity and "mixed-race" Identity', in H.S. Mirza, *Black British Feminism: A Reader*. London: Routledge.

Ifekwunigwe, J. (1999) 'Old Whine, New Vassals: Are Diaspora and Hybridity Postmodern Inventions?', in P. Cohen (ed.) *New Ethnicities, Old Racisms?* London: Zed Books.

Ifekwunigwe, J. (2000) *Scattered Be-longings: Cultural Paradoxes of 'Race', Nation, and Gender*. London: Routledge.

Ihihimaera, W. (ed.) (1998) *Growing Up Maori*. Auckland: New Zealand.

Jackson, M. (1994) *The Real Facts Of Life: Feminism and The Politics Of Sexuality, c. 1850-1940*. London: Taylor and Francis.

Jackson, S. (1993) 'Even Sociologists Fall in Love: An Exploration in the Sociology of the Emotions', *Sociology*, 27 (2): 201–220.

Jackson, S. and Scott, S. (1996) *Feminism and Sexuality: A Reader*. Edinburgh: Edinburgh University Press.

Jacobs, J.D. (1992) 'Identity Development in Biracial Children', in M.P.P. Root (ed.) (1992) .

Jagger, G. and Wright, C. (eds) (1999) *Changing Family Values: Feminist Perspectives*. London: Routledge.

James, S. and Busia, A. (eds) *Theorising Black Feminisms: The Visionary Pragmatism of Black Women*. London: Routledge.

Jensen, J. (1992) 'Fandom as Pathology: The Consequences of Characterisation', in L.A. Lewis (ed.) (1992) *The Adoring Audience: Fan Culture and Popular Media*. London: Routledge.

Johnson, R. (1983) 'What is Cultural Studies Anyway?', in J. Munns G. Rajan (eds) (1995) *A Cultural Studies Reader: History, Theory, Practice*. London and New York: Longman.

Jones, L. (1994) *Bullet-proof Diva*. Harmondsworth: Penguin.

Jones, S. (1988) *Black Culture, White Youth: The Reggae Tradition from JA to UK*. Basingstoke: Macmillan Education.

Jordan, J. (1983) 'Love is Not the Problem', in *Moving Towards Home: Political Essays*. London: Virago.

Joseph, G. (1981) 'Black Mothers and Daughters: Their Roles and Functions in American Society', in G. Joseph and J. Lewis, *Common Differences: Conflicts in Black and White Feminism*. Boston, Mass.: South End Press.

Joseph, G. and Lewis, J. (1981) *Common Differences: Conflicts in Black and White Feminism*. Boston, Mass.: South End Press.

Katz, I. (1996) *The Construction of Racial Identity in Children of Mixed-Parentage: Mixed Metaphors*, London and Bristol: Jessica Kingsley Publishers.

Kehily, M. (1995) 'Self Narration: Autobiography and Identity Construction', *Gender and Education*, 7 (1).

Kehily, M.J. and Nayak, A. (1996) '"The Christmas Kiss": Sexuality, Story Telling and schooling', in *Curriculum Studies*, 4 (2): 211–229.

Kelly, L. (1988) *Surviving Sexual Violence.* Cambridge: Polity Press.

Kelly, L., Reagan, L. and Burton, S. (1992) 'Defending the Indefensible? Quantitative Methods in Feminist Research', in H. Hinds, A. Phoenix and J. Stacey (eds) *Working Out: New Directions for Women's Studies.* London: Falmer Press.

Kenway, J. and Bullen, E. (2001) *Consuming Children: Education-entertainment-advertising.* Buckingham and Philadelphia: Open University Press.

Kilbourne, J. (1989) 'Beauty and the Beast of Advertising', in G. Dines and J.M. Humez (1995) *Gender, Race and Class: A Text Reader.* Thousand Oaks, Calif.: Sage.

Kirton, D. (2000) *'Race', Ethnicity and Adoption.* Buckingham: Open University Press.

Kress, G. (1987) 'Genre in a Social Theory of Language: A Reply to John Dixon', in I. Reid (ed.) *The Place of Genre in Learning: Current Debates.* Victoria, Australia: Centre for Studies in Literary Education, Deakin University.

Kress, G. (1989) *Linguistic Process in Socio-Cultural Practice* (2nd) edition. Oxford: Oxford University Press.

Kuhn, A. (1995) *Family Secrets: Acts of Memory and Imagination.* London: Verso.

Labyani, J. (2000) 'Miscegenation, Nation Formation and Cross-racial Identifications in the Early Francoist Folklore Musical', in A. Brah and A. Coombes (eds) *Hybridity and Its Discontents: Politics, Science, Culture.* London: Sage.

Lal, B.B. (2001) 'Learning to Do Ethnic Identity: The Transracial/Transethnic Adoptive Family as Site and Context', in D. Parker and M. Song (2001).

Lawler, S. (2000) *Mothering the Self: Mothers, Daughters, Subjects.* London and New York: Routledge.

Lawrence, E. (1982) 'In the Abundance of Water the Fool is Thirsty: Sociology and Black Pathology', in Centre for Contemporary Cultural Studies, *The Empire Strikes Back: Race and Racism in '70s Britain.* Rougledge, in association with the University of Birmingham Centre for Contemporary Cultural Studies.

Leonard, D. and Adkins, L. (eds) (1996) *Sex in Question: French Materialist Feminism.* London: Routledge.

Leonardo, M. di (1987) 'The Female World of Cards and Holidays: Women, Families and the World of Kinship', *Signs: Journal of Women in Culture and Society*, 12 (3): 440–453.

Lewis, L.A. (ed.) (1992) *The Adoring Audience: Fan Culture and Popular Media.* London: Routledge.

Liddle, J. and Rai, S. (1993) 'Between Feminism and Orientalism', in M. Kennedy, C. Lubelska and V. Walsh (eds) *Making Connections: Women's Studies, Women's Movements, Women's Lives.* London: Taylor and Francis.

Lieblich, A., Tuval-Mashiach, R. and Zilmar, T. (1998) *Narrative Research: Reading, Analysis and Interpretation.* Applied Social Research Methods: Volume 47. Thousand Oaks (Calif.), London and New Dehli: Sage Publications.

Lorde, A. (1984) 'An Open Letter to Mary Daly', in A. Lorde, *Sister/Outsider: Essays and Speeches By Audre Lorde.* Freedom, Canada: The Crossing Press.

Luke, C. (1994) 'Interracial Families: Some Reflections on Hybridization, Feminine Identities, and Racialized Othering', Paper presented at the TASA Conference at Deakin University, Geelong Victoria.

Lury, C. (1997) *Prosthetic Culture: Photography, Memory and Identity.* London and New York: Routledge.

Mac an Ghaill, M. (1994) *The Making of Men: Masculinities, Sexuality and Schooling.* Buckingham: Open University Press.

Mac an Ghaill, M. (ed.) (1996) *Understanding Masculinities.* Buckingham: Open University Press.

Mac an Ghaill, M. (1999*) Contemporary Racisms and Ethnicities: Social and Cultural Transformations.* Buckingham: Open University Press.

Mama, A. (1989) *The Hidden Struggle: Statutory and Voluntary Sector Responses to Violence Against Black Women in the Home.* London: London Race and Housing Unit.

Marcus, L. (1991) 'The Face of Autobiography', in J. Swindells (ed.) *The Uses of Autobiography.* London: Taylor and Francis.

Martinez-Alier, V. (1974) *Marriage, Class and Colour in Nineteenth Century Cuba: A Study of Attitudes and Values in a Slave Society.* Cambridge: Cambridge University Press.

Mason-John, V. (ed.) (1995) *Talking Black: Lesbians of African and Asian Descent Speak Out.* London: Cassell.

Mason-John, V. and Khambatta, A. (1993) *Lesbians Talk: Making Black Waves.* London: Scarlet Press.

Mauthner, M. (1997) 'Methodological Aspects of Collecting Data from Children: Lessons from Three Research Projects', *Children and Society*, 11: 16–28.

Mauthner, M. (1998) 'Bringing Silent Voices into a public Discourse: Researching Accounts of Sister Relationships', in J. Ribbens and R. Edwards (eds*) Feminist Dilemmas in Qualitative Resarch: Public Knowledge and Private Lives.* London: Sage.

May, T. (1993) *Social Research: Issues Methods and Process.* Buckingham: Open University Press.

Mayall, B. (ed.) (1994) *Children's Childhoods: Observed and Experienced.* London: Falmer Press.

Maybin, J. (1993) 'Children's Voices: Talk, Knowledge, Identity', in D. Graddol, J. Maybin and B. Stierer (eds) *Researching Language and Literacy in Social Context.* Milton Keynes: Open University Press.

Maynard, M. (1994) 'Methods, Practice and Epistemology: The Debate About Feminism and Research', in M. Maynard and J. Purvis (eds) *Researching Women's Lives from a Feminist Perspective.* London: Taylor and Francis.

McGuigan, T. (ed.) (1997) *Cultural Methodologies.* London: Sage.

McRobbie, A. (1991) *Feminism and Youth Culture: From Jackie to Just Seventeen.* Basingstoke: Macmillan.

Mercer, K. (1994) 'Black Hair/Style Politics', in K. Mercer, *Welcome to the Jungle: New Positions in Black Cultural Studies.* London and New York: Routledge.

Miles, R. (1989) *Racism.* London: Routledge.

Mirza, H.S. (1992) *Young, Female and Black.* London: Routledge.

Mirza, H. (1995) 'Life in the Classroom', in J. Holland, M. Blair and S. Sheldon (eds) *Debates and Issues in Feminist Research and Pedagogy: A Reader.* Avon: Multilingual Matters Ltd. in association with the Open University.

Mirza, H. (ed.) (1997) *Black British Feminism: A Reader.* London: Routledge.

Modood, T. (1988) 'Black Racial Equality and Asian Identity', *New Community*, 14 (3): 307–404.

Moraga, C. and Anzaldúa, G. (eds) 'Foreword', in T.C. Bambara *This Bridge Called My Back: Writings By Radical Women Of Color.* New York: Kitchen Table/Women of Color Press.

Morgan, D. (1996) *Family Connections: An Introduction to Family Studies.* Cambridge: Polity Press.

Morrison, T. (1994) *The Bluest Eye.* London: Picador.

Mulvey, L. (1975) 'Visual Pleasure and Narrative Cinema', in *Screen*, 16 (3) 6–18.

Munns, J. and Rajan, G. (eds) (1995) *A Cultural Studies Reader: History, Theory, Practice.* London and New York: Longman.

Nayak, A. (1993) Narratives of Racism', in *Cultural Studies from Birmingham*, Volume 2 Birmingham: University of Birmingham Press, pp. 124–54.

Nayak, A. (1999) '"Pale Warriors": Skinhead Culture and the Embodiment of White Masculinites', in A. Brah, M.J. Hickman and M. Mac an Ghaill (eds) *Thinking Identities: Ethnicity, Racism and Culture.* London: Macmillan Press.

Nayak, A. and Kehily, M. (1997) 'Why are Young Men So Homophobic?', in D.L. Steinberg, E. Epstein and R. Johnson (1997*) Border Patrols: Policing the Boundaries of Heterosexuality.* London: Cassell.

Nicholson, L. (ed.) (1990) *Feminism/Postmodernism.* London and New York: Routledge.

Nicholson, L. (ed.) (1997) *The Second Wave: A Reader in Feminist Theory*. London and NewYork: Routledge.

Non-Aligned Productions (1988) *Coffee Coloured Children*. (Video). London: Albany Video Distribution.

Oakley, A. (1974) *The Sociology of Housework*. London: Robertson.

Oakley, A. (2000) *Experiments in Knowing: Gender and Method in the Social Sciences*. Cambridge: Polity Press in association with Blackwell.

Olumide, J. (2002) *Raiding the Gene Pool: The Social Construction of Mixed-Race*. London and Stirling, Victoria: Pluto Press.

Olumide, J. (1996) 'The Social Construction of Mixed Race: An Enquiry into the Experiences of those Designated Mixed-race and into the Professional Cultures in the Production of Racialised Social Ascriptions.' Unpublished Ph.D. Thesis, University of Bradford.

Omi, M. and Winant, H. (1986) *Racial Formulation in the United States*. London: Routledge and Kegan Paul.

Opitz, M., Oguntoye, K. and Schultz, D. (eds) (1992) *Showing Our Colours/Afro-German Women Speak Out*. London: Open Letters Press.

Oster, A. (1997) *The Education and Careers of Black Teachers: Changing Identities, Changing Lives*. Buckingham: Open University Press.

Owen, C. (2001) '"Mixed Race" in Official Statistics', in D. Parker and M. Song (eds) *Rethinking 'Mixed-Race'*. London and Stirling, Victoria: Pluto Press.

Owen, G. and Gill, B. (1983) *Adoption and Race: Black, Asian and Mixed Race Children In White Families*. London: Batsford Academic and Educational in association with British Agencies for Adoption & Fostering,

Parker, D. and Song, M. (eds) (2001) *Rethinking 'Mixed-Race'*. London and Stirling, Vicoria: Pluto Press.

Parmar, P. (1982) 'Gender, Race and Class: Asian Women in Resistance', in Centre for Contemporary Cultural Studies. *The Empire Strikes Back: Race and Racism in '70s Britain*. London: Routledge in association with the University of Birmingham Centre for Contemporary Cultural Studies.

Parmar, P. (1990) 'Black Feminism: The Politics of Articulation', in J. Rutherford (ed.) *Community, Culture, Difference*. London: Lawrence and Wishart.

Patel, P. (1999) 'Difficult Alliances: Treading the Minefield of Identity and Solidarity Politics', *Soundings: A Journal of Politics and Culture*, no. 12 Summer.

Phoenix, A. (1989) 'Theories of Gender in Black Families', in G. Weiner and M. Arnot (eds) *Gender Under Scrutiny*. London: Hutchinson, in association with the Open University Press.

Phoenix, A. (1996) 'Black, White or Mixed Race?', Seminar paper presented at Birkbeck College, University of London, June.

Phoenix, A. (1997) 'Theories of Gender in Black Families', in H. Mirza (ed.) *Black British Feminism: A Reader*. London and New York: Routledge.

Phoenix, A. and Owen, C. (2000) 'From Miscegenation to Hybridity: Mixed Relationships and Mixed Parentage in Profile', in A. Brah and A. Coombes (eds) *Hybridity and its Discontents: Politics, Science, Culture*. London and New York: Routledge.

Phoenix, A., Woollett, A. and Lloyd, E. (1991*) Motherhood: Meanings, Practices and Ideologies*. London: Sage.

Piper, A. (1998) 'Passing for White, Passing for Black', in N. Mirzoeff (ed.) *The Visual Culture Reader*. London and New York: Routledge.

Plummer, K. (1995) *Telling Sexual Stories: Power, Change and Social Worlds*. London and New York: Routledge.

Polkinghorne, D.E. (1995) 'Narrative Configuration in Qualitative Analysis', in J.A. Hatch and R. Wisniewski (eds) *Life History and Narrative*. London: Falmer Press.

Postman, N. (1994) *The Disappearance of Childhood*. New York: Vintage Books.

Rattansi, A. (1992) 'Changing the Subject? Racism, Culture and Education', in J. Donald and A. Rattansi (eds) (1992) *'Race', Culture, Difference*. London: Sage/Oxford University Press.

Reay, D. (1995) 'Using Habitus to Look at "Race" and Class in Primary School Classrooms', in M. Griffiths and B. Troyna (eds) *Antiracism, Culture and Social Justice in Education*. London: Taylor and Francis.

Reay, D. (1997) 'Feminist Theory, Habitus and Social Class: Disrupting Notions of Classlessness', *Women's Studies International Forum*, 20 (2): 225–233.

Reay, D. (1998*) Class Work: Mother's Involvement in their Children's Primary Schooling*. London: UCL Press.

Reynolds, T. (2000) 'Black Women and Social Class Identities', in S. Munt (ed.) *Cultural Studies and the Working Class*. London: Cassell.

Ribbens, J. (1993) 'Fact or Fiction? Aspects of the use of Autobiographical Writing in Undergraduate Sociology', in *Sociology*, 27 (1): 81–92.

Ricoeur, P. (1984) *Time and Narrative*, Vol. 1 (translated by K. McLaughlin and D. Pelluaer). Chicago: University of Chicago Press (original work published in 1983).

Ricoeur, P. (1992) *Oneself as Another*. London and Chicago: University of Chicago Press.

Riessman, C.K. (1993) *Narrative Analysis*. London: Sage.

Robinson, V. and Richardson, D. (eds) (1993) *Introducing Women's Studies* (2nd edition). Basingstoke: Macmillan.

Roediger, D. (1992) *The Making of Whiteness: Race and the Making of the American Working Class*. London: Verso.

Roediger, D. (1994) *Towards the Abolition of Whiteness*. London: Verso.

Root, M.P.P. (ed.) (1992) *Racially Mixed People in America.* New York: Sage Publications.

Root, M.P.P. (ed.) (1996) *The Multiracial Experience: Racial Borders as the New Frontier.* New York: Sage.

Rose, S., Lewontin, R.C. and Kamin, L. (1984) *Not in Our Genes: Biology, Ideology and Human Nature.* London: Penguin.

Rose, T. (1995) 'Fear of a Black Planet! Rap Music and Black Cultural Politics in the 1990s', in G. Dines and J.M. Humez (eds) *Gender, Race and Class: A Text Reader.* Thousand Oaks, Calif.: Sage.

Rosie, A. (1993) ' "He's a Liar, I'm Afraid": Truth and Lies in a Narrative Account', in *Sociology,* 27: (Special Issue on Auto/Biography): 144–152.

Rutherford, J. (ed.) (1990) *Identity: Community, Culture Difference.* London: Lawrence and Wishart.

Sayers, J. (1982) *Biological Politics: Feminist and Anti-Feminist Perspectives.* London: Tavistock.

Schultze, L., Barton White, A. and Brown, J.D. (1993) ' "A Sacred Monster in her Prime": Audience Construction of Madonna as Low-Other', in C. Schwichtenberg (1993) *The Madonna Connection: Representational Politics, Subcultural Identities and Cultural Theory.* Boulder (Colo.) and San Francisco (Calif.): Westview Press.

Schwichtenberg, C. (ed.) (1993) *The Madonna Connection: Representational Politics, Subcultural Identities and Cultural Theory.* Boulder (Colo.) and San Francisco (Calif.): Westview Press.

Scott, J. (1992) 'Experience', in J. Butler and J. Scott (eds) *Feminists Theorise the Political.* New York and London: Routledge.

Scott, R.B. (1993) 'Images of Race and Religion in Madonna's video *Like a Prayer*: Prayer and Praise', in C. Schwichtenberg (ed.) *The Madonna Connection: Representational Politics, Subcultural Identities and Cultural Theory.* Boulder (Colo.) and San Francisco (Calif.): Westview Press.

Seabrook, J. (1991) 'My Life is in that Box', in P. Holland and J. Spence (1991) *Family Snaps: The Meanings of Domestic Photography.* London: Virago.

Segal, L. and MacIntosh, M. (1992) *Sex Exposed: Sexuality and the Pornography Debate.* London: Virago.

Shohat, E. and Stam, R. (1998) 'Narrativising Visual Culture: Towards a Polycentric Aesthetics', in N. Mirzoff (ed.) *The Visual Culture Reader.* London: Sage.

Simmonds, F.N. (1996) 'Naming and Identity', in D. Jarrett-Macauley (ed.) *Reconstructing Womanhood, Reconstructing Feminism: Writings on Black Women.* London: Routledge.

Sivanandan, A. (1990) *Communities of Resistance. Writings on Black Struggles for Socialism.* London: Verso.

Skeggs, B. (1994) 'Situating the Production of Feminist Ethnography', in M.

Maynard and J. Purvis (eds) *Researching Women's Lives from a Feminist Perspective*. London: Taylor and Francis.

Skeggs, B. (1997) *Formations of Class and Gender*. London: Sage.

Smith, Z. (2000) *White Teeth*. London: Picador.

Solomos, J. and Back, L. (eds) (1995) *Racism and Society*. London: Macmillan.

Spence, J. (1986) *Putting Myself in the Picture: A Political, Personal and Photographic Autobiography*. London: Camden Press.

Spence, J. (1991) 'Shame Work: Thoughts on Family Snaps and Fractured Identities', in P. Holland and J. Spence (1991) *Family Snaps: The Meanings of Domestic Photography*. London: Virago.

Spickard, P.R. (1992) 'The Illogic of American Racial Categories', in M.P.P. Root (ed.) *Racially Mixed People in America*. New York: Sage Publications.

Spickard, P.R. (2001) 'The Subject is Mixed-Race: The Boom in Biracial Biography', in D. Parker and M. Song (eds) *Rethinking 'Mixed-Race'*. London and Stirling, Victoria: Pluto Press.

Stanley, L. (ed.) (1990) *Feminist Praxi: Research, Theory And Epistemology in Feminist Sociology*. London: Routledge.

Stanley, L. (1992) *The Auto/biographical I; The theory and Practice of Feminist Autobiography*. Manchester: Manchester University Press.

Stanley, L. and Wise, S. (1993) *Breaking Out Again: Feminist Ontology and Epistemology*. London: Routledge.

Steedman, C. (1997) 'Writing the Self: The End of the Scholarship Girl', in T. May (ed.) *Cultural Methodologies*. London: Sage.

Steinberg, D.L., Epstein, D. and Johnson, R. (eds) (1997) *Border Patrols: Policing the Boundaries of Heterosexuality*. London: Cassell.

Stoler, A.L. (2000) 'Sexual Affronts and Racial Frontiers: European Identities and the Cultural Politics of Exclusion in Colonial Southeast Asia', in A. Brah and A. Coombes *Hybridity and Its Discontents: Politics, Science, Culture*. London: Sage.

Stonequist, E. (1937) *The Marginal Man: A Study of Personality and Culture*. New York: Russell and Russell.

Swindells, J. (ed.) (1995) *The Uses of Autobiography*. London: Taylor and Francis.

Suriya, T.K. (2000) *'Mixed Race' Issues: A Bibliography and Glossary*. Dept. of Anthropology, SOAS, University of London for the Zeena Ralf Memorial Fund.

Tanesini, A. (1991) *An Introduction to Feminist Epistemologies*. London: Blackwell.

Thorne, B. (1992) *Gender Play: Boys and Girls at School*. Buckingham: Open University Press.

Threadgold, T. (1988) 'The Immanence of Discursive Contradictions', *Cultural Studies*, 3 (1): 101–127.

Tizard, B. and Phoenix, A. (1993) *Black, White or Mixed Race: Race and Racism in the Lives of Young People.* London: Routledge.

Tong, R. (1992) *Feminist Thought: A Comprehensive Introduction.* London: Routledge.

Troyna, B. and Hatcher, R. (1992) *Racism in Children's Lives: A Study of Mainly-white Primary Schools.* London: Routledge in association with the National Children's Bureau.

Tyler, C.A. (1994) 'Passing: Narcissism, Identity and Difference', *Differences*, 6: 2–3.

Unterhalter, E. (2000) 'Gendered Diaspora Identities: South African Women, Exile and Migration (c. 1960–65)', in S. Ali *et al., Global Feminist Politics: Identities in a Changing World.* London and New York: Routledge.

Usher, R. (1998) 'Autobiographical Accounts of PhD Students', in M. Erben (1998) *Biography and Education: A Reader.* London: Falmer Press.

Van Zoonen, L. (1994) *Feminist Media Studies.* London: Sage.

Wade. A (1999) '"Who Says What a Family Should Be Like?" Children's Concepts of Family after Divorce', Paper Presented at ESRC Seminar Group 5 'Postmodern' Kinship: Changing Families/Changing Childhoods, University of Leeds, December.

Walkerdine, V. (1996) 'Popular Culture and the Eroticization of Little Girls', in J. Curran, D. Morley and V. Walkerdine (eds) *Cultural Studies and Communications.* London: Arnold.

Walkerdine, V. (1997) *Daddy's Girl: Young Girls and Popular Culture.* Basingstoke: Macmillan.

Walkerdine, V., Lucey, H. and Melody, J. (2001) *Growing Up Girl: Psychosocial Explorations into Gender and Class.* London and New York: Palgrave.

Ware, V. (1992) *Beyond the Pale: White Women, Racism and History.* London: Verso.

Ware, V. and Back, L. (2002) *Out of Whiteness: Color, Politics and Culture.* Chicago: University of Chicago Press.

Weekes, D. (1997) 'Shades of Blackness: Young Female Constructions of Beauty', in H.S. Mirza (ed.) *Black British Feminism.* London: Routledge.

Weston, K. (1997) *Families We Choose: Lesbians, Gays, Kinship.* New York: Columbia University Press.

Wilkinson, S. and Kitzinger, C. (eds) (1993) *Heterosexuality: A Feminism and Psychology Reader.* London: Sage.

Wilson, A. (1987) *Mixed Race Children: A Study of Identity.* London: Allen and Unwin.

Willis, P. (1975) *Learning To Labour: How Working Class Kids Get Working Class Jobs.* Birmingham: University of Birmingham Centre for Contemporary Cultural Studies.

Willis, P. (1993) 'Symbolic Work', in A. Gray and J. McGuigan (1993) *Studying Culture: An Introductory Reader.* London and New York: Edward Arnold.

Willis, P., with Jones, S., Canaan, J. and Hurd, G. (1990) *Common Culture: Symbolic Work at Play in the Everyday Cultures of the Young.* Milton Keynes: Open University Press.

Winship, J. (1987) *Inside Women's Magazines.* London: Pandora.

Wright, C., Weekes, D. and McGaughlin, A. (2000) *'Race', Class and Gender in Exclusion From School.* London: Falmer.

Young, L. (1996) *Fear of the Dark : 'Race', Gender and Sexuality in the Cinema.* London: Routledge.

Yuval-Davis, N. (1996) 'Women, Ethnicity and Empowerment', in K. Bhavnani and A. Phoenix (eds) *Shifting Identities: Shifting Racisms. A Feminism and Psychology Reader.* London: Sage.

Yuval-Davis, N. and Anthias, F. (1989) *Woman–Nation–State.* London: Macmillan.

Zack, N. (ed.) (1993) *Race and Mixed-Race.* Philadelphia, Pa.: Temple University Press.

Zack, N. (ed.) (1995) *American Mixed Race: The Culture of Microdiversity.* Lanham, Md. and London: Rowman and Littlefield Publishers, Inc.

Index